TA...

DATE	TOP...

JANUARY

1	Abilities	1
2	Abortion	2
3	Abundance	3
4	Abuse	4
5	Access	5
6	Accountability	6
7	Achievements	7
8	Addictions	8
9	Adultery	9
10	Adversity	10
11	Aging	11
12	Agreement	12
13	Alcoholism	13
14	Angels	14
15	Anger	15
16	Anointing	16
17	Appearance	17
18	Appointments	18
19	Armorbearers	19
20	Art of Celebrating	20
21	Art of Receiving	21
22	Assignment	22
23	Associations	23
24	Astrology	24
25	Atheism	25
26	Atmosphere	26
27	Attitude	27
28	Authority	28
29	Backsliding	29
30	Bankruptcy	30
31	Baptism of The Holy Spirit	31

	The Spirit	
2	Believing	33
3	Betrayal	34
4	Bitterness	35
5	Blessings	36
6	Blood of Jesus	37
7	Body of Christ	38
8	Boldness	39
9	Books	40
10	Borrowing	41
11	Burnout	42
12	Business	43
13	Busyness	44
14	Calvary	45
15	Career Success	46
16	Change	47
17	Character	48
18	Chastisement of God	49
19	Cheerfulness	50
20	Children	51
21	Choices	52
22	Christmas	53
23	Church	54
24	Commitment	55
25	Compassion	56
26	Complaining	57
27	Confession	58
28	Confidentiality	59

Date	Topic	Page	Date	Topic	Page
MARCH			**APRIL**		
1	Conflict	60	1	Desires	91
2	Confrontation	61	2	Determination	92
3	Confusion	62	3	Diligence	93
4	Conquering	63	4	Diplomacy	94
5	Conscience	64	5	Disappointment	95
6	Contentment	65	6	Discipleship	96
7	Conversation Skills	66	7	Discipline	97
8	Conviction	67	8	Discouragement	98
9	Correction	68	9	Discretion	99
10	Counseling	69	10	Disloyalty	100
11	Courage	70	11	Disobedience	101
12	Covenant	71	12	Disorder	102
13	Covetousness	72	13	Distractions	103
14	Creativity	73	14	Divorce	104
15	Credibility	74	15	Doubts	105
16	Crisis	75	16	Dreams	106
17	Criticism	76	17	Easter	107
18	Crucifixion of Jesus	77	18	Endurance	108
19	Dangerous Relationships	78	19	Enemies	109
20	Dating	79	20	Enthusiasm	110
21	Deadlines	80	21	Envy	111
22	Death	81	22	Ethics	112
23	Debt	82	23	Etiquette	113
24	Deception	83	24	Evangelism	114
25	Decision For Christ	84	25	Excellence	115
26	Decision-Making	85	26	Expectation	116
27	Delegation	86	27	Failure	117
28	Deliverance	87	28	Faith	118
29	Demon Spirits	88	29	Faith-Talk	119
30	Dependability	89	30	Faithfulness	120
31	Depression	90			

Date	Topic	Page	Date	Topic	Page
MAY			**JUNE**		
1	False Accusation	121	1	Habits	152
2	Fame	122	2	Happiness	153
3	Family	123	3	Harvest	154
4	Fasting	124	4	Hatred	155
5	Fathers	125	5	Healing	156
6	Fatigue	126	6	Health	157
7	Fault-Finding	127	7	Heartache	158
8	Favor	128	8	Heaven	159
9	Fear	129	9	Hell	160
10	Fear of God	130	10	Holy Spirit	161
11	Fear of Man	131	11	Home	162
12	Financial Breakthrough	132	12	Honor	163
			13	Honoring Your Parents	164
13	Flattery	133			
14	Focus	134	14	Hope	165
15	Fools	135	15	Hospitality	166
16	Forgetting The Past	136	16	Humility	167
17	Forgiveness	137	17	Hundredfold Return	168
18	Freedom	138			
19	Friendship	139	18	Hurrying	169
20	Fruit of The Spirit	140	19	Hypocrisy	170
21	Gift Giving	141	20	Ideas	171
22	Giving	142	21	Ignorance	172
23	Goal-Setting	143	22	Imagination	173
24	God	144	23	Impatience	174
25	Goodness of God	145	24	Increase	175
26	Gratitude	146	25	Influence	176
27	Greatness	147	26	Injustice	177
28	Greed	148	27	Integrity	178
29	Grief	149	28	Integrity of God	179
30	Guidance	150	29	Intercession	180
31	Guilt	151	30	Jealousy	181

Date	Topic	Page	Date	Topic	Page
JULY			**AUGUST**		
1	Jesus	182	1	Ministers	213
2	Job	183	2	Miracles	214
3	Journalizing	184	3	Missions	215
4	Joy	185	4	Mistakes	216
5	Judgments of God	186	5	Misunderstandings	217
6	Kindness	187	6	Money	218
7	Knowledge	188	7	Moods	219
8	Laughter	189	8	Mothers	220
9	Lawlessness	190	9	Motivating Yourself	221
10	Laziness	191	10	Music	222
11	Leadership	192	11	Negotiation	223
12	Learning	193	12	Networking	224
13	Letter Writing	194	13	Obedience	225
14	Life	195	14	Occults	226
15	Listening	196	15	Offenses	227
16	Loneliness	197	16	Offerings	228
17	Longevity	198	17	Order	229
18	Longsuffering	199	18	Overcoming	230
19	Loss	200	19	Overload	231
20	Love	201	20	Pain	232
21	Love of God	202	21	Parenting	233
22	Loyalty	203	22	Passion	234
23	Lust	204	23	Patience	235
24	Lying	205	24	Peace	236
25	Marriage	206	25	Peacemakers	237
26	Meditation	207	26	People-Pressure	238
27	Memorizing Scriptures	208	27	Persecution	239
28	Mentorship	209	28	Pitfalls	240
29	Mercy	210	29	Planning	241
30	Millionaire Mentality	211	30	Poverty	242
31	Ministry	212	31	Power	243

Date	Topic	Page	Date	Topic	Page
SEPTEMBER			**OCTOBER**		
1	Power of God	244	1	Reputation	274
2	Praise	245	2	Respect	275
3	Prayer	246	3	Rest	276
4	Prayer Language	247	4	Restitution	277
5	Prejudice	248	5	Restoration	278
6	Presence of God	249	6	Resurrection of Christ	279
7	Pride	250	7	Revenge	280
8	Problem People	251	8	Revival	281
9	Problem-Solving	252	9	Rewards	282
10	Productivity	253	10	Rewards of Ritual	283
11	Promises of God	254	11	Righteousness of God	284
12	Promotion	255			
13	Prosperity	256	12	Romance	285
14	Protection of God	257	13	Salvation	286
15	Protégés	258	14	Satan	287
16	Protocol	259	15	Satanism	288
17	Purity	260	16	Schedules	289
18	Quitting	261	17	Seasons	290
19	Racism	262	18	Second Coming of Christ	291
20	Rapture	263			
21	Reading	264	19	Seducing Spirits	292
22	Rebellion	265	20	Seed-Faith	293
23	Reconciliation	266	21	Seedtime And Harvest	294
24	Recovery	267			
25	Regrets	268	22	Self-Confidence	295
26	Rejection	269	23	Self-Control	296
27	Relationships	270	24	Selfishness	297
28	Remembering	271	25	Servanthood	298
29	Renewing of The Mind	272	26	Sex	299
			27	Silence	300
			28	Sin	301
			29	Singing	302
30	Repentance	273	30	Slander	303
			31	Solitude	304

V

Date	Topic	Page	Date	Topic	Page
NOVEMBER			**DECEMBER**		
1	Sorrow	305	1	Timing	335
2	Soul-Winning	306	2	Tithing	336
3	Spirit of Error	307	3	Tragedy	337
4	Spiritual Warfare	308	4	Trouble	338
5	Strength	309	5	Trust	339
6	Stress	310	6	Truth	340
7	Strife	311	7	Understanding	341
8	Struggle	312	8	Unity	342
9	Studying Your Bible	313	9	Unthankfulness	343
10	Submission	314	10	Victory	344
11	Success	315	11	Violence	345
12	Suffering	316	12	Vision	346
13	Suicidal Thoughts	317	13	Visualization	347
14	Survival	318	14	Voice of God	348
15	Talents And Skills	319	15	Vows	349
16	Talking	320	16	Waiting On God	350
17	Teaching	321	17	Walking In The Spirit	351
18	Teamwork	322	18	Water Baptism	352
19	Tears	323	19	Weakness	353
20	Temptation	324	20	Wealth	354
21	Ten Commandments	325	21	Will of God	355
22	Terrorism	326	22	Winning	356
23	Testings	327	23	Wisdom	357
24	Thanksgiving	328	24	Witchcraft	358
25	The Cross	329	25	Witnessing	359
26	The Secret Place	330	26	Word of God	360
27	The Tongue	331	27	Words	361
28	Thought-Life	332	28	Work	362
29	Time	333	29	Worry	363
30	Time-Management	334	30	Worship	364
			31	Zeal	365

Abilities

January 1

"Not by might, nor by power, but by My Spirit, saith the Lord of hosts." *Zechariah 4:6*

"For verily I say unto you, That whosoever shall say unto this mountain, Be thou removed, and be thou cast into the sea; and shall not doubt in his heart, but shall believe that those things which he saith shall come to pass; he shall have whatsoever he saith." *Mark 11:23*

"Verily, verily, I say unto you, He that believeth on Me, the works that I do shall he do also; and greater works than these shall he do; because I go unto My Father." *John 14:12*

"What shall we then say to these things? If God be for us, who can be against us?" *Romans 8:31*

"I can do all things through Christ which strengtheneth me." *Philippians 4:13*

"...because greater is He that is in you, than he that is in the world." *1 John 4:4*

"Your Significance Is Not In Your Similarity To Another...But In Your Point of Difference From Another."

-MIKE MURDOCK

READ THE BIBLE THROUGH IN ONE YEAR: Genesis 1-3

Abortion

January 2

"Thou shalt not kill." *Exodus 20:13*

"Yea, they sacrificed their sons and their daughters unto devils, And shed innocent blood, even the blood of their sons and of their daughters, whom they sacrificed unto the idols of Canaan: and the land was polluted with blood." *Psalm 106:37-38*

"I will praise Thee; for I am fearfully and wonderfully made: marvellous are Thy works; and that my soul knoweth right well." *Psalm 139:14*

"Before I formed thee in the belly, I knew thee; and before thou camest forth out of the womb I sanctified thee." *Jeremiah 1:5*

"And He saith unto them, Is it lawful to do good on the sabbath days, or to do evil? to save life, or to kill? But they held their peace." *Mark 3:4*

"Abortion Is A Satanic Strategy To Prevent The Entry of A Champion Into A Generation."

-MIKE MURDOCK

READ THE BIBLE THROUGH IN ONE YEAR: Genesis 4-6

Abundance — January 3

"The Lord God of your fathers make you a thousand times so many more as ye are, and bless you, as He hath promised you!" *Deuteronomy 1:11*

"And the Lord thy God will make thee plenteous in every work of thine hand, in the fruit of thy body, and in the fruit of thy cattle, and in the fruit of thy land, for good: for the Lord will again rejoice over thee for good, as He rejoiceth over thy fathers."
Deuteronomy 30:9

"The righteous shall flourish like the palm tree: he shall grow like a cedar in Lebanon." *Psalm 92:12*

"Bring ye all the tithes into the storehouse, that there may be meat in Mine house, and prove Me now herewith, saith the Lord of hosts, if I will not open you the windows of Heaven, and pour you out a blessing, that there shall not be room enough to receive it."
Malachi 3:10

"If God Is Holding Your Seed, Today Is The Poorest You Will Ever Be."

-MIKE MURDOCK

READ THE BIBLE THROUGH IN ONE YEAR: Genesis 7-9

Abuse

January 4

"When my father and my mother forsake me, then the Lord will take me up." *Psalm 27:10*

"In God have I put my trust: I will not be afraid what man can do unto me." *Psalm 56:11*

"And it shall come to pass in the day that the Lord shall give thee rest from thy sorrow, and from thy fear, and from the hard bondage wherein thou wast made to serve." *Isaiah 14:3*

"But whoso shall offend one of these little ones which believe in Me, it were better for him that a millstone were hanged about his neck, and that he were drowned in the depth of the sea. Even so it is not the will of your Father which is in Heaven, that one of these little ones should perish." *Matthew 18:6, 14*

"Who shall separate us from the love of Christ? shall tribulation, or distress, or persecution, or famine, or nakedness, or peril, or sword? Nay, in all these things we are more than conquerors through Him that loved us." *Romans 8:35, 37*

"Your Self-Portrait Determines What You Are Willing To Endure."

-MIKE MURDOCK

READ THE BIBLE THROUGH IN ONE YEAR: Genesis 10-14

Access

January 5

"The king's favour is toward a wise servant: but his wrath is against him that causeth shame."
Proverbs 14:35

"Righteous lips are the delight of kings; and they love him that speaketh right." *Proverbs 16:13*

"A man's gift maketh room for him, and bringeth him before great men." *Proverbs 18:16*

"A man that hath friends must shew himself friendly: and there is a friend that sticketh closer than a brother."
Proverbs 18:24

"Many will intreat the favour of the prince: and every man is a friend to him that giveth gifts." *Proverbs 19:6*

"For every one that asketh receiveth; and he that seeketh findeth; and to him that knocketh it shall be opened."
Matthew 7:8

"For through Him we both have access by one Spirit unto the Father." *Ephesians 2:18*

"Access Is The Gift That Is A Continual Test."
-*MIKE MURDOCK*

READ THE BIBLE THROUGH IN ONE YEAR: Genesis 15-17

Accountability — January 6

"Be thou diligent to know the state of thy flocks, and look well to thy herds." *Proverbs 27:23*

"So then every one of us shall give account of himself to God." *Romans 14:12*

"Moreover it is required in stewards, that a man be found faithful." *1 Corinthians 4:2*

"But He that knew not, and did commit things worthy of stripes, shall be beaten with few stripes. For unto whomsoever much is given, of him shall be much required: and to whom men have committed much, of him they will ask the more." *Luke 12:48*

"And I saw the dead, small and great, stand before God; and the books were opened: and another book was opened, which is the book of life: and the dead were judged out of those things which were written in the books, according to their works." *Revelation 20:12*

"Those Who Create Your Provision Are Authorized To Require Accountability For It."

-MIKE MURDOCK

READ THE BIBLE THROUGH IN ONE YEAR: Genesis 18-20

Achievements — January 7

"Ask of Me, and I shall give thee the heathen for thine inheritance, and the uttermost parts of the earth for thy possession." *Psalm 2:8*

"...but the people that do know their God shall be strong, and do exploits." *Daniel 11:32*

"Therefore I say unto you, What things soever ye desire, when ye pray, believe that ye receive them, and ye shall have them." *Mark 11:24*

"Verily, verily, I say unto you, He that believeth on Me, the works that I do shall he do also; and greater works than these shall he do; because I go unto My Father." *John 14:12*

"I can do all things through Christ which strengtheneth me." *Philippians 4:13*

"When Your Heart Decides The Destination, Your Mind Will Design The Map To Reach It."

-MIKE MURDOCK

READ THE BIBLE THROUGH IN ONE YEAR: Genesis 21-23

Addictions

January 8

"He sent His word, and healed them, and delivered them from their destructions." *Psalm 107:20*

"Is not this the fast that I have chosen? to loose the bands of wickedness, to undo the heavy burdens, and to let the oppressed go free, and that ye break every yoke?" *Isaiah 58:6*

"Behold, the Lord's hand is not shortened, that it cannot save; neither His ear heavy, that it cannot hear." *Isaiah 59:1*

"And ye shall know the truth, and the truth shall make you free." *John 8:32*

"What? know ye not that your body is the temple of the Holy Ghost which is in you, which ye have of God, and ye are not your own?" *1 Corinthians 6:19*

"You Can Only Conquer Something You Hate."

-MIKE MURDOCK

READ THE BIBLE THROUGH IN ONE YEAR: Genesis 24-26

Adultery

January 9

"Thou shalt not commit adultery." *Exodus 20:14*

"Let thy fountain be blessed: and rejoice with the wife of thy youth. Let her be as the loving hind and pleasant roe; let her breasts satisfy thee at all times; and be thou ravished always with her love."
Proverbs 5:18-19

"But whoso committeth adultery with a woman lacketh understanding: he that doeth it destroyeth his own soul." *Proverbs 6:32*

"What? know ye not that your body is the temple of the Holy Ghost which is in you, which ye have of God, and ye are not your own? For ye are bought with a price: therefore glorify God in your body, and in your spirit, which are God's."
1 Corinthians 6:19-20

"Marriage is honourable in all, and the bed undefiled: but whoremongers and adulterers God will judge."
Hebrews 13:4

"What You Fail To Conquer Will Eventually Conquer You."

-MIKE MURDOCK

READ THE BIBLE THROUGH IN ONE YEAR: Genesis 27-29

Adversity

January 10

"For in the time of trouble He shall hide me in His pavilion: in the secret of His tabernacle shall He hide me; He shall set me up upon a rock." *Psalm 27:5*

"When I cry unto Thee, then shall mine enemies turn back: this I know; for God is for me." *Psalm 56:9*

"If thou faint in the day of adversity, thy strength is small." *Proverbs 24:10*

"When thou passest through the waters, I will be with thee; and through the rivers, they shall not overflow thee: when thou walkest through the fire, thou shalt not be burned; neither shall the flame kindle upon thee."
Isaiah 43:2

"Behold, I give unto you power to tread on serpents and scorpions, and over all the power of the enemy: and nothing shall by any means hurt you." *Luke 10:19*

"Warfare Always Surrounds The Birth of A Miracle."

-MIKE MURDOCK

READ THE BIBLE THROUGH IN ONE YEAR: Genesis 30-32

Aging

January 11

"I have been young, and now am old; yet have I not seen the righteous forsaken, nor His seed begging bread."
Psalm 37:25

"O God, Thou hast taught me from my youth: and hitherto have I declared Thy wondrous works. Now also when I am old and greyheaded, O God, forsake me not; until I have shewed Thy strength unto this generation, and Thy power to every one that is to come."
Psalm 71:17-18

"With long life will I satisfy him, and shew him My salvation."
Psalm 91:16

"They shall still bring forth fruit in old age; they shall be fat and flourishing; To shew that the Lord is upright: He is my rock, and there is no unrighteousness in Him."
Psalm 92:14-15

"For he that will love life, and see good days, let him refrain his tongue from evil, and his lips that they speak no guile."
1 Peter 3:10

"A Life of No Regrets Is A Life of No Discoveries."
-MIKE MURDOCK

READ THE BIBLE THROUGH IN ONE YEAR: Genesis 33-37

Agreement January 12

"Two are better than one; because they have a good reward for their labour. For if they fall, the one will lift up his fellow: but woe to him that is alone when he falleth; for he hath not another to help him up."
Ecclesiastes 4:9-10

"Can two walk together, except they be agreed?"
Amos 3:3

"Agree with thine adversary quickly, whiles thou art in the way with him; lest at any time the adversary deliver thee to the judge, and the judge deliver thee to the officer, and thou be cast into prison." *Matthew 5:25*

"...if two of you shall agree on earth as touching any thing that they shall ask, it shall be done for them of My Father which is in Heaven." *Matthew 18:19*

"But foolish and unlearned questions avoid, knowing that they do gender strifes." *2 Timothy 2:23*

"But avoid foolish questions, and genealogies, and contentions, and strivings about the law; for they are unprofitable and vain." *Titus 3:9*

"Those Who Understand Your Pain Will Understand Your Goals."

-MIKE MURDOCK

READ THE BIBLE THROUGH IN ONE YEAR: Genesis 38-40

Alcoholism January 13

"He sent His word, and healed them, and delivered them from their destructions." *Psalm 107:20*

"Who hath woe? who hath sorrow? who hath contentions? who hath babbling? who hath wounds without cause? who hath redness of eyes? They that tarry long at the wine; they that go to seek mixed wine. Look not thou upon the wine when it is red, when it giveth his colour in the cup, when it moveth itself aright. At the last it biteth like a serpent, and stingeth like an adder."
Proverbs 23:29-32

"Woe unto them that rise up early in the morning, that they may follow strong drink; that continue until night, till wine inflame them!" *Isaiah 5:11*

"For if ye live after the flesh, ye shall die: but if ye through the Spirit do mortify the deeds of the body, ye shall live." *Romans 8:13*

"And be not drunk with wine, wherein is excess; but be filled with the Spirit." *Ephesians 5:18*

"You Cannot Correct What You Are Unwilling To Confront."

-MIKE MURDOCK

READ THE BIBLE THROUGH IN ONE YEAR: Genesis 41-43

Angels

January 14

"The angel of the Lord encampeth round about them that fear Him, and delivereth them." *Psalm 34:7*

" Then said Daniel unto the king, O king, live for ever. My God hath sent His angel, and hath shut the lions' mouths, that they have not hurt me: forasmuch as before Him innocency was found in me; and also before thee, O king, have I done no hurt." *Daniel 6:21-22*

"And He shall send His angels with a great sound of a trumpet, and they shall gather together His elect from the four winds, from one end of Heaven to the other."

Matthew 24:31

"But to which of the angels said He at any time, Sit on My right hand, until I make thine enemies thy footstool? Are they not all ministering spirits, sent forth to minister for them who shall be heirs of salvation?" *Hebrews 1:13-14*

"Be not forgetful to entertain strangers: for thereby some have entertained angels unawares." *Hebrews 13:2*

"Everything You See Was Created By Something You Don't See."

-MIKE MURDOCK

READ THE BIBLE THROUGH IN ONE YEAR: Genesis 44-46

Anger

January 15

"Cease from anger, and forsake wrath: fret not thyself in any wise to do evil." *Psalm 37:8*

"He that is slow to anger is better than the mighty; and he that ruleth his spirit than he that taketh a city."
Proverbs 16:32

"A gift in secret pacifieth anger: and a reward in the bosom strong wrath." *Proverbs 21:14*

"Blessed are the peacemakers: for they shall be called the children of God." *Matthew 5:9*

"Be ye angry, and sin not: let not the sun go down upon your wrath: Let all bitterness, and wrath, and anger, and clamour, and evil speaking, be put away from you, with all malice: And be ye kind one to another, tenderhearted, forgiving one another, even as God for Christ's sake hath forgiven you."
Ephesians 4:26, 31-32

"Anger Is Simply Passion Requiring An Appropriate Focus."

-MIKE MURDOCK

READ THE BIBLE THROUGH IN ONE YEAR: Genesis 47-49

Anointing

January 16

"Thou lovest righteousness, and hatest wickedness: therefore God, thy God, hath anointed thee with the oil of gladness above thy fellows." *Psalm 45:7*

"...Touch not Mine anointed, and do My prophets no harm." *Psalm 105:15*

"And it shall come to pass in that day, that His burden shall be taken away from off thy shoulder, and His yoke from off thy neck, and the yoke shall be destroyed because of the anointing." *Isaiah 10:27*

"The Spirit of the Lord is upon me, because He hath anointed me to preach the gospel to the poor; He hath sent me to heal the brokenhearted, to preach deliverance to the captives, and recovering of sight to the blind, to set at liberty them that are bruised." *Luke 4:18*

"But the anointing which ye have received of Him abideth in you, and ye need not that any man teach you: but as the same anointing teacheth you of all things, and is truth, and is no lie, and even as it hath taught you, ye shall abide in Him." *1 John 2:27*

"The Anointing You Respect Is The Anointing That Increases In Your Life."

-MIKE MURDOCK

READ THE BIBLE THROUGH IN ONE YEAR: Genesis 50-Exodus 2

Appearance January 17

"But the Lord said unto Samuel, Look not on his countenance, or on the height of his stature; because I have refused him: for the Lord seeth not as man seeth; for man looketh on the outward appearance, but the Lord looketh on the heart." *1 Samuel 16:7*

"A merry heart maketh a cheerful countenance."
Proverbs 15:13

"Who can find a virtuous woman? for her price is far above rubies. She maketh herself coverings of tapestry; her clothing is silk and purple. Strength and honour are her clothing; and she shall rejoice in time to come." *Proverbs 31:10, 22, 25*

"Whose adorning let it not be that outward adorning of plaiting the hair, and of wearing of gold, or of putting on of apparel; But let it be the hidden man of the heart, in that which is not corruptible, even the ornament of a meek and quiet spirit, which is in the sight of God of great price." *1 Peter 3:3-4*

"Package Yourself For Where You Are Going Instead of Where You Have Been."

-MIKE MURDOCK

READ THE BIBLE THROUGH IN ONE YEAR: Exodus 3-5

Appointments — January 18

"He that walketh with wise men shall be wise: but a companion of fools shall be destroyed." *Proverbs 13:20*

"Withdraw thy foot from thy neighbour's house; lest he be weary of thee, and so hate thee." *Proverbs 25:17*

"To every thing there is a season, and a time to every purpose under the Heaven: A time to be born, and a time to die; A time to get, and a time to lose; a time to keep, and a time to cast away; a time to keep silence, and a time to speak." *Ecclesiastes 3:1-2, 6-7*

"Write the vision, and make it plain upon tables, that he may run that readeth it." *Habakkuk 2:2*

"Be not deceived: evil communications corrupt good manners." *1 Corinthians 15:33*

"See then that ye walk circumspectly, not as fools, but as wise, Redeeming the time, because the days are evil." *Ephesians 5:15-16*

"...For what is your life? It is even a vapour, that appeareth for a little time, and then vanisheth away." *James 4:14*

"Your Respect For Time Is A Prediction of Your Financial Future."

-MIKE MURDOCK

READ THE BIBLE THROUGH IN ONE YEAR: Exodus 6-10

Armorbearers January 19

"Believe in the Lord your God, so shall ye be established; believe His prophets, so shall ye prosper."
2 Chronicles 20:20

"He that walketh with wise men shall be wise."
Proverbs 13:20

"Seest thou a man diligent in his business? he shall stand before kings; he shall not stand before mean men." *Proverbs 22:29*

"Whoso keepeth the fig tree shall eat the fruit thereof: so he that waiteth on his master shall be honoured."
Proverbs 27:18

"Two are better than one; because they have a good reward for their labour. For if they fall, the one will lift up his fellow: but woe to him that is alone when he falleth; for he hath not another to help him up."
Ecclesiastes 4:9-10

"Can two walk together, except they be agreed?"
Amos 3:3

"For we are labourers together with God: ye are God's husbandry, ye are God's building." *1 Corinthians 3:9*

"When You Are Assigned To Someone, *Their* Goals Become *Your* Goals."

-MIKE MURDOCK

READ THE BIBLE THROUGH IN ONE YEAR: Exodus 11-13

Art of Celebrating

January 20

"And Israel saw that great work which the Lord did upon the Egyptians:...Then sang Moses and the children of Israel this song unto the Lord, and spake, saying, I will sing unto the Lord, for He hath triumphed gloriously: the horse and his rider hath He thrown into the sea." *Exodus 14:31, 15:1*

"And David danced before the Lord with all his might; and David was girded with a linen ephod. So David and all the house of Israel brought up the ark of the Lord with shouting, and with the sound of the trumpet." *2 Samuel 6:14-15*

"Give unto the Lord the glory due unto His name: bring an offering, and come before Him: worship the Lord in the beauty of holiness." *1 Chronicles 16:29*

"And also that every man should eat and drink, and enjoy the good of all his labour, it is the gift of God." *Ecclesiastes 3:13*

"What You Celebrate You Will Remember."

-MIKE MURDOCK

READ THE BIBLE THROUGH IN ONE YEAR: Exodus 14-16

Art of Receiving

January 21

"And a very great multitude spread their garments in the way; others cut down branches from the trees, and strawed them in the way. And the multitudes that went before, and that followed, cried, saying, Hosanna to the Son of David: Blessed is He that cometh in the name of the Lord; Hosanna in the highest." *Matthew 21:8-9*

"And one of them, when he saw that he was healed, turned back, and with a loud voice glorified God, And fell down on his face at His feet, giving Him thanks: and he was a Samaritan." *Luke 17:15-16*

"In every thing give thanks: for this is the will of God in Christ Jesus concerning you."
1 Thessalonians 5:18

"The Ceremony of Appreciation Is The Gift of The Receiver Back To The Giver."

-MIKE MURDOCK

READ THE BIBLE THROUGH IN ONE YEAR: Exodus 17-19

Assignment January 22

"Withhold not good from them to whom it is due, when it is in the power of thine hand to do it." *Proverbs 3:27*

"A man's gift maketh room for him, and bringeth him before great men." *Proverbs 18:16*

"Then the word of the Lord came unto me, saying, Before I formed thee in the belly I knew thee; and before thou camest forth out of the womb I sanctified thee, and I ordained thee a prophet unto the nations...for thou shalt go to all that I shall send thee, and whatsoever I command thee thou shalt speak."
Jeremiah 1:4-5, 7

"Verily, verily, I say unto you, He that believeth on Me, the works that I do shall he do also; and greater works than these shall he do; because I go unto My Father."
John 14:12

"Knowing that whatsoever good thing any man doeth, the same shall he receive of the Lord, whether he be bond or free." *Ephesians 6:8*

"Your Assignment On Earth Is Simply The Problem God Created You To Solve."

-MIKE MURDOCK

READ THE BIBLE THROUGH IN ONE YEAR: Exodus 20-22

Associations January 23

"Take heed to thyself, lest thou make a covenant with the inhabitants of the land whither thou goest, lest it be for a snare in the midst of thee." *Exodus 34:12*

"He that walketh with wise men shall be wise: but a companion of fools shall be destroyed."
Proverbs 13:20

"Can two walk together, except they be agreed?"
Amos 3:3

"But now I have written unto you not to keep company, if any man that is called a brother be a fornicator, or covetous, or an idolater, or a railer, or a drunkard, or an extortioner; with such an one no not to eat." *1 Corinthians 5:11*

"Be not deceived: evil communications corrupt good manners." *1 Corinthians 15:33*

"Those Who Do Not Increase You Will Inevitably Decrease You."

-MIKE MURDOCK

READ THE BIBLE THROUGH IN ONE YEAR: Exodus 23-25

Astrology

January 24

"Ye shall not eat any thing with the blood: neither shall ye use enchantment, nor observe times."
Leviticus 19:26

"And the soul that turneth after such as have familiar spirits, and after wizards, to go a whoring after them, I will even set My face against that soul, and will cut him off from among his people." *Leviticus 20:6*

"But he did that which was evil in the sight of the Lord, ...also he observed times, and used enchantments, and used witchcraft, and dealt with a familiar spirit, and with wizards: he wrought much evil in the sight of the Lord, to provoke Him to anger." *2 Chronicles 33:22, 6*

"...I am the Lord that maketh all things; that stretcheth forth the Heavens alone; that spreadeth abroad the earth by Myself;...That frustrateth the tokens of the liars, and maketh diviners mad." *Isaiah 44:24-25*

"Stars Do Not Decide Seasons; Decisions Decide Seasons."

-MIKE MURDOCK

READ THE BIBLE THROUGH IN ONE YEAR: Exodus 26-28

Atheism January 25

"In the beginning God created the Heaven and the earth." *Genesis 1:1*

"The fool hath said in his heart, There is no God. They are corrupt, they have done abominable works, there is none that doeth good." *Psalm 14:1*

"For the invisible things of Him from the creation of the world are clearly seen, being understood by the things that are made, even His eternal power and Godhead; so that they are without excuse: Because that, when they knew God, they glorified Him not as God, neither were thankful; but became vain in their imaginations, and their foolish heart was darkened." *Romans 1:20-21*

"And even as they did not like to retain God in their knowledge, God gave them over to a reprobate mind, to do those things which are not convenient." *Romans 1:28*

"But if our gospel be hid, it is hid to them that are lost: In whom the god of this world hath blinded the minds of them which believe not, lest the light of the glorious gospel of Christ, Who is the image of God, should shine unto them." *2 Corinthians 4:3-4*

"The Evidence of God's Presence Far Outweighs The Proof of His Absence."

-MIKE MURDOCK

READ THE BIBLE THROUGH IN ONE YEAR: Exodus 29-33

Atmosphere — January 26

"And it came to pass, when the evil spirit from God was upon Saul, that David took an harp, and played with his hand: so Saul was refreshed, and was well, and the evil spirit departed from him." *1 Samuel 16:23*

"And it came to pass, when the priests were come out of the holy place, that the cloud filled the house of the Lord, So that the priests could not stand to minister because of the cloud: for the glory of the Lord had filled the house of the Lord." *1 Kings 8:10-11*

"Thou wilt shew me the path of life: in Thy presence is fulness of joy; at Thy right hand there are pleasures for evermore." *Psalm 16:11*

"...and the power of the Lord was present to heal them." *Luke 5:17*

"And when the day of Pentecost was fully come, they were all with one accord in one place. And suddenly there came a sound from Heaven as of a rushing mighty wind, and it filled all the house where they were sitting." *Acts 2:1-2*

"The Atmosphere You Create Determines The Product You Produce."

-MIKE MURDOCK

READ THE BIBLE THROUGH IN ONE YEAR: Exodus 34-36

Attitude

January 27

"The sacrifices of God are a broken spirit: a broken and a contrite heart, O God, Thou wilt not despise."
Psalm 51:17

"A merry heart maketh a cheerful countenance: but by sorrow of the heart the spirit is broken." *Proverbs 15:13*

"A merry heart doeth good like a medicine: but a broken spirit drieth the bones." *Proverbs 17:22*

"She openeth her mouth with Wisdom; and in her tongue is the law of kindness." *Proverbs 31:26*

"Then this Daniel was preferred above the presidents and princes, because an excellent spirit was in him; and the king thought to set him over the whole realm."
Daniel 6:3

"...for out of the abundance of the heart the mouth speaketh. A good man out of the good treasure of the heart bringeth forth good things: and an evil man out of the evil treasure bringeth forth evil things."
Matthew 12:34-35

"The Attitude of The Servant Controls The Atmosphere of The Palace."

-MIKE MURDOCK

READ THE BIBLE THROUGH IN ONE YEAR: Exodus 37-39

Authority

January 28

"For He taught them as one having authority, and not as the scribes." *Matthew 7:29*

"And Jesus came and spake unto them, saying, All power is given unto Me in Heaven and in earth."
Matthew 28:18

"Then He called His twelve disciples together, and gave them power and authority over all devils, and to cure diseases. And He sent them to preach the kingdom of God, and to heal the sick." *Luke 9:1-2*

"Children, obey your parents in the Lord: for this is right." *Ephesians 6:1*

"Submit yourselves to every ordinance of man for the Lord's sake: whether it be to the king, as supreme; For so is the will of God, that with well doing ye may put to silence the ignorance of foolish men." *1 Peter 2:13, 15*

"Likewise, ye younger, submit yourselves unto the elder." *1 Peter 5:5*

"The Proofs of Legitimate Authority Are Provision, Protection And Promotion!"

-MIKE MURDOCK

READ THE BIBLE THROUGH IN ONE YEAR: Exodus 40-Leviticus 2

Backsliding

January 29

"The law of his God is in his heart; none of his steps shall slide." *Psalm 37:31*

"The backslider in heart shall be filled with his own ways: and a good man shall be satisfied from himself."
Proverbs 14:14

"Return, ye backsliding children, and I will heal your backslidings. Behold, we come unto Thee; for Thou art the Lord our God." *Jeremiah 3:22*

"And Jesus said unto him, No man, having put his hand to the plough, and looking back, is fit for the kingdom of God." *Luke 9:62*

"But the Lord is faithful, Who shall stablish you, and keep you from evil." *2 Thessalonians 3:3*

"That good thing which was committed unto thee keep by the Holy Ghost which dwelleth in us." *2 Timothy 1:14*

"Now unto Him that is able to keep you from falling, and to present you faultless before the presence of His glory with exceeding joy." *Jude 1:24*

"The Gift of Choice Is More Powerful Than The Gift of Love."

-MIKE MURDOCK

READ THE BIBLE THROUGH IN ONE YEAR: Leviticus 3-5

Bankruptcy January 30

"In God have I put my trust: I will not be afraid what man can do unto me." *Psalm 56:11*

"In the day of prosperity be joyful, but in the day of adversity consider: God also hath set the one over against the other, to the end that man should find nothing after him." *Ecclesiastes 7:14*

"Remember ye not the former things, neither consider the things of old. Behold, I will do a new thing; now it shall spring forth; shall ye not know it? I will even make a way in the wilderness, and rivers in the desert." *Isaiah 43:18-19*

"And I will restore to you the years that the locust hath eaten, the cankerworm, and the caterpiller, and the palmerworm, My great army which I sent among you. And ye shall eat in plenty, and be satisfied, and praise the name of the Lord your God, that hath dealt wondrously with you: and My people shall never be ashamed." *Joel 2:25-26*

"Moreover it is required in stewards, that a man be found faithful." *1 Corinthians 4:2*

"Loss Is The First Step Toward Learning."

-MIKE MURDOCK

READ THE BIBLE THROUGH IN ONE YEAR: Leviticus 6-8

Baptism of The Holy Spirit

January 31

"For with stammering lips and another tongue will He speak to this people." *Isaiah 28:11*

"And these signs shall follow them that believe; In My name shall they cast out devils; they shall speak with new tongues." *Mark 16:17*

"For John truly baptized with water; but ye shall be baptized with the Holy Ghost not many days hence. But ye shall receive power, after that the Holy Ghost is come upon you." *Acts 1:5, 8*

"And they were all filled with the Holy Ghost, and began to speak with other tongues, as the Spirit gave them utterance." *Acts 2:4*

"And as I began to speak, the Holy Ghost fell on them, as on us at the beginning." *Acts 11:15*

"And be not drunk with wine, wherein is excess; but be filled with the Spirit." *Ephesians 5:18*

"What Peter Did Not Become Walking Beside Jesus For 3½ Years, He Became In One Day When The Holy Spirit Came."

-MIKE MURDOCK

READ THE BIBLE THROUGH IN ONE YEAR: Leviticus 9-11

Being Led By The Spirit

February 1

"And thine ears shall hear a word behind thee, saying, This is the way, walk ye in it, when ye turn to the right hand, and when ye turn to the left." *Isaiah 30:21*

"The Spirit of the Lord God is upon me; because the Lord hath anointed me to preach good tidings unto the meek; He hath sent me to bind up the brokenhearted, to proclaim liberty to the captives, and the opening of the prison to them that are bound." *Isaiah 61:1*

"And Jesus being full of the Holy Ghost returned from Jordan, and was led by the Spirit into the wilderness."
Luke 4:1

"And the Spirit bade me go with them, nothing doubting." *Acts 11:12*

"For as many as are led by the Spirit of God, they are the sons of God." *Romans 8:14*

"...But we have the mind of Christ."
1 Corinthians 2:16

"Joy Is The Divine Reward For Discerning The Divine Purpose of The Immediate Moment."

-MIKE MURDOCK

READ THE BIBLE THROUGH IN ONE YEAR: Leviticus 12-16

Believing

February 2

"...if two of you shall agree on earth as touching any thing that they shall ask, it shall be done for them of My Father which is in Heaven." *Matthew 18:19*

"And all things, whatsoever ye shall ask in prayer, believing, ye shall receive." *Matthew 21:22*

"Jesus said unto him, If thou canst believe, all things are possible to him that believeth." *Mark 9:23*

"...What things soever ye desire, when ye pray, believe that ye receive them, and ye shall have them." *Mark 11:24*

"Above all, taking the shield of faith, wherewith ye shall be able to quench all the fiery darts of the wicked."
Ephesians 6:16

"But without faith it is impossible to please Him: for he that cometh to God must believe that He is, and that He is a rewarder of them that diligently seek Him." *Hebrews 11:6*

"Whoever You Trust Controls Your Future."

-MIKE MURDOCK

READ THE BIBLE THROUGH IN ONE YEAR: Leviticus 17-19

Betrayal

February 3

"But as for you, ye thought evil against me; but God meant it unto good, to bring to pass, as it is this day, to save much people alive." *Genesis 50:20*

"For I have heard the slander of many: fear was on every side: while they took counsel together against me, they devised to take away my life. My times are in Thy hand: deliver me from the hand of mine enemies, and from them that persecute me. Make Thy face to shine upon Thy servant: save me for Thy mercies' sake."
Psalm 31:13, 15-16

"Yea, mine own familiar friend, in whom I trusted, which did eat of my bread, hath lifted up his heel against me. But Thou, O Lord, be merciful unto me, and raise me up, that I may requite them." *Psalm 41:9-10*

"The Son of man goeth as it is written of Him: but woe unto that man by whom the Son of man is betrayed! it had been good for that man if he had not been born."
Matthew 26:24

"Someone You Are Trusting Is Trusting Someone You Would Not."

-MIKE MURDOCK

READ THE BIBLE THROUGH IN ONE YEAR: Leviticus 20-22

Bitterness

February 4

"Let the words of my mouth, and the meditation of my heart, be acceptable in Thy sight, O Lord, my strength, and my Redeemer." *Psalm 19:14*

"The heart knoweth his own bitterness; and a stranger doth not intermeddle with his joy." *Proverbs 14:10*

"Wherefore putting away lying, speak every man truth with his neighbour: for we are members one of another. Be ye angry, and sin not: let not the sun go down upon your wrath: Let all bitterness, and wrath, and anger, and clamour, and evil speaking, be put away from you, with all malice: And be ye kind one to another, tenderhearted, forgiving one another, even as God for Christ's sake hath forgiven you." *Ephesians 4:25-26, 31-32*

"Follow peace with all men, and holiness, without which no man shall see the Lord: Looking diligently lest any man fail of the grace of God; lest any root of bitterness springing up trouble you, and thereby many be defiled." *Hebrews 12:14-15*

"Bitterness Is An Internal And Chosen Enemy...A Thousand Times Deadlier Than Any Injustice You Experience."

-MIKE MURDOCK

READ THE BIBLE THROUGH IN ONE YEAR: Leviticus 23-25

Blessings

February 5

"And I will make of thee a great nation, and I will bless thee, and make thy name great; and thou shalt be a blessing." *Genesis 12:2*

"Behold, I set before you this day a blessing and a curse." *Deuteronomy 11:26*

"And all these blessings shall come on thee, and overtake thee, if thou shalt hearken unto the voice of the Lord thy God." *Deuteronomy 28:2*

"The blessing of the Lord, it maketh rich, and He addeth no sorrow with it." *Proverbs 10:22*

"A faithful man shall abound with blessings: but he that maketh haste to be rich shall not be innocent." *Proverbs 28:20*

"If ye be willing and obedient, ye shall eat the good of the land." *Isaiah 1:19*

"Blessed be the God and Father of our Lord Jesus Christ, Who hath blessed us with all spiritual blessings in Heavenly places in Christ." *Ephesians 1:3*

"The Person of Jesus Creates Your Peace, The Principles of Jesus Create Your Prosperity."

-MIKE MURDOCK

READ THE BIBLE THROUGH IN ONE YEAR: Leviticus 26-Numbers 1

Blood of Jesus

February 6

"Neither by the blood of goats and calves, but by His own blood He entered in once into the holy place, having obtained eternal redemption for us. For if the blood of bulls and of goats, and the ashes of an heifer sprinkling the unclean, sanctifieth to the purifying of the flesh: How much more shall the blood of Christ, Who through the eternal Spirit offered Himself without spot to God, purge your conscience from dead works to serve the living God?" *Hebrews 9:12-14*

"And almost all things are by the law purged with blood; and without shedding of blood is no remission." *Hebrews 9:22*

"Forasmuch as ye know that ye were not redeemed with corruptible things, as silver and gold, from your vain conversation received by tradition from your fathers; But with the precious blood of Christ, as of a lamb without blemish and without spot." *1 Peter 1:18-19*

"But if we walk in the light, as He is in the light, we have fellowship one with another, and the blood of Jesus Christ His Son cleanseth us from all sin." *1 John 1:7*

"The Price God Was Willing To Pay
Reveals The Worth of The Product He Saw."

-MIKE MURDOCK

READ THE BIBLE THROUGH IN ONE YEAR: Numbers 2-4

Body of Christ

February 7

"For by one Spirit are we all baptized into one body, whether we be Jews or Gentiles, whether we be bond or free; and have been all made to drink into one Spirit." *1 Corinthians 12:13*

"If the whole body were an eye, where were the hearing? If the whole were hearing, where were the smelling?" *1 Corinthians 12:17*

"That there should be no schism in the body; but that the members should have the same care one for another." *1 Corinthians 12:25*

"For the perfecting of the saints, for the work of the ministry, for the edifying of the body of Christ."
Ephesians 4:12

"For the husband is the head of the wife, even as Christ is the head of the church: and He is the saviour of the body." *Ephesians 5:23*

"Whatever You Have Not Been Given God Has Placed In Someone Near You And Love Is The Secret Map To The Treasure."

-MIKE MURDOCK

READ THE BIBLE THROUGH IN ONE YEAR: Numbers 5-7

Boldness

February 8

"The wicked flee when no man pursueth: but the righteous are bold as a lion." *Proverbs 28:1*

"But ye shall receive power, after that the Holy Ghost is come upon you: and ye shall be witnesses unto Me both in Jerusalem, and in all Judaea, and in Samaria, and unto the uttermost part of the earth." *Acts 1:8*

"And now, Lord, behold their threatenings: and grant unto Thy servants, that with all boldness they may speak Thy word, By stretching forth Thine hand to heal; and that signs and wonders may be done by the name of Thy holy child Jesus." *Acts 4:29-30*

"Then spake the Lord to Paul in the night by a vision, Be not afraid, but speak, and hold not thy peace: For I am with thee, and no man shall set on thee to hurt thee: for I have much people in this city." *Acts 18:9-10*

"And many of the brethren in the Lord, waxing confident by my bonds, are much more bold to speak the word without fear." *Philippians 1:14*

"Let us therefore come boldly unto the throne of grace, that we may obtain mercy, and find grace to help in time of need." *Hebrews 4:16*

"The Product of Knowledge Is Persuasion;
The Product of Persuasion Is Boldness."

-MIKE MURDOCK

READ THE BIBLE THROUGH IN ONE YEAR: Numbers 8-12

Books

February 9

"And the Lord said unto Moses, Write this for a memorial in a book, and rehearse it in the ears of Joshua: for I will utterly put out the remembrance of Amalek from under Heaven." *Exodus 17:14*

"And the Lord answered me, and said, Write the vision, and make it plain upon tables, that he may run that readeth it." *Habakkuk 2:2*

"Study to shew thyself approved unto God, a workman that needeth not to be ashamed, rightly dividing the word of truth." *2 Timothy 2:15*

"Saying, I am Alpha and Omega, the first and the last: and, What thou seest, write in a book, and send it unto the seven churches which are in Asia; unto Ephesus, and unto Smyrna, and unto Pergamos, and unto Thyatira, and unto Sardis, and unto Philadelphia, and unto Laodicea. Write the things which thou hast seen, and the things which are, and the things which shall be hereafter." *Revelation 1:11, 19*

"And I went unto the angel, and said unto him, Give me the little book. And he said unto me, Take it, and eat it up; and it shall make thy belly bitter, but it shall be in thy mouth sweet as honey." *Revelation 10:9*

"God Sent His Son, But He Left His Book."

-MIKE MURDOCK

READ THE BIBLE THROUGH IN ONE YEAR: Numbers 13-15

Borrowing

February 10

"For the Lord thy God blesseth thee, as He promised thee: and thou shalt lend unto many nations, but thou shalt not borrow; and thou shalt reign over many nations, but they shall not reign over thee." *Deuteronomy 15:6*

"The Lord shall open unto thee His good treasure, the Heaven to give the rain unto thy land in His season, and to bless all the work of thine hand: and thou shalt lend unto many nations, and thou shalt not borrow."
Deuteronomy 28:12

"The wicked borroweth, and payeth not again: but the righteous sheweth mercy, and giveth." *Psalm 37:21*

"That I may cause those that love Me to inherit substance; and I will fill their treasures." *Proverbs 8:21*

"The rich ruleth over the poor, and the borrower is servant to the lender." *Proverbs 22:7*

"Owe no man any thing, but to love one another: for he that loveth another hath fulfilled the law." *Romans 13:8*

"The Proof of Blessing Is The *Ability To Lend,*
The Proof of Impatience Is The Willingness
To *Borrow*."

-MIKE MURDOCK

READ THE BIBLE THROUGH IN ONE YEAR: Numbers 16-18

Burnout

February 11

"Why art thou cast down, O my soul? and why art thou disquieted in me? hope thou in God: for I shall yet praise Him for the help of His countenance." *Psalm 42:5*

"For a just man falleth seven times, and riseth up again." *Proverbs 24:16*

"And he shall speak great words against the most High, and shall wear out the saints of the most High, and think to change times and laws: and they shall be given into his hand until a time and times and the dividing of time." *Daniel 7:25*

"And He said unto them, Come ye yourselves apart into a desert place, and rest a while: for there were many coming and going, and they had no leisure so much as to eat. And they departed into a desert place by ship privately." *Mark 6:31-32*

"And let us not be weary in well doing: for in due season we shall reap, if we faint not." *Galatians 6:9*

"You Cannot Give Away What You Have Not Yet Received."

-MIKE MURDOCK

READ THE BIBLE THROUGH IN ONE YEAR: Numbers 19-21

Business

February 12

"They that go down to the sea in ships, that do business in great waters; These see the works of the Lord, and His wonders in the deep." *Psalm 107:23-24*

"Seest thou a man diligent in his business? he shall stand before kings; he shall not stand before mean men."
Proverbs 22:29

"Thus saith the Lord, thy Redeemer, the Holy One of Israel; I am the Lord thy God which teacheth thee to profit, which leadeth thee by the way that thou shouldest go." *Isaiah 48:17*

"And he said unto them, How is it that ye sought me? wist ye not that I must be about my Father's business?"
Luke 2:49

"Not slothful in business." *Romans 12:11*

"And that ye study to be quiet, and to do your own business, and to work with your own hands, as we commanded you." *1 Thessalonians 4:11*

"Business Is Simply Solving A Problem For An Agreed Reward."

-MIKE MURDOCK

READ THE BIBLE THROUGH IN ONE YEAR: Numbers 22-24

Busyness

February 13

"Be still, and know that I am God: I will be exalted among the heathen, I will be exalted in the earth."
Psalm 46:10

"Better is an handful with quietness, than both the hands full with travail and vexation of spirit."
Ecclesiastes 4:6

"And He said unto them, Come ye yourselves apart into a desert place, and rest a while: for there were many coming and going, and they had no leisure so much as to eat. And they departed into a desert place by ship privately." *Mark 6:31-32*

"And Jesus answered and said unto her, Martha, Martha, thou art careful and troubled about many things: But one thing is needful: and Mary hath chosen that good part, which shall not be taken away from her." *Luke 10:41-42*

"There remaineth therefore a rest to the people of God. For he that is entered into his rest, he also hath ceased from his own works, as God did from his. Let us labour therefore to enter into that rest, lest any man fall after the same example of unbelief." *Hebrews 4:9-11*

"The Command To Rest Is Equal To The Command To Work."

-MIKE MURDOCK

READ THE BIBLE THROUGH IN ONE YEAR: Numbers 25-27

Calvary

February 14

"Greater love hath no man than this, that a man lay down his life for his friends." *John 15:13*

"And He bearing His cross went forth into a place called the place of a skull, which is called in the Hebrew Golgotha: Where they crucified Him, and two other with Him, on either side one, and Jesus in the midst. And Pilate wrote a title, and put it on the cross. And the writing was, JESUS OF NAZARETH THE KING OF THE JEWS." *John 19:17-19*

"For the preaching of the cross is to them that perish foolishness; but unto us which are saved it is the power of God." *1 Corinthians 1:18*

"But we preach Christ crucified, unto the Jews a stumblingblock, and unto the Greeks foolishness; But unto them which are called, both Jews and Greeks, Christ the power of God, and the Wisdom of God."
1 Corinthians 1:23-24

"For I determined not to know any thing among you, save Jesus Christ, and Him crucified." *1 Corinthians 2:2*

"Calvary Created A Debt That Atheists Cannot Bear."
-MIKE MURDOCK

READ THE BIBLE THROUGH IN ONE YEAR: Numbers 28-30

Career Success

February 15

"This book of the law shall not depart out of thy mouth; but thou shalt meditate therein day and night, that thou mayest observe to do according to all that is written therein: for then thou shalt make thy way prosperous, and then thou shalt have good success." *Joshua 1:8*

"Let them shout for joy, and be glad, that favour My righteous cause: yea, let them say continually, Let the Lord be magnified, which hath pleasure in the prosperity of His servant." *Psalm 35:27*

"Without counsel purposes are disappointed: but in the multitude of counsellors they are established."
Proverbs 15:22

"Thus saith the Lord, thy Redeemer, the Holy One of Israel; I am the Lord thy God which teacheth thee to profit, which leadeth thee by the way that thou shouldest go." *Isaiah 48:17*

"If any of you lack Wisdom, let him ask of God, that giveth to all men liberally, and upbraideth not; and it shall be given him." *James 1:5*

"You Will Only Succeed With That Which Becomes An Obsession."

-MIKE MURDOCK

READ THE BIBLE THROUGH IN ONE YEAR: Numbers 31-35

Change

February 16

"And I will restore to you the years that the locust hath eaten, the cankerworm, and the caterpillar, and the palmerworm, My great army which I sent among you."
Joel 2:25

"And as He prayed, the fashion of His countenance was altered, and His raiment was white and glistering."
Luke 9:29

"Behold, I shew you a mystery; We shall not all sleep, but we shall all be changed, In a moment, in the twinkling of an eye, at the last trump: for the trumpet shall sound, and the dead shall be raised incorruptible, and we shall be changed." *1 Corinthians 15:51-52*

"Therefore if any man be in Christ, he is a new creature: old things are passed away; behold, all things are become new." *2 Corinthians 5:17*

"And have put on the new man, which is renewed in knowledge after the image of Him that created him."
Colossians 3:10

"Change Is Always Proportionate To Your Knowledge."

-MIKE MURDOCK

READ THE BIBLE THROUGH IN ONE YEAR: Numbers 36-Deuteronomy 2

Character

February 17

"There is none greater in this house than I; neither hath he kept back any thing from me but thee, because thou art his wife: how then can I do this great wickedness, and sin against God?" *Genesis 39:9*

"Withhold not good from them to whom it is due, when it is in the power of thine hand to do it." *Proverbs 3:27*

"For nothing is secret, that shall not be made manifest; neither any thing hid, that shall not be known and come abroad." *Luke 8:17*

"Neither is there any creature that is not manifest in His sight: but all things are naked and opened unto the eyes of Him with Whom we have to do." *Hebrews 4:13*

"But be ye doers of the word, and not hearers only, deceiving your own selves." *James 1:22*

"For in many things we offend all. If any man offend not in word, the same is a perfect man, and able also to bridle the whole body." *James 3:2*

"What You Are Will Outlast What Men Say You Are."
-MIKE MURDOCK

READ THE BIBLE THROUGH IN ONE YEAR: Deuteronomy 3-5

Chastisement of God

February 18

"Behold, happy is the man whom God correcteth: therefore despise not thou the chastening of the Almighty." *Job 5:17*

"Blessed is the man whom Thou chastenest, O Lord, and teachest him out of Thy law." *Psalm 94:12*

"My son, despise not the chastening of the Lord; neither be weary of His correction." *Proverbs 3:11*

"For whom the Lord loveth He chasteneth, and scourgeth every son whom He receiveth. If ye endure chastening, God dealeth with you as with sons; for what son is he whom the father chasteneth not?"
Hebrews 12:6-7

"For they verily for a few days chastened us after their own pleasure; but He for our profit, that we might be partakers of His holiness. Now no chastening for the present seemeth to be joyous, but grievous: nevertheless afterward it yieldeth the peaceable fruit of righteousness unto them which are exercised thereby."
Hebrews 12:10-11

"The Proof of Love Is The Willingness To Correct."

-MIKE MURDOCK

READ THE BIBLE THROUGH IN ONE YEAR: Deuteronomy 6-8

Cheerfulness — February 19

"Happy is the man that findeth Wisdom, and the man that getteth understanding." *Proverbs 3:13*

"A merry heart maketh a cheerful countenance: but by sorrow of the heart the spirit is broken." *Proverbs 15:13*

"A merry heart doeth good like a medicine: but a broken spirit drieth the bones." *Proverbs 17:22*

"These things have I spoken unto you, that My joy might remain in you, and that your joy might be full." *John 15:11*

"Every man according as he purposeth in his heart, so let him give; not grudgingly, or of necessity: for God loveth a cheerful giver." *2 Corinthians 9:7*

"My brethren, count it all joy when ye fall into divers temptations." *James 1:2*

"Is any among you afflicted? let him pray. Is any merry? let him sing psalms." *James 5:13*

"There Is Something More Important Than Appearance—The Way Someone Feels In Your Presence."

-MIKE MURDOCK

READ THE BIBLE THROUGH IN ONE YEAR: Deuteronomy 9-11

Children February 20

"And these words, which I command thee this day, shall be in thine heart: And thou shalt teach them diligently unto thy children, and shalt talk of them when thou sittest in thine house, and when thou walkest by the way, and when thou liest down, and when thou risest up."

Deuteronomy 6:6-7

"Lo, children are an heritage of the Lord: and the fruit of the womb is his reward. As arrows are in the hand of a mighty man; so are children of the youth. Happy is the man that hath his quiver full of them: they shall not be ashamed, but they shall speak with the enemies in the gate." *Psalm 127:3-5*

"Train up a child in the way he should go: and when he is old, he will not depart from it." *Proverbs 22:6*

"Children, obey your parents in the Lord: for this is right. Honour thy father and mother; which is the first commandment with promise; That it may be well with thee, and thou mayest live long on the earth. And, ye fathers, provoke not your children to wrath: but bring them up in the nurture and admonition of the Lord."

Ephesians 6:1-4

"Your Reaction To The Word of God Determines God's Reaction To Your Children."

-MIKE MURDOCK

READ THE BIBLE THROUGH IN ONE YEAR: Deuteronomy 12-14

Choices

February 21

"I call Heaven and earth to record this day against you, that I have set before you life and death, blessing and cursing: therefore choose life, that both thou and thy seed may live." *Deuteronomy 30:19*

"And if it seem evil unto you to serve the Lord, choose you this day whom ye will serve; whether the gods which your fathers served that were on the other side of the flood, or the gods of the Amorites, in whose land ye dwell: but as for me and my house, we will serve the Lord." *Joshua 24:15*

"Let us choose to us judgment: let us know among ourselves what is good." *Job 34:4*

"If ye be willing and obedient, ye shall eat the good of the land: But if ye refuse and rebel, ye shall be devoured with the sword: for the mouth of the Lord hath spoken it."
Isaiah 1:19-20

"And thine ears shall hear a word behind thee, saying, This is the way, walk ye in it, when ye turn to the right hand, and when ye turn to the left." *Isaiah 30:21*

"Choice Is The Divine Paint Brush God Gives Every Man To Design His Own World."

-MIKE MURDOCK

READ THE BIBLE THROUGH IN ONE YEAR: Deuteronomy 15-17

Christmas February 22

"Now the birth of Jesus Christ was on this wise: When as His mother Mary was espoused to Joseph, before they came together, she was found with child of the Holy Ghost...Joseph, thou son of David, fear not to take unto thee Mary thy wife: for that which is conceived in her is of the Holy Ghost." *Matthew 1:18, 20*

"And she brought forth her firstborn son, and wrapped Him in swaddling clothes, and laid Him in a manger; because there was no room for them in the inn. And the angel said unto them, Fear not: for, behold, I bring you good tidings of great joy, which shall be to all people. For unto you is born this day in the city of David a Saviour, which is Christ the Lord. And this shall be a sign unto you; Ye shall find the babe wrapped in swaddling clothes, lying in a manger. And suddenly there was with the angel a multitude of the Heavenly host praising God, and saying, Glory to God in the highest, and on earth peace, good will toward men. And they came with haste, and found Mary, and Joseph, and the babe lying in a manger." *Luke 2:7, 10-14, 16*

"For God so loved the world, that He gave His only begotten Son, that whosoever believeth in Him should not perish, but have everlasting life." *John 3:16*

"God Had A Son But Wanted A Family; He Sowed His Son To Create That Family."

-MIKE MURDOCK

READ THE BIBLE THROUGH IN ONE YEAR: Deuteronomy 18-22

Church

February 23

"And let them make Me a sanctuary; that I may dwell among them." *Exodus 25:8*

"One thing have I desired of the Lord, that will I seek after; that I may dwell in the house of the Lord all the days of my life, to behold the beauty of the Lord, and to enquire in His temple." *Psalm 27:4*

"I was glad when they said unto me, Let us go into the house of the Lord." *Psalm 122:1*

"Keep thy foot when thou goest to the house of God, and be more ready to hear, than to give the sacrifice of fools: for they consider not that they do evil." *Ecclesiastes 5:1*

"For where two or three are gathered together in My name, there am I in the midst of them." *Matthew 18:20*

"Not forsaking the assembling of ourselves together, as the manner of some is; but exhorting one another: and so much the more, as ye see the day approaching."
Hebrews 10:25

"Where You Are Determines What Grows Inside You."
-MIKE MURDOCK

READ THE BIBLE THROUGH IN ONE YEAR: Deuteronomy 23-25

Commitment February 24

"Commit thy way unto the Lord; trust also in Him; and He shall bring it to pass." *Psalm 37:5*

"Commit thy works unto the Lord, and thy thoughts shall be established." *Proverbs 16:3*

"And Jesus said unto him, No man, having put his hand to the plough, and looking back, is fit for the kingdom of God." *Luke 9:62*

"And let us not be weary in well doing: for in due season we shall reap, if we faint not." *Galatians 6:9*

"...this one thing I do, forgetting those things which are behind, and reaching forth unto those things which are before, I press toward the mark for the prize of the high calling of God in Christ Jesus." *Philippians 3:13-14*

"I have fought a good fight, I have finished my course, I have kept the faith." *2 Timothy 4:7*

"The Best Way To Distract A Man With A Goal Is To Give Him Another One."

-MIKE MURDOCK

READ THE BIBLE THROUGH IN ONE YEAR: Deuteronomy 26-28

Compassion — February 25

"But He, being full of compassion, forgave their iniquity, and destroyed them not: yea, many a time turned He His anger away, and did not stir up all His wrath." *Psalm 78:38*

"Can a woman forget her sucking child, that she should not have compassion on the son of her womb? yea, they may forget, yet will I not forget thee."

Isaiah 49:15

"And Jesus, when He came out, saw much people, and was moved with compassion toward them, because they were as sheep not having a shepherd: and He began to teach them many things." *Mark 6:34*

"Finally, be ye all of one mind, having compassion one of another, love as brethren, be pitiful, be courteous."

1 Peter 3:8

"But whoso hath this world's good, and seeth his brother have need, and shutteth up his bowels of compassion from him, how dwelleth the love of God in him?" *1 John 3:17*

"Those Who Unlock Your Compassion Are Those To Whom You Have Been Assigned."

-MIKE MURDOCK

READ THE BIBLE THROUGH IN ONE YEAR: Deuteronomy 29-31

Complaining — February 26

"And Pharaoh said unto Joseph, Forasmuch as God hath shewed thee all this, there is none so discreet and wise as thou art: Thou shalt be over my house, and according unto thy word shall all my people be ruled: only in the throne will I be greater than thou."
Genesis 41:39-40

"What shall we then say to these things? If God be for us, who can be against us?" *Romans 8:31*

"Let no corrupt communication proceed out of your mouth, but that which is good to the use of edifying, that it may minister grace unto the hearers. And grieve not the Holy Spirit of God, whereby ye are sealed unto the day of redemption." *Ephesians 4:29-30*

"Do all things without murmurings and disputings."
Philippians 2:14

"...for I have learned, in whatsoever state I am, therewith to be content." *Philippians 4:11*

"In every thing give thanks: for this is the will of God in Christ Jesus concerning you." *1 Thessalonians 5:18*

"Losers Discuss What They Are Going Through, Champions Discuss What They Are Going To."

-MIKE MURDOCK

READ THE BIBLE THROUGH IN ONE YEAR: Deuteronomy 32-34

Confession February 27

"If My people, which are called by My name, shall humble themselves, and pray, and seek My face, and turn from their wicked ways; then will I hear from Heaven, and will forgive their sin, and will heal their land." *2 Chronicles 7:14*

"Death and life are in the power of the tongue: and they that love it shall eat the fruit thereof." *Proverbs 18:21*

"He that covereth his sins shall not prosper: but whoso confesseth and forsaketh them shall have mercy." *Proverbs 28:13*

"For with the heart man believeth unto righteousness; and with the mouth confession is made unto salvation." *Romans 10:10*

"If we confess our sins, He is faithful and just to forgive us our sins, and to cleanse us from all unrighteousness." *1 John 1:9*

"What You Keep Saying You Eventually Believe."
  -MIKE MURDOCK

READ THE BIBLE THROUGH IN ONE YEAR: Joshua 1-3

Confidentiality — February 28

"And Pharaoh said unto Joseph, Forasmuch as God hath shewed thee all this, there is none so discreet and wise as thou art: Thou shalt be over my house, and according unto thy word shall all my people be ruled: only in the throne will I be greater than thou." *Genesis 41:39-40*

"A good man sheweth favour, and lendeth: he will guide his affairs with discretion." *Psalm 112:5*

"Discretion shall preserve thee, understanding shall keep thee." *Proverbs 2:11*

"Debate thy cause with thy neighbour himself; and discover not a secret to another." *Proverbs 25:9*

"Therefore the prudent shall keep silence in that time; for it is an evil time." *Amos 5:13*

"To be discreet, chaste, keepers at home, good, obedient to their own husbands, that the word of God be not blasphemed." *Titus 2:5*

"Never Discuss Your Problem With Someone Incapable of Solving It."

-MIKE MURDOCK

READ THE BIBLE THROUGH IN ONE YEAR: Joshua 4-6

Conflict

March 1

"For the Lord your God is He that goeth with you, to fight for you against your enemies, to save you."
Deuteronomy 20:4

"Strive not with a man without cause, if he have done thee no harm." *Proverbs 3:30*

"A soft answer turneth away wrath: but grievous words stir up anger." *Proverbs 15:1*

"Can two walk together, except they be agreed?"
Amos 3:3

"We are troubled on every side, yet not distressed; we are perplexed, but not in despair; Persecuted, but not forsaken; cast down, but not destroyed."
2 Corinthians 4:8-9

"Casting all your care upon Him; for He careth for you." *1 Peter 5:7*

"You Can Only Conquer What You Are Willing To Confront."

-MIKE MURDOCK

READ THE BIBLE THROUGH IN ONE YEAR: Joshua 7-11

Confrontation — March 2

"A soft answer turneth away wrath: but grievous words stir up anger." *Proverbs 15:1*

"Therefore if thou bring thy gift to the altar, and there rememberest that thy brother hath ought against thee; Leave there thy gift before the altar, and go thy way; first be reconciled to thy brother, and then come and offer thy gift." *Matthew 5:23-24*

"For I will give you a mouth and Wisdom, which all your adversaries shall not be able to gainsay nor resist." *Luke 21:15*

"If it be possible, as much as lieth in you, live peaceably with all men." *Romans 12:18*

"Rebuke not an elder, but intreat him as a father; and the younger men as brethren; Against an elder receive not an accusation, but before two or three witnesses." *1 Timothy 5:1, 19*

"Them that sin rebuke before all, that others also may fear." *1 Timothy 5:20*

"Wherefore, my beloved brethren, let every man be swift to hear, slow to speak, slow to wrath." *James 1:19*

"You Can Never Correct What You Are Unwilling To Confront."

-MIKE MURDOCK

READ THE BIBLE THROUGH IN ONE YEAR: Joshua 12-14

Confusion

March 3

"In Thee, O Lord, do I put my trust: let me never be put to confusion." *Psalm 71:1*

"Trust in the Lord with all thine heart; and lean not unto thine own understanding. In all thy ways acknowledge Him, and He shall direct thy paths."
Proverbs 3:5-6

"For the Lord God will help me; therefore shall I not be confounded: therefore have I set my face like a flint, and I know that I shall not be ashamed."
Isaiah 50:7

"For God is not the author of confusion, but of peace, as in all churches of the saints." *1 Corinthians 14:33*

"For where envying and strife is, there is confusion and every evil work." *James 3:16*

"He that believeth on Him shall not be confounded."
1 Peter 2:6

"Confusion Is The Proof of Rejected Truth."

-MIKE MURDOCK

READ THE BIBLE THROUGH IN ONE YEAR: Joshua 15-17

Conquering — March 4

"And such as do wickedly against the covenant shall he corrupt by flatteries: but the people that do know their God shall be strong, and do exploits."
Daniel 11:32

"Nay, in all these things we are more than conquerors through Him that loved us." *Romans 8:37*

"...greater is He that is in you, than he that is in the world." *1 John 4:4*

"For whatsoever is born of God overcometh the world: and this is the victory that overcometh the world, even our faith. Who is he that overcometh the world, but he that believeth that Jesus is the Son of God?" *1 John 5:4-5*

"And I saw, and behold a white horse: and he that sat on him had a bow; and a crown was given unto him: and he went forth conquering, and to conquer."
Revelation 6:2

"You Cannot Conquer What You Refuse To Hate."
-MIKE MURDOCK

READ THE BIBLE THROUGH IN ONE YEAR: Joshua 18-20

Conscience March 5

"And herein do I exercise myself, to have always a conscience void of offence toward God, and toward men." *Acts 24:16*

"Now the end of the commandment is charity out of a pure heart, and of a good conscience, and of faith unfeigned." *1 Timothy 1:5*

"Unto the pure all things are pure: but unto them that are defiled and unbelieving is nothing pure; but even their mind and conscience is defiled." *Titus 1:15*

"How much more shall the blood of Christ, Who through the eternal Spirit offered Himself without spot to God, purge your conscience from dead works to serve the living God?" *Hebrews 9:14*

"For this is thankworthy, if a man for conscience toward God endure grief, suffering wrongfully." *1 Peter 2:19*

"Having a good conscience; that, whereas they speak evil of you, as of evildoers, they may be ashamed that falsely accuse your good conversation in Christ."
1 Peter 3:16

"Your Conscience Is The Invisible Reference Within You, Discomforting You When You Break A Divine Rule or Law."

-MIKE MURDOCK

READ THE BIBLE THROUGH IN ONE YEAR: Joshua 21-23

Contentment — March 6

"Great peace have they which love Thy law: and nothing shall offend them." *Psalm 119:165*

"But seek ye first the kingdom of God, and His righteousness; and all these things shall be added unto you. Take therefore no thought for the morrow: for the morrow shall take thought for the things of itself. Sufficient unto the day is the evil thereof."
Matthew 6:33-34

"For I have learned, in whatsoever state I am, therewith to be content." *Philippians 4:11*

"But godliness with contentment is great gain."
1 Timothy 6:6

"And having food and raiment let us be therewith content." *1 Timothy 6:8*

"Let your conversation be without covetousness; and be content with such things as ye have: for He hath said, I will never leave thee, nor forsake thee."
Hebrews 13:5

"Contentment Is The Reward For Being Thankful."
-MIKE MURDOCK

READ THE BIBLE THROUGH IN ONE YEAR: Joshua 24-Judges 2

Conversation Skills

March 7

"Whoso offereth praise glorifieth Me: and to him that ordereth his conversation aright will I shew the salvation of God." *Psalm 50:23*

"The tongue of the wise useth knowledge aright: but the mouth of fools poureth out foolishness." *Proverbs 15:2*

"Death and life are in the power of the tongue: and they that love it shall eat the fruit thereof." *Proverbs 18:21*

"That ye put off concerning the former conversation the old man, which is corrupt according to the deceitful lusts." *Ephesians 4:22*

"Only let your conversation be as it becometh the gospel of Christ." *Philippians 1:27*

"But as He which hath called you is holy, so be ye holy in all manner of conversation." *1 Peter 1:15*

"Who is a wise man and endued with knowledge among you? let him shew out of a good conversation his works with meekness of Wisdom." *James 3:13*

"Those Who Ask The Questions Determine The Quality of The Conversation."

-MIKE MURDOCK

READ THE BIBLE THROUGH IN ONE YEAR: Judges 3-5

Conviction March 8

"Now when Ezra had prayed, and when he had confessed, weeping and casting himself down before the house of God, there assembled unto him out of Israel a very great congregation of men and women and children: for the people wept very sore." *Ezra 10:1*

"And he would fain have filled his belly with the husks that the swine did eat: and no man gave unto him. And when he came to himself, he said, How many hired servants of my father's have bread enough and to spare, and I perish with hunger! I will arise and go to my father, and will say unto him, Father, I have sinned against Heaven, and before thee." *Luke 15:16-18*

"And he fell to the earth, and heard a voice saying unto him, Saul, Saul, why persecutest thou Me? And he said, Who art Thou, Lord? And the Lord said, I am Jesus Whom thou persecutest: it is hard for thee to kick against the pricks. And he trembling and astonished said, Lord, what wilt Thou have me to do? And the Lord said unto him, Arise, and go into the city, and it shall be told thee what thou must do." *Acts 9:4-6*

"What You Hear Determines What You Feel."
-MIKE MURDOCK

READ THE BIBLE THROUGH IN ONE YEAR: Judges 6-10

Correction

March 9

"...rebuke a wise man, and he will love thee."
Proverbs 9:8

"He is in the way of life that keepeth instruction: but he that refuseth reproof erreth." *Proverbs 10:17*

"Poverty and shame shall be to him that refuseth instruction: but he that regardeth reproof shall be honoured." *Proverbs 13:18*

"A fool despiseth his father's instruction: but he that regardeth reproof is prudent. Correction is grievous unto him that forsaketh the way: and he that hateth reproof shall die. The ear that heareth the reproof of life abideth among the wise. He that refuseth instruction despiseth his own soul: but he that heareth reproof getteth understanding." *Proverbs 15:5, 10, 31-32*

"The rod and reproof give Wisdom." *Proverbs 29:15*

"Correct thy son, and he shall give thee rest; yea, he shall give delight unto thy soul." *Proverbs 29:17*

"All scripture is given by inspiration of God, and is profitable for doctrine, for reproof, for correction, for instruction in righteousness." *2 Timothy 3:16*

"The Difference Between The Wise And A Fool...Is Revealed By Their Reaction To Correction."

-MIKE MURDOCK

READ THE BIBLE THROUGH IN ONE YEAR: Judges 11-13

Counseling March 10

"Blessed is the man that walketh not in the counsel of the ungodly, nor standeth in the way of sinners, nor sitteth in the seat of the scornful. But his delight is in the law of the Lord; and in His law doth he meditate day and night. And he shall be like a tree planted by the rivers of water, that bringeth forth his fruit in his season; his leaf also shall not wither; and whatsoever he doeth shall prosper." *Psalm 1:1-3*

"Thou shalt guide me with Thy counsel."
Psalm 73:24

"Where no counsel is, the people fall: but in the multitude of counsellors there is safety."
Proverbs 11:14

"Without counsel purposes are disappointed: but in the multitude of counsellors they are established."
Proverbs 15:22

"Woe to the rebellious children, saith the Lord, that take counsel, but not of Me." *Isaiah 30:1*

"You Are Never Responsible For The Pain of Those Who Have Rejected Your Counsel."

-MIKE MURDOCK

READ THE BIBLE THROUGH IN ONE YEAR: Judges 14-16

Courage

March 11

"Be strong and of a good courage, fear not, nor be afraid of them: for the Lord thy God, He it is that doth go with thee; He will not fail thee, nor forsake thee."
Deuteronomy 31:6

"Have not I commanded thee? Be strong and of a good courage; be not afraid, neither be thou dismayed: for the Lord thy God is with thee whithersoever thou goest." *Joshua 1:9*

"Be of good courage, and He shall strengthen your heart, all ye that hope in the Lord." *Psalm 31:24*

"Fear thou not; for I am with thee: be not dismayed; for I am thy God: I will strengthen thee; yea, I will help thee; yea, I will uphold thee with the right hand of My righteousness." *Isaiah 41:10*

"I can do all things through Christ which strengtheneth me." *Philippians 4:13*

"Courage Is Proportionate To Your Passion."

-*MIKE MURDOCK*

READ THE BIBLE THROUGH IN ONE YEAR: Judges 17-19

Covenant

March 12

"Take heed unto yourselves, lest ye forget the covenant of the Lord your God, which He made with you, and make you a graven image, or the likeness of any thing, which the Lord thy God hath forbidden thee. For the Lord thy God is a consuming fire, even a jealous God." *Deuteronomy 4:23-24*

"I have made a covenant with My chosen, I have sworn unto David My servant, My covenant will I not break, nor alter the thing that is gone out of My lips." *Psalm 89:3, 34*

"If thy children will keep My covenant and My testimony that I shall teach them, their children shall also sit upon thy throne for evermore." *Psalm 132:12*

"Verily I say unto you, Whatsoever ye shall bind on earth shall be bound in Heaven: and whatsoever ye shall loose on earth shall be loosed in Heaven. Again I say unto you, That if two of you shall agree on earth as touching any thing that they shall ask, it shall be done for them of My Father which is in Heaven." *Matthew 18:18-19*

"When You Get Involved With God's Dream, He Will Get Involved With Your Dream."

-MIKE MURDOCK

READ THE BIBLE THROUGH IN ONE YEAR: Judges 20-Ruth 1

Covetousness — March 13

"Thou shalt not covet thy neighbour's house, thou shalt not covet thy neighbour's wife, nor his manservant, nor his maidservant, nor his ox, nor his ass, nor any thing that is thy neighbour's."

Exodus 20:17

"Incline my heart unto thy testimonies, and not to covetousness." *Psalm 119:36*

"And he said unto them, Take heed, and beware of covetousness: for a man's life consisteth not in the abundance of the things which he possesseth."

Luke 12:15

"For the love of money is the root of all evil: which while some coveted after, they have erred from the faith, and pierced themselves through with many sorrows." *1 Timothy 6:10*

"Let your conversation be without covetousness; and be content with such things as ye have: for he hath said, I will never leave thee, nor forsake thee."

Hebrews 13:5

"Covetousness Is The Pursuit of Something That You Have Not Yet Earned."

-MIKE MURDOCK

READ THE BIBLE THROUGH IN ONE YEAR: Ruth 2-4

Creativity

March 14

"I will praise Thee; for I am fearfully and wonderfully made: marvellous are Thy works; and that my soul knoweth right well. My substance was not hid from Thee, when I was made in secret, and curiously wrought in the lowest parts of the earth." *Psalm 139:14-15*

"Trust in the Lord with all thine heart; and lean not unto thine own understanding. In all thy ways acknowledge Him, and He shall direct thy paths." *Proverbs 3:5-6*

"I Wisdom dwell with prudence, and find out knowledge of witty inventions." *Proverbs 8:12*

"Sing unto the Lord a new song, and His praise from the end of the earth, ye that go down to the sea, and all that is therein." *Isaiah 42:10*

"Behold, I will do a new thing; now it shall spring forth; shall ye not know it?" *Isaiah 43:19*

"...I have shewed thee new things from this time, even hidden things, and thou didst not know them." *Isaiah 48:6*

"God Has Never Stopped Creating;
He Merely Rested On The Seventh Day."

-MIKE MURDOCK

READ THE BIBLE THROUGH IN ONE YEAR: 1 Samuel 1-3

Credibility

March 15

"And the Lord said unto Moses, Lo, I come unto thee in a thick cloud, that the people may hear when I speak with thee, and believe thee for ever." *Exodus 19:9*

"Believe in the Lord your God, so shall ye be established; believe His prophets, so shall ye prosper."
2 Chronicles 20:20

"A good name is rather to be chosen than great riches, and loving favour rather than silver and gold."
Proverbs 22:1

"Let your light so shine before men, that they may see your good works, and glorify your Father which is in Heaven." *Matthew 5:16*

"But I have greater witness than that of John: for the works which the Father hath given Me to finish, the same works that I do, bear witness of Me, that the Father hath sent Me." *John 5:36*

"Believe Me that I am in the Father, and the Father in Me: or else believe Me for the very works' sake."
John 14:11

"What You Are Will Outlast What Men Think You Are."

-MIKE MURDOCK

READ THE BIBLE THROUGH IN ONE YEAR: 1 Samuel 4-8

Crisis March 16

"Yea, though I walk through the valley of the shadow of death, I will fear no evil: for Thou art with me; Thy rod and Thy staff they comfort me." *Psalm 23:4*

"For in the time of trouble He shall hide me in His pavilion: in the secret of His tabernacle shall He hide me; He shall set me up upon a rock." *Psalm 27:5*

"God is our refuge and strength, a very present help in trouble. Therefore will not we fear, though the earth be removed, and though the mountains be carried into the midst of the sea; Though the waters thereof roar and be troubled, though the mountains shake with the swelling thereof." *Psalm 46:1-3*

"The Lord is on my side; I will not fear: what can man do unto me?" *Psalm 118:6*

"When thou passest through the waters, I will be with thee; and through the rivers, they shall not overflow thee: when thou walkest through the fire, thou shalt not be burned; neither shall the flame kindle upon thee."
Isaiah 43:2

"Crisis Always Occurs At The Curve of Change."
-*MIKE MURDOCK*

READ THE BIBLE THROUGH IN ONE YEAR: 1 Samuel 9-11

Criticism

March 17

"Thou shalt hide them in the secret of Thy presence from the pride of man: Thou shalt keep them secretly in a pavilion from the strife of tongues." *Psalm 31:20*

"My tongue also shall talk of Thy righteousness all the day long: for they are confounded, for they are brought unto shame, that seek my hurt." *Psalm 71:24*

"The Lord is on my side; I will not fear: what can man do unto me?" *Psalm 118:6*

"There is that speaketh like the piercings of a sword: but the tongue of the wise is health." *Proverbs 12:18*

"A soft answer turneth away wrath: but grievous words stir up anger." *Proverbs 15:1*

"Blessed are ye, when men shall revile you, and persecute you, and shall say all manner of evil against you falsely, for My sake." *Matthew 5:11*

"Never Spend More Time On A Critic Than You Would Give To A Friend."

-MIKE MURDOCK

READ THE BIBLE THROUGH IN ONE YEAR: 1 Samuel 12-14

Crucifixion of Jesus

March 18

"Saying, The Son of man must be delivered into the hands of sinful men, and be crucified, and the third day rise again." *Luke 24:7*

"And I, if I be lifted up from the earth, will draw all men unto Me." *John 12:32*

"And He bearing His cross went forth into a place called the place of a skull, which is called in the Hebrew Golgotha: Where they crucified Him, and two other with Him, on either side one, and Jesus in the midst. And Pilate wrote a title, and put it on the cross. And the writing was, JESUS OF NAZARETH THE KING OF THE JEWS. This title then read many of the Jews: for the place where Jesus was crucified was nigh to the city: and it was written in Hebrew, and Greek, and Latin." *John 19:17-20*

"Much more then, being now justified by His blood, we shall be saved from wrath through Him." *Romans 5:9*

"And almost all things are by the law purged with blood; and without shedding of blood is no remission." *Hebrews 9:22*

"The Proof of Love Is The Desire To Give."

-MIKE MURDOCK

READ THE BIBLE THROUGH IN ONE YEAR: 1 Samuel 15-17

Dangerous Relationships

March 19

"Go from the presence of a foolish man, when thou perceivest not in him the lips of knowledge."

Proverbs 14:7

"Where no wood is, there the fire goeth out: so where there is no talebearer, the strife ceaseth." *Proverbs 26:20*

"Be ye not unequally yoked together with unbelievers: for what fellowship hath righteousness with unrighteousness? and what communion hath light with darkness?" *2 Corinthians 6:14*

"And have no fellowship with the unfruitful works of darkness, but rather reprove them." *Ephesians 5:11*

"Perverse disputings of men of corrupt minds, and destitute of the truth, supposing that gain is godliness: from such withdraw thyself." *1 Timothy 6:5*

"Every Strong Relationship In Your Life Is A Miracle or A Mistake."

-MIKE MURDOCK

READ THE BIBLE THROUGH IN ONE YEAR: 1 Samuel 18-20

Dating

March 20

"Who can find a virtuous woman? for her price is far above rubies." *Proverbs 31:10*

"Two are better than one; because they have a good reward for their labour. For if they fall, the one will lift up his fellow: but woe to him that is alone when he falleth; for he hath not another to help him up. Again, if two lie together, then they have heat: but how can one be warm alone? And if one prevail against him, two shall withstand him; and a threefold cord is not quickly broken." *Ecclesiastes 4:9-12*

"Can two walk together, except they be agreed?"
Amos 3:3

"Neither yield ye your members as instruments of unrighteousness unto sin: but yield yourselves unto God, as those that are alive from the dead, and your members as instruments of righteousness unto God."
Romans 6:13

"Time Will Expose What Interrogation Cannot."
-*MIKE MURDOCK*

READ THE BIBLE THROUGH IN ONE YEAR: 1 Samuel 21-23

Deadlines

March 21

"To every thing there is a season, and a time to every purpose under the Heaven." *Ecclesiastes 3:1*

"Lest haply, after he hath laid the foundation and is not able to finish it, all that behold it begin to mock him, Saying, This man began to build, and was not able to finish." *Luke 14:29-30*

"Jesus saith unto them, My meat is to do the will of Him that sent Me, and to finish His work." *John 4:34*

"For He will finish the work, and cut it short in righteousness: because a short work will the Lord make upon the earth." *Romans 9:28*

"Redeeming the time, because the days are evil."

Ephesians 5:16

"Brethren, I count not myself to have apprehended: but this one thing I do, forgetting those things which are behind, and reaching forth unto those things which are before." *Philippians 3:13*

"Do thy diligence to come shortly unto me."

2 Timothy 4:9

"What You Finish Is More Important Than What You Begin."

-MIKE MURDOCK

READ THE BIBLE THROUGH IN ONE YEAR: 1 Samuel 24-26

Death March 22

"Yea, though I walk through the valley of the shadow of death, I will fear no evil: for Thou art with me; Thy rod and Thy staff they comfort me." *Psalm 23:4*

"Precious in the sight of the Lord is the death of His saints." *Psalm 116:15*

"There is no man that hath power over the spirit to retain the spirit." *Ecclesiastes 8:8*

"If in this life only we have hope in Christ, we are of all men most miserable." *1 Corinthians 15:19*

"The last enemy that shall be destroyed is death. So when this corruptible shall have put on incorruption, and this mortal shall have put on immortality, then shall be brought to pass the saying that is written, Death is swallowed up in victory. O death, where is thy sting? O grave, where is thy victory?" *1 Corinthians 15:26, 54-55*

"We are confident, I say, and willing rather to be absent from the body, and to be present with the Lord." *2 Corinthians 5:8*

"Death For The Believer Is Simply The End of Pain."
-MIKE MURDOCK

READ THE BIBLE THROUGH IN ONE YEAR: 1 Samuel 27-31

Debt

March 23

"For the Lord thy God blesseth thee, as He promised thee: and thou shalt lend unto many nations, but thou shalt not borrow; and thou shalt reign over many nations, but they shall not reign over thee."

Deuteronomy 15:6

"The Lord shall open unto thee His good treasure, the Heaven to give the rain unto thy land in His season, and to bless all the work of thine hand: and thou shalt lend unto many nations, and thou shalt not borrow."

Deuteronomy 28:12

"The wicked borroweth, and payeth not again: but the righteous sheweth mercy, and giveth." *Psalm 37:21*

"The rich ruleth over the poor, and the borrower is servant to the lender." *Proverbs 22:7*

"Owe no man any thing, but to love one another."

Romans 13:8

"But my God shall supply all your need according to His riches in glory by Christ Jesus." *Philippians 4:19*

"Beloved, I wish above all things that thou mayest prosper and be in health, even as thy soul prospereth."

3 John 1:2

"Debt Is Birthed By A Spirit That Wants A Harvest It Has Not Yet Earned."

-MIKE MURDOCK

READ THE BIBLE THROUGH IN ONE YEAR: 2 Samuel 1-3

Deception

March 24

"And Jesus answered and said unto them, Take heed that no man deceive you." *Matthew 24:4*

"For there is nothing covered, that shall not be revealed; neither hid, that shall not be known." *Luke 12:2*

"Let no man deceive you with vain words: for because of these things cometh the wrath of God upon the children of disobedience." *Ephesians 5:6*

"For there are many unruly and vain talkers and deceivers, specially they of the circumcision." *Titus 1:10*

"Neither is there any creature that is not manifest in His sight: but all things are naked and opened unto the eyes of Him with Whom we have to do." *Hebrews 4:13*

"And the great dragon was cast out, that old serpent, called the devil, and satan, which deceiveth the whole world: he was cast out into the earth, and his angels were cast out with him." *Revelation 12:9*

"Patience Is The Weapon That Forces Deception To Reveal Itself."

-MIKE MURDOCK

READ THE BIBLE THROUGH IN ONE YEAR: 2 Samuel 4-6

Decision For Christ

March 25

"I call Heaven and earth to record this day against you, that I have set before you life and death, blessing and cursing: therefore choose life, that both thou and thy seed may live." *Deuteronomy 30:19*

"Let us hear the conclusion of the whole matter: Fear God, and keep His commandments: for this is the whole duty of man. For God shall bring every work into judgment, with every secret thing, whether it be good, or whether it be evil." *Ecclesiastes 12:13-14*

"For all have sinned, and come short of the glory of God." *Romans 3:23*

"For the wages of sin is death; but the gift of God is eternal life through Jesus Christ our Lord." *Romans 6:23*

"That if thou shalt confess with thy mouth the Lord Jesus, and shalt believe in thine heart that God hath raised Him from the dead, thou shalt be saved. For with the heart man believeth unto righteousness; and with the mouth confession is made unto salvation."
Romans 10:9-10

"When You Ignore God, You Schedule A Tragedy."
-MIKE MURDOCK

READ THE BIBLE THROUGH IN ONE YEAR: 2 Samuel 7-9

Decision-Making

March 26

"Blessed is the man that walketh not in the counsel of the ungodly, nor standeth in the way of sinners, nor sitteth in the seat of the scornful." *Psalm 1:1*

"For the Lord giveth Wisdom: out of His mouth cometh knowledge and understanding." *Proverbs 2:6*

"Trust in the Lord with all thine heart; and lean not unto thine own understanding. In all thy ways acknowledge Him, and He shall direct thy paths." *Proverbs 3:5-6*

"Where no counsel is, the people fall: but in the multitude of counsellors there is safety." *Proverbs 11:14*

"And thine ears shall hear a word behind thee, saying, This is the way, walk ye in it, when ye turn to the right hand, and when ye turn to the left." *Isaiah 30:21*

"This I say then, Walk in the Spirit, and ye shall not fulfil the lust of the flesh." *Galatians 5:16*

"As we have therefore opportunity, let us do good unto all men, especially unto them who are of the household of faith." *Galatians 6:10*

"Champions Make Decisions That Create *The Future* They Desire, While Losers Make Decisions That Create *The Present* They Desire."

-MIKE MURDOCK

READ THE BIBLE THROUGH IN ONE YEAR: 2 Samuel 10-12

Delegation March 27

"Heal the sick, cleanse the lepers, raise the dead, cast out devils: freely ye have received, freely give."

Matthew 10:8

"His lord said unto him, Well done, thou good and faithful servant: thou hast been faithful over a few things, I will make thee ruler over many things: enter thou into the joy of thy lord." *Matthew 25:21*

"And if ye have not been faithful in that which is another man's, who shall give you that which is your own?" *Luke 16:12*

"And the things that thou hast heard of Me among many witnesses, the same commit thou to faithful men, who shall be able to teach others also."

2 Timothy 2:2

"Wherefore, holy brethren, partakers of the Heavenly calling, consider the Apostle and High Priest of our profession, Christ Jesus; Who was faithful to Him that appointed him, as also Moses was faithful in all his house. For this man was counted worthy of more glory than Moses, inasmuch as he who hath builded the house hath more honour than the house."

Hebrews 3:1-3

"Delegation Is Permitting Others To Create A Success Experience For Themselves."

-MIKE MURDOCK

READ THE BIBLE THROUGH IN ONE YEAR: 2 Samuel 13-15

Deliverance — March 28

"Bow down Thine ear to me; deliver me speedily: be Thou my strong rock, for an house of defence to save me." *Psalm 31:2*

"Thou art my hiding place; Thou shalt preserve me from trouble; Thou shalt compass me about with songs of deliverance." *Psalm 32:7*

"I sought the Lord, and He heard me, and delivered me from all my fears." *Psalm 34:4*

"...but transgressors shall be taken in their own naughtiness." *Proverbs 11:6*

"And it shall come to pass, that whosoever shall call on the name of the Lord shall be delivered." *Joel 2:32*

"And ye shall know the truth, and the truth shall make you free." *John 8:32*

"Now the Lord is that Spirit: and where the Spirit of the Lord is, there is liberty." *2 Corinthians 3:17*

"Who hath delivered us from the power of darkness, and hath translated us into the kingdom of his dear Son." *Colossians 1:13*

"What You Cannot Hate, You Cannot Conquer."

-MIKE MURDOCK

READ THE BIBLE THROUGH IN ONE YEAR: 2 Samuel 16-18

Demon Spirits

March 29

"And it came to pass, when the evil spirit from God was upon Saul, that David took an harp, and played with his hand: so Saul was refreshed, and was well, and the evil spirit departed from him." *1 Samuel 16:23*

"When the even was come, they brought unto Him many that were possessed with devils: and He cast out the spirits with His word, and healed all that were sick."

Matthew 8:16

"...there was a man, which had a spirit of an unclean devil, and cried out with a loud voice, Saying, Let us alone; what have we to do with Thee, Thou Jesus of Nazareth? art Thou come to destroy us? I know Thee who Thou art; the Holy One of God. And Jesus rebuked him, saying, Hold thy peace, and come out of him. And when the devil had thrown him in the midst, he came out of him, and hurt him not." *Luke 4:33-35*

"Resist the devil, and he will flee from you." *James 4:7*

"Ye are of God, little children, and have overcome them: because greater is He that is in you, than he that is in the world." *1 John 4:4*

"Anything Good Is Hated By Everything Evil."

-MIKE MURDOCK

READ THE BIBLE THROUGH IN ONE YEAR: 2 Samuel 19-23

Dependability — March 30

"God is not a man, that He should lie; neither the son of man, that He should repent: hath He said, and shall He not do it? or hath He spoken, and shall He not make it good?" *Numbers 23:19*

"Most men will proclaim every one his own goodness: but a faithful man who can find?" *Proverbs 20:6*

"Seest thou a man diligent in his business? he shall stand before kings; he shall not stand before mean men." *Proverbs 22:29*

"Confidence in an unfaithful man in time of trouble is like a broken tooth, and a foot out of joint." *Proverbs 25:19*

"His lord said unto him, Well done, thou good and faithful servant: thou hast been faithful over a few things, I will make thee ruler over many things: enter thou into the joy of thy lord." *Matthew 25:21*

"Moreover it is required in stewards, that a man be found faithful." *1 Corinthians 4:2*

"And the things that thou hast heard of Me among many witnesses, the same commit thou to faithful men, who shall be able to teach others also." *2 Timothy 2:2*

"Dependability Is Knowing That The First Instruction Will Never Require Follow-Up."

-MIKE MURDOCK

READ THE BIBLE THROUGH IN ONE YEAR: 2 Samuel 24-1 Kings 2

Depression — March 31

"And it came to pass, when the evil spirit from God was upon Saul, that David took an harp, and played with his hand: so Saul was refreshed, and was well, and the evil spirit departed from him."
1 Samuel 16:23

"...in Thy presence is fulness of joy; at Thy right hand there are pleasures for evermore." *Psalm 16:11*

"Weeping may endure for a night, but joy cometh in the morning." *Psalm 30:5*

"Hope deferred maketh the heart sick: but when the desire cometh, it is a tree of life." *Proverbs 13:12*

"He healeth the broken in heart, and bindeth up their wounds." *Psalm 147:3*

"These things have I spoken unto you, that My joy might remain in you, and that your joy might be full."
John 15:11

"Your Present *Focus* Is Creating Your Present *Feelings*."

-MIKE MURDOCK

READ THE BIBLE THROUGH IN ONE YEAR: 1 Kings 3-5

Desires

April 1

"Delight thyself also in the Lord; and He shall give thee the desires of thine heart." *Psalm 37:4*

"Lord, all my desire is before Thee; and my groaning is not hid from Thee." *Psalm 38:9*

"...but the desire of the righteous shall be granted." *Proverbs 10:24*

"Hope deferred maketh the heart sick: but when the desire cometh, it is a tree of life." *Proverbs 13:12*

"The desire accomplished is sweet to the soul." *Proverbs 13:19*

"...What things soever ye desire, when ye pray, believe that ye receive them, and ye shall have them." *Mark 11:24*

"And whatsoever we ask, we receive of Him, because we keep His commandments, and do those things that are pleasing in His sight." *1 John 3:22*

And if we know that He hear us, whatsoever we ask, we know that we have the petitions that we desired of Him." *1 John 5:15*

"The Proof of Desire Is Pursuit."

-MIKE MURDOCK

READ THE BIBLE THROUGH IN ONE YEAR: 1 Kings 6-8

Determination — April 2

"If thou faint in the day of adversity, thy strength is small." *Proverbs 24:10*

"But they that wait upon the Lord shall renew their strength; they shall mount up with wings as eagles; they shall run, and not be weary; and they shall walk, and not faint." *Isaiah 40:31*

"And ye shall be hated of all men for My name's sake: but he that endureth to the end shall be saved." *Matthew 10:22*

"And Jesus said unto him, No man, having put his hand to the plough, and looking back, is fit for the kingdom of God." *Luke 9:62*

"...men ought always to pray, and not to faint." *Luke 18:1*

"And let us not be weary in well doing: for in due season we shall reap, if we faint not." *Galatians 6:9*

"Champions Are Willing To Do Things They Hate To Create Something Else They Love."

-MIKE MURDOCK

READ THE BIBLE THROUGH IN ONE YEAR: 1 Kings 9-11

Diligence

April 3

"He becometh poor that dealeth with a slack hand: but the hand of the diligent maketh rich. He that gathereth in summer is a wise son: but he that sleepeth in harvest is a son that causeth shame." *Proverbs 10:4-5*

"The hand of the diligent shall bear rule:...The substance of a diligent man is precious."
Proverbs 12:24, 27

"The soul of the sluggard desireth, and hath nothing: but the soul of the diligent shall be made fat."
Proverbs 13:4

"Seest thou a man diligent in his business? he shall stand before kings; he shall not stand before mean men." *Proverbs 22:29*

"Whatsoever thy hand findeth to do, do it with thy might." *Ecclesiastes 9:10*

"Or he that exhorteth, on exhortation: he that giveth, let him do it with simplicity; he that ruleth, with diligence; he that sheweth mercy, with cheerfulness."
Romans 12:8

"Diligence Is Speedy Attention To An Assigned Task."
-*MIKE MURDOCK*

READ THE BIBLE THROUGH IN ONE YEAR: 1 Kings 12-14

Diplomacy   April 4

"A soft answer turneth away wrath: but grievous words stir up anger."   *Proverbs 15:1*

"A wholesome tongue is a tree of life: but perverseness therein is a breach in the spirit."   *Proverbs 15:4*

"He that answereth a matter before he heareth it, it is folly and shame unto him. Death and life are in the power of the tongue: and they that love it shall eat the fruit thereof."   *Proverbs 18:13, 21*

"By long forbearing is a prince persuaded, and a soft tongue breaketh the bone."   *Proverbs 25:15*

"A fool uttereth all his mind: but a wise man keepeth it in till afterwards."   *Proverbs 29:11*

"Now we exhort you, brethren, warn them that are unruly, comfort the feebleminded, support the weak, be patient toward all men."   *1 Thessalonians 5:14*

"What You Respect Will Come Toward You."
                                    -MIKE MURDOCK

READ THE BIBLE THROUGH IN ONE YEAR: 1 Kings 15-17

Disappointment — April 5

"Have not I commanded thee? Be strong and of a good courage; be not afraid, neither be thou dismayed: for the Lord thy God is with thee whithersoever thou goest." *Joshua 1:9*

"...weeping may endure for a night, but joy cometh in the morning." *Psalm 30:5*

"I will lift up mine eyes unto the hills, from whence cometh my help. My help cometh from the Lord, which made Heaven and earth." *Psalm 121:1-2*

"Without counsel purposes are disappointed: but in the multitude of counsellors they are established."
Proverbs 15:22

"And we know that all things work together for good to them that love God, to them who are the called according to His purpose. What shall we then say to these things? If God be for us, who can be against us?" *Romans 8:28, 31*

"And let us not be weary in well doing: for in due season we shall reap, if we faint not." *Galatians 6:9*

"Nothing Is Ever As Bad As It First Appears."
-MIKE MURDOCK

READ THE BIBLE THROUGH IN ONE YEAR: 1 Kings 18-22

Discipleship — April 6

"And He saith unto them, Follow Me, and I will make you fishers of men. And they straightway left their nets, and followed Him." *Matthew 4:19-20*

"And He said to them all, If any man will come after Me, let him deny himself, and take up his cross daily, and follow Me." *Luke 9:23*

"And Jesus said unto him, No man, having put his hand to the plough, and looking back, is fit for the kingdom of God." *Luke 9:62*

"Then said Jesus to those Jews which believed on Him, If ye continue in My word, then are ye My disciples indeed." *John 8:31*

"By this shall all men know that ye are My disciples, if ye have love one to another." *John 13:35*

"Herein is My Father glorified, that ye bear much fruit; so shall ye be My disciples." *John 15:8*

"The Cost of Discipleship Is The Same For Everyone... *Everything.*"

-MIKE MURDOCK

READ THE BIBLE THROUGH IN ONE YEAR: 2 Kings 1-3

Discipline April 7

"Train up a child in the way he should go: and when he is old, he will not depart from it. Foolishness is bound in the heart of a child; but the rod of correction shall drive it far from him." *Proverbs 22:6, 15*

"O Lord, correct me, but with judgment; not in Thine anger, lest Thou bring me to nothing." *Jeremiah 10:24*

"And He cometh, and findeth them sleeping, and saith unto Peter, Simon, sleepest thou? couldest not thou watch one hour?" *Mark 14:37*

"Let every soul be subject unto the higher powers. For there is no power but of God: the powers that be are ordained of God." *Romans 13:1*

"For if a man know not how to rule his own house, how shall he take care of the church of God?" *1 Timothy 3:5*

"For whom the Lord loveth He chasteneth, and scourgeth every son whom He receiveth. If ye endure chastening, God dealeth with you as with sons; for what son is he whom the father chasteneth not? But if ye be without chastisement, whereof all are partakers, then are ye bastards, and not sons." *Hebrews 12:6-8*

"Behavior Permitted Is Behavior Repeated."
-MIKE MURDOCK

READ THE BIBLE THROUGH IN ONE YEAR: 2 Kings 4-6

Discouragement April 8

"Behold, the Lord thy God hath set the land before thee: go up and possess it, as the Lord God of thy fathers hath said unto thee; fear not, neither be discouraged." *Deuteronomy 1:21*

"My help cometh from the Lord, which made Heaven and earth. He will not suffer thy foot to be moved: He that keepeth thee will not slumber." *Psalm 121:2-3*

"But they that wait upon the Lord shall renew their strength; they shall mount up with wings as eagles; they shall run, and not be weary; and they shall walk, and not faint." *Isaiah 40:31*

"Fear thou not; for I am with thee: be not dismayed; for I am thy God: I will strengthen thee; yea, I will help thee; yea, I will uphold thee with the right hand of My righteousness." *Isaiah 41:10*

"Come unto Me, all ye that labour and are heavy laden, and I will give you rest." *Matthew 11:28*

"Cast not away therefore your confidence, which hath great recompence of reward." *Hebrews 10:35*

"Your Focus Determines Your Feelings."

-MIKE MURDOCK

READ THE BIBLE THROUGH IN ONE YEAR: 2 Kings 7-9

Discretion

April 9

"A good man sheweth favour, and lendeth: he will guide his affairs with discretion." *Psalm 112:5*

"Discretion shall preserve thee, understanding shall keep thee." *Proverbs 2:11*

"That thou mayest regard discretion, and that thy lips may keep knowledge." *Proverbs 5:2*

"As a jewel of gold in a swine's snout, so is a fair woman which is without discretion." *Proverbs 11:22*

"The discretion of a man deferreth his anger; and it is his glory to pass over a transgression." *Proverbs 19:11*

"Whoso keepeth his mouth and his tongue keepeth his soul from troubles." *Proverbs 21:23*

"Seest thou a man that is hasty in his words? there is more hope of a fool than of him." *Proverbs 29:20*

"Wherefore, my beloved brethren, let every man be swift to hear, slow to speak, slow to wrath."

James 1:19

"For in many things we offend all. If any man offend not in word, the same is a perfect man, and able also to bridle the whole body." *James 3:2*

"Never Discuss Your Problem With Someone Who Cannot Solve It."

-MIKE MURDOCK

READ THE BIBLE THROUGH IN ONE YEAR: 2 Kings 10-12

Disloyalty

April 10

"He that worketh deceit shall not dwell within My house: he that telleth lies shall not tarry in My sight."
Psalm 101:7

"A talebearer revealeth secrets: but he that is of a faithful spirit concealeth the matter." *Proverbs 11:13*

"Confidence in an unfaithful man in time of trouble is like a broken tooth, and a foot out of joint."
Proverbs 25:19

"And if ye have not been faithful in that which is another man's, who shall give you that which is your own?" *Luke 16:12*

"And Simon Peter stood and warmed himself. They said therefore unto him, Art not thou also one of His disciples? He denied it, and said, I am not."
John 18:25

"The Proof of Loyalty Is The Unwillingness To Betray."

-MIKE MURDOCK

READ THE BIBLE THROUGH IN ONE YEAR: 2 Kings 13-15

Disobedience April 11

"For rebellion is as the sin of witchcraft, and stubbornness is as iniquity and idolatry. Because thou hast rejected the word of the Lord, He hath also rejected thee from being king." *1 Samuel 15:23*

"If ye be willing and obedient, ye shall eat the good of the land: But if ye refuse and rebel, ye shall be devoured with the sword: for the mouth of the Lord hath spoken it." *Isaiah 1:19-20*

"Therefore thus saith the Lord; Behold, I will cast thee from off the face of the earth: this year thou shalt die, because thou hast taught rebellion against the Lord." *Jeremiah 28:16*

"For as by one man's disobedience many were made sinners, so by the obedience of one shall many be made righteous." *Romans 5:19*

"Let no man deceive you with vain words: for because of these things cometh the wrath of God upon the children of disobedience." *Ephesians 5:6*

"Submit yourselves to every ordinance of man for the Lord's sake: whether it be to the king, as supreme."
1 Peter 2:13

"The Waves of Yesterday's Disobedience Always Splash On The Shores of Today For A Season."

-MIKE MURDOCK

READ THE BIBLE THROUGH IN ONE YEAR: 2 Kings 16-18

Disorder

April 12

"And in those times there was no peace to him that went out, nor to him that came in, but great vexations were upon all the inhabitants of the countries."
2 Chronicles 15:5

"For God is not the author of confusion, but of peace, as in all churches of the saints." *1 Corinthians 14:33*

"Let all things be done decently and in order."
1 Corinthians 14:40

"For we hear that there are some which walk among you disorderly, working not at all, but are busybodies." *2 Thessalonians 3:11*

"For this cause left I thee in Crete, that thou shouldest set in order the things that are wanting, and ordain elders in every city, as I had appointed thee." *Titus 1:5*

"For where envying and strife is, there is confusion and every evil work." *James 3:16*

"Pain Is The Proof of Disorder."

-MIKE MURDOCK

READ THE BIBLE THROUGH IN ONE YEAR: 2 Kings 19-23

Distractions — April 13

"Only be thou strong and very courageous, that thou mayest observe to do according to all the law, which Moses My servant commanded thee: turn not from it to the right hand or to the left, that thou mayest prosper whithersoever thou goest." *Joshua 1:7*

"He shall not be afraid of evil tidings: his heart is fixed, trusting in the Lord." *Psalm 112:7*

"Remember ye not the former things, neither consider the things of old." *Isaiah 43:18*

"And if thy right eye offend thee, pluck it out, and cast it from thee: for it is profitable for thee that one of thy members should perish, and not that thy whole body should be cast into hell." *Matthew 5:29*

"And Jesus said unto him, No man, having put his hand to the plough, and looking back, is fit for the kingdom of God." *Luke 9:62*

"Remember Lot's wife." *Luke 17:32*

"Distractions Only Occur With Your Permission."

-*MIKE MURDOCK*

READ THE BIBLE THROUGH IN ONE YEAR: 2 Kings 24-1 Chronicles 1

Divorce April 14

"Better is it that thou shouldest not vow, than that thou shouldest vow and not pay." *Ecclesiastes 5:5*

"What therefore God hath joined together, let not man put asunder." *Mark 10:9*

"For the woman which hath an husband is bound by the law to her husband so long as he liveth; but if the husband be dead, she is loosed from the law of her husband. So then if, while her husband liveth, she be married to another man, she shall be called an adulteress: but if her husband be dead, she is free from that law; so that she is no adulteress, though she be married to another man." *Romans 7:2-3*

"If it be possible, as much as lieth in you, live peaceably with all men." *Romans 12:18*

"...Let not the wife depart from her husband: But and if she depart, let her remain unmarried, or be reconciled to her husband: and let not the husband put away his wife." *1 Corinthians 7:10-11*

"Those Who Created Yesterday's Pain Do Not Decide Tomorrow's Pleasure."

-MIKE MURDOCK

READ THE BIBLE THROUGH IN ONE YEAR: 1 Chronicles 2-4

Doubts

April 15

"...If thou canst believe, all things are possible to him that believeth. And straightway the father of the child cried out, and said with tears, Lord, I believe; help Thou mine unbelief." *Mark 9:23-24*

"For verily I say unto you, That whosoever shall say unto this mountain, Be thou removed, and be thou cast into the sea; and shall not doubt in his heart, but shall believe that those things which he saith shall come to pass; he shall have whatsoever he saith." *Mark 11:23*

"Afterward He appeared unto the eleven as they sat at meat, and upbraided them with their unbelief and hardness of heart, because they believed not them which had seen Him after He was risen." *Mark 16:14*

"Take heed, brethren, lest there be in any of you an evil heart of unbelief, in departing from the living God. So we see that they could not enter in because of unbelief." *Hebrews 3:12, 19*

"But let him ask in faith, nothing wavering. For he that wavereth is like a wave of the sea driven with the wind and tossed." *James 1:6*

"One Day of Doubt Will Create 365 Days of Pain."
-MIKE MURDOCK

READ THE BIBLE THROUGH IN ONE YEAR: 1 Chronicles 5-7

Dreams — April 16

"For God speaketh once, yea twice, yet man perceiveth it not. In a dream, in a vision of the night, when deep sleep falleth upon men, in slumberings upon the bed; Then He openeth the ears of men, and sealeth their instruction, That He may withdraw man from his purpose, and hide pride from man." *Job 33:14-17*

"Behold, I am against them that prophesy false dreams, saith the Lord, and do tell them, and cause My people to err by their lies, and by their lightness; yet I sent them not, nor commanded them: therefore they shall not profit this people at all, saith the Lord."
Jeremiah 23:32

"For thus saith the Lord of hosts, the God of Israel; Let not your prophets and your diviners, that be in the midst of you, deceive you, neither hearken to your dreams which ye cause to be dreamed." *Jeremiah 29:8*

"And it shall come to pass afterward, that I will pour out My Spirit upon all flesh; and your sons and your daughters shall prophesy, your old men shall dream dreams, your young men shall see visions." *Joel 2:28*

"What You See Determines What You Are Willing To Change."

-MIKE MURDOCK

READ THE BIBLE THROUGH IN ONE YEAR: 1 Chronicles 8-10

Easter

April 17

"In the end of the sabbath, as it began to dawn toward the first day of the week, came Mary Magdalene and the other Mary to see the sepulchre. And, behold, there was a great earthquake: for the angel of the Lord descended from Heaven, and came and rolled back the stone from the door, and sat upon it. His countenance was like lightning, and his raiment white as snow: And for fear of him the keepers did shake, and became as dead men. And the angel answered and said unto the women, Fear not ye: for I know that ye seek Jesus, which was crucified. He is not here: for He is risen, as he said. Come, see the place where the Lord lay. And go quickly, and tell His disciples that He is risen from the dead; and, behold, He goeth before you into Galilee; there shall ye see Him: lo, I have told you. And they departed quickly from the sepulchre with fear and great joy; and did run to bring His disciples word. And as they went to tell His disciples, behold, Jesus met them, saying, All hail. And they came and held Him by the feet, and worshipped Him." *Matthew 28:1-9*

"Jesus said unto her, I am the resurrection, and the life: he that believeth in Me, though he were dead, yet shall he live." *John 11:25*

"God's Only Pain Is To Be Doubted—God's Only Pleasure Is To Be Believed."

-MIKE MURDOCK

READ THE BIBLE THROUGH IN ONE YEAR: 1 Chronicles 11-13

Endurance April 18

"...for the joy of the Lord is your strength."
Nehemiah 8:10

"A wise man is strong; yea, a man of knowledge increaseth strength." *Proverbs 24:5*

"For a just man falleth seven times, and riseth up again." *Proverbs 24:16*

"But they that wait upon the Lord shall renew their strength; they shall mount up with wings as eagles; they shall run, and not be weary; and they shall walk, and not faint." *Isaiah 40:31*

"And ye shall be hated of all men for My name's sake: but he that endureth to the end shall be saved."
Matthew 10:22

"And let us not be weary in well doing: for in due season we shall reap, if we faint not." *Galatians 6:9*

"Blessed is the man that endureth temptation: for when he is tried, he shall receive the crown of life, which the Lord hath promised to them that love Him."
James 1:12

"He that overcometh shall inherit all things; and I will be his God, and he shall be My son." *Revelation 21:7*

"You Have No Right To Anything You Have Not Pursued."

-MIKE MURDOCK

READ THE BIBLE THROUGH IN ONE YEAR: 1 Chronicles 14-16

Enemies

April 19

"But if thou shalt indeed obey his voice, and do all that I speak; then I will be an enemy unto thine enemies, and an adversary unto thine adversaries."
Exodus 23:22

"Thou through Thy commandments hast made me wiser than mine enemies: for they are ever with me."
Psalm 119:98

"But I say unto you, Love your enemies, bless them that curse you, do good to them that hate you, and pray for them which despitefully use you, and persecute you." *Matthew 5:44*

"That we should be saved from our enemies, and from the hand of all that hate us." *Luke 1:71*

"Behold, I give unto you power to tread on serpents and scorpions, and over all the power of the enemy: and nothing shall by any means hurt you." *Luke 10:19*

"The Size of Your Enemy Determines The Size of Your Reward."

-MIKE MURDOCK

READ THE BIBLE THROUGH IN ONE YEAR: 1 Chronicles 17-21

Enthusiasm April 20

"...for this day is holy unto our Lord: neither be ye sorry; for the joy of the Lord is your strength."
Nehemiah 8:10

"Blessed is the people that know the joyful sound: they shall walk. O Lord, in the light of Thy countenance." *Psalm 89:15*

"Serve the Lord with gladness: come before His presence with singing." *Psalm 100:2*

"They that sow in tears shall reap in joy. He that goeth forth and weepeth, bearing precious seed, shall doubtless come again with rejoicing, bringing his sheaves with him." *Psalm 126:5-6*

"A merry heart maketh a cheerful countenance."
Proverbs 15:13

"A man hath joy by the answer of his mouth: and a word spoken in due season, how good is it!"
Proverbs 15:23

"The Atmosphere You Permit Determines The Product You Produce."

-MIKE MURDOCK

READ THE BIBLE THROUGH IN ONE YEAR: 1 Chronicles 22-24

Envy

April 21

"For he had possession of flocks, and possession of herds, and great store of servants: and the Philistines envied him." *Genesis 26:14*

"A sound heart is the life of the flesh: but envy the rottenness of the bones." *Proverbs 14:30*

"Wrath is cruel, and anger is outrageous; but who is able to stand before envy?" *Proverbs 27:4*

"Again, I considered all travail, and every right work, that for this a man is envied of his neighbour. This is also vanity and vexation of spirit." *Ecclesiastes 4:4*

"Being filled with all unrighteousness, fornication, wickedness, covetousness, maliciousness; full of envy, murder, debate, deceit, malignity; whisperers." *Romans 1:29*

"For ye are yet carnal: for whereas there is among you envying, and strife, and divisions, are ye not carnal, and walk as men?" *1 Corinthians 3:3*

"Wherefore laying aside all malice, and all guile, and hypocrisies, and envies, and all evil speakings." *1 Peter 2:1*

"Envy Is When Someone Has Something You Believe Belongs To You."

-MIKE MURDOCK

READ THE BIBLE THROUGH IN ONE YEAR: 1 Chronicles 25-27

Ethics

April 22

"Thou shalt not bear false witness against thy neighbour." *Exodus 20:16*

"Therefore I esteem all Thy precepts concerning all things to be right; and I hate every false way."
Psalm 119:128

"The integrity of the upright shall guide them."
Proverbs 11:3

"A false witness shall not be unpunished, and he that speaketh lies shall perish." *Proverbs 19:9*

"The just man walketh in his integrity: his children are blessed after him." *Proverbs 20:7*

"Recompense to no man evil for evil. Provide things honest in the sight of all men." *Romans 12:17*

"Receive us; we have wronged no man, we have corrupted no man, we have defrauded no man."
2 Corinthians 7:2

"What You Are Is Revealed By What You Do.
What You Do Reveals What You Really Believe."
-MIKE MURDOCK

READ THE BIBLE THROUGH IN ONE YEAR: 1 Chronicles 28-2 Chronicles 1

Etiquette

April 23

"Then Pharaoh sent and called Joseph, and they brought him hastily out of the dungeon: and he shaved himself, and changed his raiment, and came in unto Pharaoh." *Genesis 41:14*

"And put a knife to thy throat, if thou be a man given to appetite." *Proverbs 23:2*

"Put not forth thyself in the presence of the king, and stand not in the place of great men: For better it is that it be said unto thee, Come up hither; than that thou shouldest be put lower in the presence of the prince whom thine eyes have seen." *Proverbs 25:6-7*

"Withdraw thy foot from thy neighbour's house; lest he be weary of thee, and so hate thee."

Proverbs 25:17

"Let all things be done decently and in order."
1 Corinthians 14:40

"Every Environment Requires A Code of Conduct For Entering or Remaining In It."

-MIKE MURDOCK

READ THE BIBLE THROUGH IN ONE YEAR: 2 Chronicles 2-4

Evangelism — April 24

"...and he that winneth souls is wise." *Proverbs 11:30*

"Then saith He unto His disciples, The harvest truly is plenteous, but the labourers are few." *Matthew 9:37*

"Go ye therefore, and teach all nations, baptizing them in the name of the Father, and of the Son, and of the Holy Ghost: Teaching them to observe all things whatsoever I have commanded you: and, lo, I am with you alway, even unto the end of the world. Amen." *Matthew 28:19-20*

"And He said unto them, Go ye into all the world, and preach the gospel to every creature." *Mark 16:15*

"How then shall they call on Him in Whom they have not believed? and how shall they believe in Him of Whom they have not heard? and how shall they hear without a preacher? And how shall they preach, except they be sent? as it is written, How beautiful are the feet of them that preach the gospel of peace, and bring glad tidings of good things!" *Romans 10:14-15*

"Your Understanding of God Determines Your Message To Men."

-MIKE MURDOCK

READ THE BIBLE THROUGH IN ONE YEAR: 2 Chronicles 5-7

Excellence

April 25

"Hear; for I will speak of excellent things; and the opening of my lips shall be right things." *Proverbs 8:6*

"The righteous is more excellent than his neighbour: but the way of the wicked seduceth them."
Proverbs 12:26

"He that hath knowledge spareth his words: and a man of understanding is of an excellent spirit."
Proverbs 17:27

"The north wind driveth away rain: so doth an angry countenance a backbiting tongue." *Proverbs 25:23*

"A faithful man shall abound with blessings: but he that maketh haste to be rich shall not be innocent."
Proverbs 28:20

"Then this Daniel was preferred above the presidents and princes, because an excellent spirit was in him; and the king thought to set him over the whole realm."
Daniel 6:3

"You Will Only Have Significant Success With Something That Is An Obsession."

-MIKE MURDOCK

READ THE BIBLE THROUGH IN ONE YEAR: 2 Chronicles 8-10

Expectation — April 26

"My soul wait thou only upon God; for my expectation is from Him." *Psalm 62:5*

"For she said within herself, If I may but touch His garment, I shall be whole." *Matthew 9:21*

"...If thou canst believe, all things are possible to him that believeth." *Mark 9:23*

"And Peter, fastening his eyes upon him with John, said, Look on us. And he gave heed unto them, expecting to receive something of them. Then Peter said, Silver and gold have I none; but such as I have give I thee: In the name of Jesus Christ of Nazareth rise up and walk." *Acts 3:4-6*

"Cast not away therefore your confidence, which hath great recompence of reward." *Hebrews 10:35*

"Beloved, if our heart condemn us not, then have we confidence toward God. And whatsoever we ask, we receive of Him, because we keep His commandments, and do those things that are pleasing in His sight."
1 John 3:21-22

"The Seasons of Your Life Will Change Every Time You Decide To Use Your Faith."

-MIKE MURDOCK

READ THE BIBLE THROUGH IN ONE YEAR: 2 Chronicles 11-15

Failure

April 27

"Come now, and let us reason together, saith the Lord: though your sins be as scarlet, they shall be as white as snow; though they be red like crimson, they shall be as wool." *Isaiah 1:18*

"Cast thy burden upon the Lord, and He shall sustain thee: He shall never suffer the righteous to be moved." *Psalm 55:22*

"For a just man falleth seven times, and riseth up again: but the wicked shall fall into mischief."
Proverbs 24:16

"And I will restore to you the years that the locust hath eaten, the cankerworm, and the caterpillar, and the palmerworm, My great army which I sent among you." *Joel 2:25*

"Brethren, if a man be overtaken in a fault, ye which are spiritual, restore such an one in the spirit of meekness; considering thyself, lest thou also be tempted. Bear ye one another's burdens, and so fulfil the law of Christ." *Galatians 6:1-2*

"Men Don't Drown By Falling In The Water, But By Staying There."

-MIKE MURDOCK

READ THE BIBLE THROUGH IN ONE YEAR: 2 Chronicles 16-18

Faith

April 28

"And all things, whatsoever ye shall ask in prayer, believing, ye shall receive." *Matthew 21:22*

"Jesus said unto him, If thou canst believe, all things are possible to him that believeth." *Mark 9:23*

"...What things soever ye desire, when ye pray, believe that ye receive them, and ye shall have them."
Mark 11:24

"But what saith it? The word is nigh thee, even in thy mouth, and in thy heart: that is, the word of faith, which we preach." *Romans 10:8*

"So then faith cometh by hearing, and hearing by the word of God." *Romans 10:17*

"For we walk by faith, not by sight." *2 Corinthians 5:7*

"For by grace are ye saved through faith; and that not of yourselves: it is the gift of God." *Ephesians 2:8*

"But without faith it is impossible to please Him: for he that cometh to God must believe that He is, and that He is a rewarder of them that diligently seek Him."
Hebrews 11:6

"God Never Responds To Your Need—He Only Responds To Your Faith."

-MIKE MURDOCK

READ THE BIBLE THROUGH IN ONE YEAR: 2 Chronicles 19-21

Faith-Talk

April 29

"For the eyes of the Lord run to and fro throughout the whole earth, to shew Himself strong in the behalf of them whose heart is perfect toward Him. Herein thou hast done foolishly: therefore from henceforth thou shalt have wars." *2 Chronicles 16:9*

"I will meditate also of all Thy work, and talk of Thy doings." *Psalm 77:12*

"I will greatly praise the Lord with my mouth; yea, I will praise Him among the multitude." *Psalm 109:30*

"Set a watch, O Lord, before my mouth; keep the door of my lips." *Psalm 141:3*

"Death and life are in the power of the tongue: and they that love it shall eat the fruit thereof."
Proverbs 18:21

"...The word is nigh thee, even in thy mouth, and in thy heart: that is, the word of faith, which we preach."
Romans 10:8

"Your Mouth Is The Multiplier of Whatever Is In Your Heart."

-MIKE MURDOCK

READ THE BIBLE THROUGH IN ONE YEAR: 2 Chronicles 22-24

Faithfulness — April 30

"A faithful man shall abound with blessings: but he that maketh haste to be rich shall not be innocent."
Proverbs 28:20

"His lord said unto him, Well done, good and faithful servant; thou hast been faithful over a few things, I will make thee ruler over many things: enter thou into the joy of thy lord."
Matthew 25:23

"And if ye have not been faithful in that which is another man's, who shall give you that which is your own?"
Luke 16:12

"And the things that thou hast heard of Me among many witnesses, the same commit thou to faithful men, who shall be able to teach others also."
2 Timothy 2:2

"If we believe not, yet he abideth faithful: he cannot deny himself."
2 Timothy 2:13

"I have fought a good fight, I have finished my course, I have kept the faith."
2 Timothy 4:7

"Uncommon Men Do Daily What Common Men Do Occasionally."

-MIKE MURDOCK

READ THE BIBLE THROUGH IN ONE YEAR: 2 Chronicles 25-27

False Accusation May 1

"Thou shalt not bear false witness against thy neighbour." *Exodus 20:16*

"A false witness that speaketh lies." *Proverbs 6:19*

"...he that uttereth a slander, is a fool." *Proverbs 10:18*

"A false witness shall not be unpunished, and he that speaketh lies shall perish." *Proverbs 19:9*

"Now the chief priests, and elders, and all the council, sought false witness against Jesus, to put Him to death." *Matthew 26:59*

"...Do violence to no man, neither accuse any falsely; and be content with your wages." *Luke 3:14*

"And Zacchaeus stood, and said unto the Lord: Behold, Lord, the half of my goods I give to the poor; and if I have taken any thing from any man by false accusation, I restore him fourfold." *Luke 19:8*

"False Accusation Is The Last Stage Before Supernatural Promotion."

-MIKE MURDOCK

READ THE BIBLE THROUGH IN ONE YEAR: 2 Chronicles 28-30

Fame

May 2

"Better is a little with righteousness than great revenues without right." *Proverbs 16:8*

"Many will intreat the favour of the prince: and every man is a friend to him that giveth gifts." *Proverbs 19:6*

"A good name is better than precious ointment; and the day of death than the day of one's birth."

Ecclesiastes 7:1

"But so much the more went there a fame abroad of Him: and great multitudes came together to hear, and to be healed by Him of their infirmities. And He withdrew Himself into the wilderness, and prayed."

Luke 5:15-16

"...For unto whomsoever much is given, of him shall be much required: and to whom men have committed much, of him they will ask the more." *Luke 12:48*

"Fame Creates Pursuit; Pursuit Creates Demand; Demand Increases Distraction."

-MIKE MURDOCK

READ THE BIBLE THROUGH IN ONE YEAR: 2 Chronicles 31-33

Family — May 3

"Lo, children are an heritage of the Lord: and the fruit of the womb is his reward. Happy is the man that hath his quiver full of them." *Psalm 127:3, 5*

"Through Wisdom is an house builded; and by understanding it is established." *Proverbs 24:3*

"Two are better than one; because they have a good reward for their labour." *Ecclesiastes 4:9*

"And all thy children shall be taught of the Lord; and great shall be the peace of thy children."

Isaiah 54:13

"And if a house be divided against itself, that house cannot stand." *Mark 3:25*

"And, ye fathers, provoke not your children to wrath: but bring them up in the nurture and admonition of the Lord." *Ephesians 6:4*

"But if any provide not for his own, and specially for those of his own house, he hath denied the faith, and is worse than an infidel." *1 Timothy 5:8*

"The Proof of Love Is The Desire To Protect."

-MIKE MURDOCK

READ THE BIBLE THROUGH IN ONE YEAR: 2 Chronicles 34-Ezra 2

Fasting

May 4

"Go, gather together all the Jews that are present in Shushan, and fast ye for me, and neither eat nor drink three days, night or day: I also and my maidens will fast likewise; and so will I go in unto the king, which is not according to the law: and if I perish, I perish."
Esther 4:16

"Is not this the fast that I have chosen? to loose the bands of wickedness, to undo the heavy burdens, and to let the oppressed go free, and that ye break every yoke?" *Isaiah 58:6*

"Therefore also now, saith the Lord, turn ye even to Me with all your heart, and with fasting, and with weeping, and with mourning." *Joel 2:12*

"Then was Jesus led up of the Spirit into the wilderness to be tempted of the devil. And when He had fasted forty days and forty nights, He was afterward an hungered." *Matthew 4:1-2*

"And He said unto them, This kind can come forth by nothing, but by prayer and fasting." *Mark 9:29*

"What You Are Willing To Walk Away From Determines What God Will Bring To You."

-*MIKE MURDOCK*

READ THE BIBLE THROUGH IN ONE YEAR: Ezra 3-5

Fathers

May 5

"When my father and my mother forsake me, then the Lord will take me up." *Psalm 27:10*

"Train up a child in the way he should go: and when he is old, he will not depart from it." *Proverbs 22:6*

"The father of the righteous shall greatly rejoice: and he that begetteth a wise child shall have joy of him." *Proverbs 23:24*

"For though ye have ten thousand instructors in Christ, yet have ye not many fathers: for in Christ Jesus I have begotten you through the gospel." *1 Corinthians 4:15*

"And, ye fathers, provoke not your children to wrath: but bring them up in the nurture and admonition of the Lord." *Ephesians 6:4*

"Fathers, provoke not your children to anger, lest they be discouraged." *Colossians 3:21*

"But if any provide not for his own, and specially for those of his own house, he hath denied the faith, and is worse than an infidel." *1 Timothy 5:8*

"The Purpose of Authority Is Order."

-MIKE MURDOCK

READ THE BIBLE THROUGH IN ONE YEAR: Ezra 6-8

Fatigue

May 6

"It is a sign between Me and the children of Israel for ever: for in six days the Lord made Heaven and earth, and on the seventh day He rested, and was refreshed."
Exodus 31:17

"But they that wait upon the Lord shall renew their strength; they shall mount up with wings as eagles; they shall run, and not be weary; and they shall walk, and not faint." *Isaiah 40:31*

"Come unto Me, all ye that labour and are heavy laden, and I will give you rest. For My yoke is easy, and My burden is light." *Matthew 11:28, 30*

"And He said unto them, Come ye yourselves apart into a desert place, and rest a while: for there were many coming and going, and they had no leisure so much as to eat." *Mark 6:31*

"There remaineth therefore a rest to the people of God."
Hebrews 4:9

"When Fatigue Walks In, Faith Walks Out."

-*MIKE MURDOCK*

READ THE BIBLE THROUGH IN ONE YEAR: Ezra 9-Nehemiah 1

Fault-Finding

May 7

"And why beholdest thou the mote that is in thy brother's eye, but considerest not the beam that is in thine own eye? Thou hypocrite, first cast out the beam out of thine own eye; and then shalt thou see clearly to cast out the mote out of thy brother's eye."
Matthew 7:3, 5

"...He that is without sin among you, let him first cast a stone at her." *John 8:7*

"Brethren, if a man be overtaken in a fault, ye which are spiritual, restore such an one in the spirit of meekness; considering thyself, lest thou also be tempted." *Galatians 6:1*

"Let no corrupt communication proceed out of your mouth, but that which is good to the use of edifying, that it may minister grace unto the hearers. Let all bitterness, and wrath, and anger, and clamour, and evil speaking, be put away from you, with all malice: And be ye kind one to another, tenderhearted, forgiving one another, even as God for Christ's sake hath forgiven you." *Ephesians 4:29, 31-32*

"Go Where You Are Celebrated Instead of Where You Are Tolerated."

-MIKE MURDOCK

READ THE BIBLE THROUGH IN ONE YEAR: Nehemiah 2-4

Favor

May 8

"A good man sheweth favour, and lendeth: he will guide his affairs with discretion." *Psalm 112:5*

"He that diligently seeketh good procureth favour." *Proverbs 11:27*

"A good man obtaineth favour of the Lord." *Proverbs 12:2*

"Good understanding giveth favour." *Proverbs 13:15*

"The king's favour is toward a wise servant." *Proverbs 14:35*

"Many will intreat the favour of the prince: and every man is a friend to him that giveth gifts." *Proverbs 19:6*

"A good name is rather to be chosen than great riches, and loving favour rather than silver and gold." *Proverbs 22:1*

"Every man shall kiss his lips that giveth a right answer." *Proverbs 24:26*

"Now God had brought Daniel into favour and tender love with the prince of the eunuchs." *Daniel 1:9*

"And Jesus increased in Wisdom and stature, and in favour with God and man." *Luke 2:52*

"One Day of Favor Is Worth A Lifetime of Labor."

-MIKE MURDOCK

READ THE BIBLE THROUGH IN ONE YEAR: Nehemiah 5-7

Fear

May 9

"Be strong and of a good courage, fear not, nor be afraid of them: for the Lord thy God, He it is that doth go with thee; He will not fail thee, nor forsake thee."
Deuteronomy 31:6

"Hear the right, O Lord, attend unto my cry, give ear unto my prayer, that goeth not out of feigned lips. Thou hast proved mine heart; Thou hast visited me in the night; Thou hast tried me, and shalt find nothing; I am purposed that my mouth shall not transgress." *Psalm 17:1, 3*

"Fear thou not; for I am with thee: be not dismayed; for I am thy God: I will strengthen thee; yea, I will help thee; yea, I will uphold thee with the right hand of My righteousness." *Isaiah 41:10*

"For God hath not given us the spirit of fear; but of power; and of love, and of a sound mind." *2 Timothy 1:7*

"So that we may boldly say, The Lord is my helper, and I will not fear what man shall do unto me." *Hebrews 13:6*

"There is no fear in love; but perfect love casteth out fear: because fear hath torment. He that feareth is not made perfect in love." *1 John 4:18*

"The Reward of Love Is The Absence of Fear."

-MIKE MURDOCK

READ THE BIBLE THROUGH IN ONE YEAR: Nehemiah 8-10

Fear of God

May 10

"And Moses said unto the people, Fear not: for God is come to prove you, and that His fear may be before your faces, that ye sin not." *Exodus 20:20*

"That thou mightest fear the Lord thy God, to keep all His statutes and His commandments, which I command thee, thou, and thy son, and thy son's son, all the days of thy life; and that thy days may be prolonged."
Deuteronomy 6:2

"The fear of the Lord is the beginning of Wisdom: a good understanding have all they that do His commandments: His praise endureth for ever." *Psalm 111:10*

"The fear of the Lord is to hate evil." *Proverbs 8:13*

"Let us hear the conclusion of the whole matter: Fear God, and keep His commandments: for this is the whole duty of man. For God shall bring every work into judgment, with every secret thing, whether it be good, or whether it be evil." *Ecclesiastes 12:13-14*

"If You Never Saw God's Wrath How Could You Believe In His Rewards."

-MIKE MURDOCK

BIBLE THROUGH IN ONE YEAR: Nehemiah 11-Esther 2

Fear of Man

May 11

"Ye shall not fear them: for the Lord your God He shall fight for you." *Deuteronomy 3:22*

"The Lord is my light and my salvation; whom shall I fear? the Lord is the strength of my life; of whom shall I be afraid? When the wicked, even mine enemies and my foes, came upon me to eat up my flesh, they stumbled and fell. Though an host should encamp against me, my heart shall not fear: though war should rise against me, in this will I be confident." *Psalm 27:1-3*

"The Lord is on my side; I will not fear: what can man do unto me?" *Psalm 118:6*

"No weapon that is formed against thee shall prosper; and every tongue that shall rise against thee in judgment thou shalt condemn. This is the heritage of the servants of the Lord, and their righteousness is of Me, saith the Lord." *Isaiah 54:17*

"For God hath not given us the spirit of fear; but of power, and of love, and of a sound mind." *2 Timothy 1:7*

"Your Success Is Determined By What You Are Willing To Ignore."

-MIKE MURDOCK

READ THE BIBLE THROUGH IN ONE YEAR: Esther 3-5

Financial Breakthrough

May 12

"But thou shalt remember the Lord thy God: for it is He that giveth thee power to get wealth, that He may establish His covenant which He sware unto thy fathers, as it is this day." *Deuteronomy 8:18*

"...Let the Lord be magnified, which hath pleasure in the prosperity of His servant." *Psalm 35:27*

"Praise ye the Lord. Blessed is the man that feareth the Lord, that delighteth greatly in His commandments. His seed shall be mighty upon earth: the generation of the upright shall be blessed. Wealth and riches shall be in his house: and his righteousness endureth for ever." *Psalm 112:1-3*

"That I may cause those that love Me to inherit substance; and I will fill their treasures." *Proverbs 8:21*

"Give, and it shall be given unto you; good measure, pressed down, and shaken together, and running over, shall men give into your bosom. For with the same measure that ye mete withal it shall be measured to you again." *Luke 6:38*

"What A Financial Deliverer Begins—A Financial Mentor Completes."

-MIKE MURDOCK

THE BIBLE THROUGH IN ONE YEAR: Esther 6-8

Flattery

May 13

"He that speaketh flattery to his friends, even the eyes of his children shall fail." *Job 17:5*

"To keep thee from the evil woman, from the flattery of the tongue of a strange woman." *Proverbs 6:24*

"With her much fair speech she caused him to yield, with the flattering of her lips she forced him." *Proverbs 7:21*

"...meddle not with him that flattereth with his lips." *Proverbs 20:19*

"A lying tongue hateth those that are afflicted by it; and a flattering mouth worketh ruin." *Proverbs 26:28*

"He that rebuketh a man afterwards shall find more favour than he that flattereth with the tongue." *Proverbs 28:23*

"A man that flattereth his neighbour spreadeth a net for his feet." *Proverbs 29:5*

"These are murmurers, complainers, walking after their own lusts; and their mouth speaketh great swelling words, having men's persons in admiration because of advantage." *Jude 1:16*

"Flattery Is A Wrong Heart...Speaking Right Things."
-*MIKE MURDOCK*

READ THE BIBLE THROUGH IN ONE YEAR: Esther 9-Job 1

Focus

May 14

"Only be thou strong and very courageous, that thou mayest observe to do according to all the law, which Moses My servant commanded thee: turn not from it to the right hand or to the left, that thou mayest prosper whithersoever thou goest." *Joshua 1:7*

"Remember ye not the former things, neither consider the things of old." *Isaiah 43:18*

"And Jesus said unto him, No man, having put his hand to the plough, and looking back, is fit for the kingdom of God." *Luke 9:62*

"Remember Lot's wife." *Luke 17:32*

"Brethren, I count not myself to have apprehended: but this one thing I do, forgetting those things which are behind, and reaching forth unto those things which are before, I press toward the mark for the prize of the high calling of God in Christ Jesus." *Philippians 3:13-14*

"Looking unto Jesus the author and finisher of our faith; Who for the joy that was set before Him endured the cross, despising the shame, and is set down at the right hand of the throne of God." *Hebrews 12:2*

"The Only Reason Men Fail Is Broken Focus."

-MIKE MURDOCK

READ THE BIBLE THROUGH IN ONE YEAR: Job 2-4

Fools

May 15

"The fool hath said in his heart, There is no God." *Psalm 14:1*

"The fear of the Lord is the beginning of knowledge: but fools despise Wisdom and instruction." *Proverbs 1:7*

"...he that uttereth a slander, is a fool." *Proverbs 10:18*

"He that walketh with wise men shall be wise: but a companion of fools shall be destroyed."
Proverbs 13:20

"Go from the presence of a foolish man, when thou perceivest not in him the lips of knowledge."
Proverbs 14:7

"Fools make a mock at sin." *Proverbs 14:9*

"A fool uttereth all his mind: but a wise man keepeth it in till afterwards." *Proverbs 29:11*

"When You Open Your Mouth I Know Your I.Q."
-MIKE MURDOCK

READ THE BIBLE THROUGH IN ONE YEAR: Job 5-7

Forgetting The Past

May 16

"As far as the east is from the west, so far hath He removed our transgressions from us." *Psalm 103:12*

"Remember ye not the former things, neither consider the things of old." *Isaiah 43:18*

"A new heart also will I give you, and a new spirit will I put within you: and I will take away the stony heart out of your flesh, and I will give you an heart of flesh." *Ezekiel 36:26*

"Brethren, I count not myself to have apprehended: but this one thing I do, forgetting those things which are behind, and reaching forth unto those things which are before, I press toward the mark for the prize of the high calling of God in Christ Jesus." *Philippians 3:13-14*

"For I will be merciful to their unrighteousness, and their sins and their iniquities will I remember no more." *Hebrews 8:12*

"And He that sat upon the throne said, Behold, I make all things new." *Revelation 21:5*

"Stop Discussing What You Want Others To Forget."

-MIKE MURDOCK

READ THE BIBLE THROUGH IN ONE YEAR: Job 8-10

Forgiveness — May 17

"For Thou, Lord, art good, and ready to forgive; and plenteous in mercy unto all them that call upon Thee."
Psalm 86:5

"As far as the east is from the west, so far hath He removed our transgressions from us." *Psalm 103:12*

"The discretion of a man deferreth his anger; and it is his glory to pass over a transgression." *Proverbs 19:11*

"But if ye forgive not men their trespasses, neither will your Father forgive your trespasses." *Matthew 6:15*

"And when ye stand praying, forgive, if ye have ought against any: that your Father also which is in Heaven may forgive you your trespasses." *Mark 11:25*

"...condemn not, and ye shall not be condemned: forgive, and ye shall be forgiven." *Luke 6:37*

"If we confess our sins, He is faithful and just to forgive us our sins, and to cleanse us from all unrighteousness." *1 John 1:9*

"Forgiveness Must Become Your Seed Before You Reap It As A Harvest."

-MIKE MURDOCK

READ THE BIBLE THROUGH IN ONE YEAR: Job 11-15

Freedom

May 18

"And I will walk at liberty: for I seek Thy precepts."
Psalm 119:45

"And ye shall know the truth, and the truth shall make you free. If the Son therefore shall make you free, ye shall be free indeed." *John 8:32, 36*

"Being then made free from sin, ye became the servants of righteousness." *Romans 6:18*

"But now being made free from sin, and become servants to God, ye have your fruit unto holiness, and the end everlasting life." *Romans 6:22*

"For the law of the Spirit of life in Christ Jesus hath made me free from the law of sin and death."
Romans 8:2

"Now the Lord is that Spirit: and where the Spirit of the Lord is, there is liberty." *2 Corinthians 3:17*

"Stand fast therefore in the liberty wherewith Christ hath made us free, and be not entangled again with the yoke of bondage." *Galatians 5:1*

"The Difference Between Servanthood And Slavery Is Choice."

-MIKE MURDOCK

READ THE BIBLE THROUGH IN ONE YEAR: Job 16-18

Friendship

May 19

"A friend loveth at all times, and a brother is born for adversity." *Proverbs 17:17*

"A man that hath friends must shew himself friendly: and there is a friend that sticketh closer than a brother." *Proverbs 18:24*

"Many will intreat the favour of the prince: and every man is a friend to him that giveth gifts." *Proverbs 19:6*

"Faithful are the wounds of a friend; but the kisses of an enemy are deceitful. Ointment and perfume rejoice the heart: so doth the sweetness of a man's friend by hearty counsel. Thine own friend, and thy father's friend, forsake not; neither go into thy brother's house in the day of thy calamity: for better is a neighbour that is near than a brother far off." *Proverbs 27:6, 9-10*

"Greater love hath no man than this, that a man lay down his life for his friends. Ye are my friends, if ye do whatsoever I command you." *John 15:13-14*

"And have no fellowship with the unfruitful works of darkness, but rather reprove them." *Ephesians 5:11*

"When God Wants To Bless You He Brings A Person Into Your Life."

-MIKE MURDOCK

READ THE BIBLE THROUGH IN ONE YEAR: Job 19-21

Fruit of The Spirit

May 20

"A good tree cannot bring forth evil fruit, neither can a corrupt tree bring forth good fruit." *Matthew 7:18*

"Herein is My Father glorified, that ye bear much fruit; so shall ye be My disciples." *John 15:8*

"Ye have not chosen Me, but I have chosen you, and ordained you, that ye should go and bring forth fruit, and that your fruit should remain: that whatsoever ye shall ask of the Father in My name, He may give it you." *John 15:16*

"And hope maketh not ashamed; because the love of God is shed abroad in our hearts by the Holy Ghost which is given unto us." *Romans 5:5*

"But the fruit of the Spirit is love, joy, peace, longsuffering, gentleness, goodness, faith, Meekness, temperance: against such there is no law." *Galatians 5:22-23*

"For the fruit of the Spirit is in all goodness and righteousness and truth." *Ephesians 5:9*

"What You Do Reveals What You Are."

-MIKE MURDOCK

READ THE BIBLE THROUGH IN ONE YEAR: Job 22-24

Gift Giving May 21

"Thou shalt not wrest judgment; thou shalt not respect persons, neither take a gift: for a gift doth blind the eyes of the wise, and pervert the words of the righteous."
Deuteronomy 16:19

"A gift is as a precious stone in the eyes of him that hath it: whithersoever it turneth, it prospereth." *Proverbs 17:8*

"A wicked man taketh a gift out of the bosom to pervert the ways of judgment." *Proverbs 17:23*

"A man's gift maketh room for him, and bringeth him before great men." *Proverbs 18:16*

"...every man is a friend to him that giveth gifts."
Proverbs 19:6

"If ye then, being evil, know how to give good gifts unto your children, how much more shall your Father which is in Heaven give good things to them that ask Him?" *Matthew 7:11*

"Give, and it shall be given unto you; good measure, pressed down, and shaken together, and running over, shall men give into your bosom. For with the same measure that ye mete withal it shall be measured to you again." *Luke 6:38*

"The Ungodly Give Gifts To Control Decision-Makers; The Godly Give Gifts To Reward Problem-Solvers."

-MIKE MURDOCK

READ THE BIBLE THROUGH IN ONE YEAR: Job 25-27

Giving

May 22

"Many will intreat the favour of the prince: and every man is a friend to him that giveth gifts." *Proverbs 19:6*

"If ye then, being evil, know how to give good gifts unto your children, how much more shall your Father which is in Heaven give good things to them that ask Him?" *Matthew 7:11*

"Heal the sick, cleanse the lepers, raise the dead, cast out devils: freely ye have received, freely give." *Matthew 10:8*

"Give, and it shall be given unto you; good measure, pressed down, and shaken together, and running over, shall men give into your bosom. For with the same measure that ye mete withal it shall be measured to you again." *Luke 6:38*

"...It is more blessed to give than to receive." *Acts 20:35*

"Every man according as he purposeth in his heart, so let him give; not grudgingly, or of necessity: for God loveth a cheerful giver." *2 Corinthians 9:7*

"Ecstasy To A Giver Is Discovering Someone Qualified To Receive."

-MIKE MURDOCK

READ THE BIBLE THROUGH IN ONE YEAR: Job 28-30

Goal-Setting — May 23

"In all thy ways acknowledge Him, and He shall direct thy paths." *Proverbs 3:6*

"Remember ye not the former things, neither consider the things of old." *Isaiah 43:18*

"And the Lord answered me, and said, Write the vision, and make it plain upon tables, that he may run that readeth it." *Habakkuk 2:2*

"For which of you, intending to build a tower, sitteth not down first, and counteth the cost, whether he have sufficient to finish it? Lest haply, after he hath laid the foundation, and is not able to finish it, all that behold it begin to mock him, Saying, This man began to build, and was not able to finish. Or what king, going to make war against another king, sitteth not down first, and consulteth whether he be able with ten thousand to meet him that cometh against him with twenty thousand? Or else, while the other is yet a great way off, he sendeth an ambassage, and desireth conditions of peace." *Luke 14:28-32*

"The Clearer Your Goals, The Greater Your Faith."
                                    -MIKE MURDOCK

READ THE BIBLE THROUGH IN ONE YEAR: Job 31-33

God

May 24

"In the beginning God created the Heaven and the earth." *Genesis 1:1*

"In the beginning was the Word, and the Word was with God, and the Word was God. The same was in the beginning with God." *John 1:1-2*

"For it is written, As I live, saith the Lord, every knee shall bow to Me, and every tongue shall confess to God. So then every one of us shall give account of himself to God." *Romans 14:11-12*

"For by Him were all things created, that are in Heaven, and that are in earth, visible and invisible, whether they be thrones, or dominions, or principalities, or powers: all things were created by Him, and for Him: And He is before all things, and by Him all things consist." *Colossians 1:16-17*

"And a voice came out of the throne, saying, Praise our God, all ye His servants, and ye that fear Him, both small and great." *Revelation 19:5*

"The Evidence of God's Presence Far Outweighs The Proof of His Absence."

-MIKE MURDOCK

READ THE BIBLE THROUGH IN ONE YEAR: Job 34-38

Goodness of God

May 25

"O give thanks unto the Lord; for He is good; for His mercy endureth for ever." *1 Chronicles 16:34*

"O taste and see that the Lord is good: blessed is the man that trusteth in Him." *Psalm 34:8*

"Why boastest thou thyself in mischief, O mighty man? the goodness of God endureth continually." *Psalm 52:1*

"For Thou, Lord, art good, and ready to forgive; and plenteous in mercy unto all them that call upon Thee." *Psalm 86:5*

"For the Lord is good; His mercy is everlasting; and His truth endureth to all generations." *Psalm 100:5*

"The Lord is good to all: and His tender mercies are over all His works." *Psalm 145:9*

"Or despisest thou the riches of His goodness and forbearance and longsuffering; not knowing that the goodness of God leadeth thee to repentance?" *Romans 2:4*

"God Is In Continuous Search For Someone Qualified To Receive."

-MIKE MURDOCK

READ THE BIBLE THROUGH IN ONE YEAR: Job 39-41

Gratitude

May 26

"It is a good thing to give thanks unto the Lord, and to sing praises unto Thy name, O most High." *Psalm 92:1*

"Enter into His gates with thanksgiving, and into His courts with praise: be thankful unto Him, and bless His name." *Psalm 100:4*

"I will praise thee with uprightness of heart, when I shall have learned Thy righteous judgments." *Psalm 119:7*

"Cease not to give thanks for you, making mention of you in my prayers." *Ephesians 1:16*

"Giving thanks always for all things unto God and the Father in the name of our Lord Jesus Christ."
Ephesians 5:20

"In every thing give thanks: for this is the will of God in Christ Jesus concerning you." *1 Thessalonians 5:18*

"I exhort therefore, that, first of all, supplications, prayers, intercessions, and giving of thanks, be made for all men." *1 Timothy 2:1*

"Gratitude Is Your Gift Back To A Giver."

-MIKE MURDOCK

READ THE BIBLE THROUGH IN ONE YEAR: Job 42-Psalms 2

Greatness

May 27

"And I will make of thee a great nation, and I will bless thee, and make thy name great; and thou shalt be a blessing." *Genesis 12:2*

"Keep therefore and do them; for this is your Wisdom and your understanding in the sight of the nations, which shall hear all these statutes, and say, Surely this great nation is a wise and understanding people."

Deuteronomy 4:6

"Whosoever therefore shall break one of these least commandments, and shall teach men so, he shall be called the least in the kingdom of Heaven: but whosoever shall do and teach them, the same shall be called great in the kingdom of Heaven." *Matthew 5:19*

"But he that is greatest among you shall be your servant." *Matthew 23:11*

"And I saw the dead, small and great, stand before God; and the books were opened: and another book was opened, which is the book of life: and the dead were judged out of those things which were written in the books, according to their works." *Revelation 20:12*

"Greatness Is Not The Absence of A Flaw, But The Ability To Survive Your Flaw."

-MIKE MURDOCK

READ THE BIBLE THROUGH IN ONE YEAR: Psalms 3-5

Greed

May 28

"He that is greedy of gain troubleth his own house."
Proverbs 15:27

"...so the eyes of man are never satisfied."
Proverbs 27:20

"He that loveth silver shall not be satisfied with silver; nor he that loveth abundance with increase: this is also vanity." *Ecclesiastes 5:10*

"And He said unto them, Take heed, and beware of covetousness: for a man's life consisteth not in the abundance of the things which he possesseth. For where your treasure is, there will your heart be also."
Luke 12:15, 34

"But godliness with contentment is great gain."
1 Timothy 6:6

"Be content with such things as ye have: for He hath said, I will never leave thee, nor forsake thee."
Hebrews 13:5

"Giving Is The Only Proof You Have Conquered Greed."

-MIKE MURDOCK

READ THE BIBLE THROUGH IN ONE YEAR: Psalms 6-8

Grief

May 29

"Weeping may endure for a night, but joy cometh in the morning." *Psalm 30:5*

"He healeth the broken in heart, and bindeth up their wounds." *Psalm 147:3*

"Remember ye not the former things, neither consider the things of old. Behold, I will do a new thing; now it shall spring forth; shall ye not know it? I will even make a way in the wilderness, and rivers in the desert."

Isaiah 43:18-19

"Come unto Me, all ye that labour and are heavy laden, and I will give you rest." *Matthew 11:28*

"Blessed are they that mourn for they shall be comforted." *Matthew 5:4*

"For we have not an high priest which cannot be touched with the feeling of our infirmities; but was in all points tempted like as we are, yet without sin."

Hebrews 4:15

"And God shall wipe away all tears from their eyes; and there shall be no more death, neither sorrow, nor crying, neither shall there be any more pain: for the former things are passed away." *Revelation 21:4*

"Loss Is The First Step Toward Discovering God."

-MIKE MURDOCK

READ THE BIBLE THROUGH IN ONE YEAR: Psalms 9-11

Guidance

May 30

"For Thou art my rock and my fortress; therefore for Thy name's sake lead me, and guide me." *Psalm 31:3*

"I will instruct thee and teach thee in the way which thou shalt go: I will guide thee with Mine eye."
Psalm 32:8

"For by wise counsel thou shalt make thy war: and in multitude of counsellors there is safety." *Proverbs 24:6*

"And thine ears shall hear a word behind thee, saying, This is the way, walk ye in it, when ye turn to the right hand, and when ye turn to the left." *Isaiah 30:21*

"And the Lord shall guide thee continually, and satisfy thy soul in drought, and make fat thy bones: and thou shalt be like a watered garden, and like a spring of water, whose waters fail not." *Isaiah 58:11*

"Wilt thou not from this time cry unto Me, My father, Thou art the guide of my youth?" *Jeremiah 3:4*

"Howbeit when He, the Spirit of truth, is come, He will guide you into all truth: for He shall not speak of Himself; but whatsoever He shall hear, that shall He speak: and He will shew you things to come." *John 16:13*

"The Proof of Humility Is The Willingness To Ask."
-MIKE MURDOCK

READ THE BIBLE THROUGH IN ONE YEAR: Psalms 12-14

Guilt

May 31

"Come now, and let us reason together, saith the Lord: though your sins be as scarlet, they shall be as white as snow; though they be red like crimson, they shall be as wool." *Isaiah 1:18*

"For God sent not His Son into the world to condemn the world; but that the world through Him might be saved." *John 3:17*

"There is therefore now no condemnation to them which are in Christ Jesus, who walk not after the flesh, but after the Spirit." *Romans 8:1*

"Who shall lay any thing to the charge of God's elect? It is God that justifieth. Who is he that condemneth? It is Christ that died, yea rather, that is risen again, Who is even at the right hand of God, Who also maketh intercession for us." *Romans 8:33-34*

"If we confess our sins, He is faithful and just to forgive us our sins, and to cleanse us from all unrighteousness." *1 John 1:9*

"For if our heart condemn us, God is greater than our heart, and knoweth all things. Beloved, if our heart condemn us not, then have we confidence toward God." *1 John 3:20-21*

"The Instant Cure For Guilt Is Confession."

-MIKE MURDOCK

READ THE BIBLE THROUGH IN ONE YEAR: Psalms 15-19

Habits

June 1

"So will I sing praise unto Thy name forever, that I may daily perform my vows." *Psalm 61:8*

"Mine eye mourneth by reason of affliction: Lord, I have called daily upon Thee, I have stretched out my hands unto Thee." *Psalm 88:9*

"Seven times a day do I praise Thee because of Thy righteous judgments." *Psalm 119:164*

"Yet they seek Me daily, and delight to know My ways, as a nation that did righteousness, and forsook not the ordinance of their God: they ask of Me the ordinances of justice; they take delight in approaching to God." *Isaiah 58:2*

"Now when Daniel knew that the writing was signed, he went into his house; and his windows being open in his chamber toward Jerusalem, he kneeled upon his knees three times a day, and prayed, and gave thanks before his God, as he did aforetime." *Daniel 6:10*

"These were more noble than those in Thessalonica, in that they received the word with all readiness of mind, and searched the scriptures daily, whether those things were so." *Acts 17:11*

"Successful Men Do Daily What Unsuccessful Men Do Occasionally."

-MIKE MURDOCK

READ THE BIBLE THROUGH IN ONE YEAR: Psalms 20-22

Happiness

June 2

"Thou hast put gladness in my heart, more than in the time that their corn and their wine increased."

Psalm 4:7

"For thou shalt eat the labour of thine hands: happy shalt thou be, and it shall be well with thee." *Psalm 128:2*

"Happy is that people, that is in such a case: yea, happy is that people, whose God is the Lord." *Psalm 144:15*

"Happy is the man that findeth Wisdom, and the man that getteth understanding." *Proverbs 3:13*

"He that handleth a matter wisely shall find good: and whoso trusteth in the Lord, happy is he."

Proverbs 16:20

"He that keepeth the law, happy is he."

Proverbs 29:18

"Your Present Focus Determines Your Present Feelings."

-MIKE MURDOCK

READ THE BIBLE THROUGH IN ONE YEAR: Psalms 23-25

Harvest

June 3

"While the earth remaineth, seedtime and harvest, and cold and heat, and summer and winter, and day and night shall not cease." *Genesis 8:22*

"Give, and it shall be given unto you; good measure, pressed down, and shaken together, and running over, shall men give into your bosom. For with the same measure that ye mete withal it shall be measured to you again." *Luke 6:38*

"But this I say, He which soweth sparingly shall reap also sparingly; and he which soweth bountifully shall reap also bountifully." *2 Corinthians 9:6*

"Be not deceived; God is not mocked: for whatsoever a man soweth, that shall he also reap. For he that soweth to his flesh shall of the flesh reap corruption; but he that soweth to the Spirit shall of the Spirit reap life everlasting. And let us not be weary in well doing: for in due season we shall reap, if we faint not."

Galatians 6:7-9

"Knowing that whatsoever good thing any man doeth, the same shall he receive of the Lord, whether he be bond or free." *Ephesians 6:8*

"An Uncommon Seed Always Creates An Uncommon Harvest."

-MIKE MURDOCK

READ THE BIBLE THROUGH IN ONE YEAR: Psalms 26-28

Hatred

June 4

"He that is slow to anger is better than the mighty; and he that ruleth his spirit than he that taketh a city."
Proverbs 16:32

"A time to love, and a time to hate; a time of war, and a time of peace." *Ecclesiastes 3:8*

"Ye have heard that it hath been said, Thou shalt love thy neighbour, and hate thine enemy. But I say unto you, Love your enemies, bless them that curse you, do good to them that hate you, and pray for them which despitefully use you, and persecute you." *Matthew 5:43-44*

"And when ye stand praying, forgive, if ye have ought against any: that your Father also which is in Heaven may forgive you your trespasses." *Mark 11:25*

"But I say unto you which hear, Love your enemies, do good to them which hate you." *Luke 6:27*

"By this shall all men know that ye are My disciples, if ye have love one to another." *John 13:35*

"Be ye angry, and sin not: let not the sun go down upon your wrath." *Ephesians 4:26*

"Marvel not, my brethren, if the world hate you."
1 John 3:13

"Anything Good Is Hated By Everything Evil."

-*MIKE MURDOCK*

READ THE BIBLE THROUGH IN ONE YEAR: Psalms 29-31

Healing

June 5

"I will put none of these diseases upon thee, which I have brought upon the Egyptians: for I am the Lord that healeth thee." *Exodus 15:26*

"For the Lord God is a sun and shield: the Lord will give grace and glory: no good thing will He withhold from them that walk uprightly." *Psalm 84:11*

"Bless the Lord, O my soul, and forget not all His benefits: Who forgiveth all thine iniquities; Who healeth all thy diseases." *Psalm 103:2-3*

"For I will restore health unto thee, and I will heal thee of thy wounds, saith the Lord." *Jeremiah 30:17*

"How God anointed Jesus of Nazareth with the Holy Ghost and with power: Who went about doing good, and healing all that were oppressed of the devil; for God was with Him." *Acts 10:38*

"Beloved, I wish above all things that thou mayest prosper and be in health, even as thy soul prospereth." *3 John 1:2*

"Anything Broken Can Be Repaired."

-MIKE MURDOCK

READ THE BIBLE THROUGH IN ONE YEAR: Psalms 32-34

Health

June 6

"He healeth the broken in heart, and bindeth up their wounds." *Psalm 147:3*

"Be not wise in thine own eyes: fear the Lord, and depart from evil. It shall be health to thy navel, and marrow to thy bones." *Proverbs 3:7-8*

"My son, attend to my words; incline thine ear unto my sayings. Let them not depart from thine eyes; keep them in the midst of thine heart. For they are life unto those that find them, and health to all their flesh." *Proverbs 4:20-22*

"Pleasant words are as an honeycomb, sweet to the soul, and health to the bones." *Proverbs 16:24*

"For I will restore health unto thee, and I will heal thee of thy wounds, saith the Lord; because they called thee an Outcast, saying, This is Zion, whom no man seeketh after." *Jeremiah 30:17*

"Beloved, I wish above all things that thou mayest prosper and be in health, even as thy soul prospereth." *3 John 1:2*

"The Secret of Your Health Is Hidden In Your Daily Routine."

-MIKE MURDOCK

READ THE BIBLE THROUGH IN ONE YEAR: Psalms 35-37

Heartache

June 7

"...weeping may endure for a night, but joy cometh in the morning." *Psalm 30:5*

"The Lord is nigh unto them that are of a broken heart; and saveth such as be of a contrite spirit." *Psalm 34:18*

"The sacrifices of God are a broken spirit: a broken and a contrite heart, O God, Thou wilt not despise." *Psalm 51:17*

"They that sow in tears shall reap in joy. He that goeth forth and weepeth, bearing precious seed, shall doubtless come again with rejoicing, bringing his sheaves with him." *Psalm 126:5-6*

"He healeth the broken in heart, and bindeth up their wounds." *Psalm 147:3*

"Heaviness in the heart of man maketh it stoop: but a good word maketh it glad." *Proverbs 12:25*

"Painful Memories Birth Great Decisions."

-MIKE MURDOCK

READ THE BIBLE THROUGH IN ONE YEAR: Psalms 38-42

Heaven
June 8

"In My Father's house are many mansions: if it were not so, I would have told you. I go to prepare a place for you. And if I go and prepare a place for you, I will come again, and receive you unto Myself; that where I am, there ye may be also." *John 14:2-3*

"And the city lieth foursquare, and the length is as large as the breadth: and he measured the city with the reed, twelve thousand furlongs. The length and the breadth and the height of it are equal. And the building of the wall of it was of jasper: and the city was pure gold, like unto clear glass. And the twelve gates were twelve pearls; every several gate was of one pearl: and the street of the city was pure gold, as it were transparent glass. And the city had no need of the sun, neither of the moon, to shine in it: for the glory of God did lighten it, and the Lamb is the light thereof. And the gates of it shall not be shut at all by day: for there shall be no night there. And there shall in no wise enter into it any thing that defileth, neither whatsoever worketh abomination, or maketh a lie: but they which are written in the Lamb's book of life." *Revelation 21:16, 18, 21, 23, 25, 27*

"God Made Places Before He Made People."
-MIKE MURDOCK

READ THE BIBLE THROUGH IN ONE YEAR: Psalms 43-45

Hell

June 9

"The way of life is above to the wise, that he may depart from hell beneath." *Proverbs 15:24*

"And fear not them which kill the body, but are not able to kill the soul: but rather fear him which is able to destroy both soul and body in hell."

Matthew 10:28

"Then shall He say also unto them on the left hand, Depart from Me, ye cursed, into everlasting fire, prepared for the devil and his angels: And these shall go away into everlasting punishment; but the righteous into life eternal." *Matthew 25:41, 46*

"And if thine eye offend thee, pluck it out: it is better for thee to enter into the kingdom of God with one eye, than having two eyes to be cast into hell fire: Where their worm dieth not, and the fire is not quenched." *Mark 9:47-48*

"Disobedience Will Always Cost More Than Obedience."

-MIKE MURDOCK

READ THE BIBLE THROUGH IN ONE YEAR: Psalms 46-48

Holy Spirit

June 10

"If ye then, being evil, know how to give good gifts unto your children: how much more shall your Heavenly Father give the Holy Spirit to them that ask Him?" *Luke 11:13*

"And I will pray the Father, and He shall give you another Comforter, that He may abide with you for ever; Even the Spirit of truth; Whom the world cannot receive, because it seeth Him not, neither knoweth Him: but ye know Him; for He dwelleth with you, and shall be in you." *John 14:16-17*

"Howbeit when He, the Spirit of truth, is come, He will guide you into all truth: for He shall not speak of Himself; but whatsoever He shall hear, that shall He speak: and He will shew you things to come." *John 16:13*

"And it shall come to pass in the last days, saith God, I will pour out of My Spirit upon all flesh: and your sons and your daughters shall prophesy, and your young men shall see visions, and your old men shall dream dreams." *Acts 2:17*

"The Presence of God Is The Only Place Where Your Weakness Will Die."

-MIKE MURDOCK

READ THE BIBLE THROUGH IN ONE YEAR: Psalms 49-51

Home

June 11

"Every wise woman buildeth her house: but the foolish plucketh it down with her hands." *Proverbs 14:1*

"The house of the wicked shall be overthrown: but the tabernacle of the upright shall flourish." *Proverbs 14:11*

"In the house of the righteous is much treasure: but in the revenues of the wicked is trouble." *Proverbs 15:6*

"Better is a dry morsel, and quietness therewith, than an house full of sacrifices with strife." *Proverbs 17:1*

"Through Wisdom is an house builded; and by understanding it is established: And by knowledge shall the chambers be filled with all precious and pleasant riches." *Proverbs 24:3-4*

"Or else how can one enter into a strong man's house, and spoil his goods, except he first bind the strong man? and then he will spoil his house." *Matthew 12:29*

"To be discreet, chaste, keepers at home, good, obedient to their own husbands, that the word of God be not blasphemed." *Titus 2:5*

"Home Should Be The Nest Without Thorns."

-MIKE MURDOCK

READ THE BIBLE THROUGH IN ONE YEAR: Psalms 52-54

Honor

June 12

"He hath dispersed, He hath given to the poor; His righteousness endureth for ever; His horn shall be exalted with honour." *Psalm 112:9*

"...and before honour is humility." *Proverbs 15:33*

"It is an honour for a man to cease from strife: but every fool will be meddling." *Proverbs 20:3*

"He that followeth after righteousness and mercy findeth life, righteousness, and honour." *Proverbs 21:21*

"By humility and the fear of the Lord are riches, and honour, and life." *Proverbs 22:4*

"Honour all men. Love the brotherhood. Fear God. Honour the king." *1 Peter 2:17*

"Likewise, ye husbands, dwell with them according to knowledge, giving honour unto the wife, as unto the weaker vessel, and as being heirs together of the grace of life; that your prayers be not hindered." *1 Peter 3:7*

"Honor Must Become Your Seed Before It Becomes Your Harvest."

-MIKE MURDOCK

READ THE BIBLE THROUGH IN ONE YEAR: Psalms 55-57

Honoring Your Parents

June 13

"Honour thy father and thy mother: that thy days may be long upon the land which the Lord thy God giveth thee." *Exodus 20:12*

"He that wasteth his father, and chaseth away his mother, is a son that causeth shame, and bringeth reproach." *Proverbs 19:26*

"Whoso curseth his father or his mother, his lamp shall be put out in obscure darkness." *Proverbs 20:20*

"Hearken unto thy father that begat thee, and despise not thy mother when she is old." *Proverbs 23:22*

"Children, obey your parents in the Lord: for this is right." *Ephesians 6:1*

"Honour thy father and mother; (which is the first commandment with promise;) That it may be well with thee, and thou mayest live long on the earth."
Ephesians 6:2-3

"Your Reaction To Your Parents Determines God's Reaction To You."

-MIKE MURDOCK

READ THE BIBLE THROUGH IN ONE YEAR: Psalms 58-60

Hope

June 14

"Behold, the eye of the Lord is upon them that fear Him, upon them that hope in His mercy." *Psalm 33:18*

"For Thou art my hope, O Lord God: Thou art my trust from my youth." *Psalm 71:5*

"Thou wilt keep him in perfect peace, whose mind is stayed on Thee: because he trusteth in Thee." *Isaiah 26:3*

"Blessed is the man that trusteth in the Lord, and whose hope the Lord is." *Jeremiah 17:7*

"And now abideth faith, hope, charity, these three; but the greatest of these is charity." *1 Corinthians 13:13*

"If in this life only we have hope in Christ, we are of all men most miserable." *1 Corinthians 15:19*

"Cast not away therefore your confidence, which hath great recompence of reward." *Hebrews 10:35*

"...and Lord Jesus Christ, which is our hope."
1 Timothy 1:1

"But sanctify the Lord God in your hearts: and be ready always to give an answer to every man that asketh you a reason of the hope that is in you with meekness and fear." *1 Peter 3:15*

"The Most Dangerous Relationship In Your Life Is The Person Who Destroys Your Hope."

-MIKE MURDOCK

READ THE BIBLE THROUGH IN ONE YEAR: Psalms 61-65

Hospitality June 15

"Distributing to the necessity of saints; given to hospitality." *Romans 12:13*

"A bishop then must be blameless, the husband of one wife, vigilant, sober, of good behaviour, given to hospitality, apt to teach." *1 Timothy 3:2*

"Well reported of for good works; if she have brought up children, if she have lodged strangers, if she have washed the saints' feet, if she have relieved the afflicted, if she have diligently followed every good work." *1 Timothy 5:10*

"But a lover of hospitality, a lover of good men, sober, just, holy, temperate." *Titus 1:8*

"Be not forgetful to entertain strangers: for thereby some have entertained angels unawares." *Hebrews 13:2*

"Use hospitality one to another without grudging." *1 Peter 4:9*

"The Proof of Caring Is The Attention To Detail."
  -MIKE MURDOCK

READ THE BIBLE THROUGH IN ONE YEAR: Psalms 66-68

Humility

June 16

"By humility and the fear of the Lord are riches, and honour, and life." *Proverbs 22:4*

"Whosoever therefore shall humble himself as this little child, the same is greatest in the kingdom of Heaven." *Matthew 18:4*

"Not that we are sufficient of ourselves to think any thing as of ourselves; but our sufficiency is of God." *2 Corinthians 3:5*

"And being found in fashion as a man, He humbled Himself, and became obedient unto death, even the death of the cross." *Philippians 2:8*

"But He giveth more grace. Wherefore He saith, God resisteth the proud, but giveth grace unto the humble. Humble yourselves in the sight of the Lord, and He shall lift you up." *James 4:6, 10*

"Humble yourselves therefore under the mighty hand of God, that He may exalt you in due time." *1 Peter 5:6*

"Recognition of Your Worth Creates Confidence—Recognition of Your Lack Creates Humility."

-*MIKE MURDOCK*

READ THE BIBLE THROUGH IN ONE YEAR: Psalms 69-71

Hundredfold Return

June 17

"Then Isaac sowed in that land, and received in the same year an hundredfold: and the Lord blessed him."
Genesis 26:12

"But other fell into good ground, and brought forth fruit, some an hundredfold, some sixtyfold, some thirtyfold."
Matthew 13:8

"But he that received seed into the good ground is he that heareth the word, and understandeth it; which also beareth fruit, and bringeth forth, some an hundredfold, some sixty, some thirty."
Matthew 13:23

"And every one that hath forsaken houses, or brethren, or sisters, or father, or mother, or wife, or children, or lands, for My name's sake, shall receive an hundredfold, and shall inherit everlasting life."
Matthew 19:29

"But he shall receive an hundredfold now in this time, houses, and brethren, and sisters, and mothers, and children, and lands, with persecutions; and in the world to come eternal life."
Mark 10:30

"Anything God Touches Multiplies."

-MIKE MURDOCK

READ THE BIBLE THROUGH IN ONE YEAR: Psalms 72-74

Hurrying

June 18

"The Lord is good unto them that wait for Him, to the soul that seeketh Him." *Lamentations 3:25*

"Wait on the Lord: be of good courage, and He shall strengthen thine heart: wait, I say, on the Lord."
Psalm 27:14

"But they that wait upon the Lord shall renew their strength; they shall mount up with wings as eagles; they shall run, and not be weary; and they shall walk, and not faint." *Isaiah 40:31*

"But if we hope for that we see not, then do we with patience wait for it." *Romans 8:25*

"And let us not be weary in well doing: for in due season we shall reap, if we faint not." *Galatians 6:9*

"Not that I speak in respect of want: for I have learned, in whatsoever state I am, therewith to be content."
Philippians 4:11

"Always Stay Long Enough In The Secret Place To Create A Memory."

-MIKE MURDOCK

READ THE BIBLE THROUGH IN ONE YEAR: Psalms 75-77

Hypocrisy

June 19

"But the Lord said unto Samuel, Look not on his countenance, or on the height of his stature; because I have refused him: for the Lord seeth not as man seeth; for man looketh on the outward appearance, but the Lord looketh on the heart." *1 Samuel 16:7*

"That the hypocrite reign not, lest the people be ensnared." *Job 34:30*

"An hypocrite with his mouth destroyeth his neighbour: but through knowledge shall the just be delivered." *Proverbs 11:9*

"Wherefore the Lord said, Forasmuch as this people draw near Me with their mouth, and with their lips do honour Me, but have removed their heart far from Me, and their fear toward Me is taught by the precept of men." *Isaiah 29:13*

"For I say unto you, That except your righteousness shall exceed the righteousness of the scribes and Pharisees, ye shall in no case enter into the kingdom of Heaven." *Matthew 5:20*

"Thou hypocrite, first cast out the beam out of thine own eye; and then shalt thou see clearly to cast out the mote out of thy brother's eye." *Matthew 7:5*

"Hypocrisy Is Requiring From Another What You Are Unwilling To Give Yourself."

-MIKE MURDOCK

READ THE BIBLE THROUGH IN ONE YEAR: Psalms 78-80

Ideas June 20

"I Wisdom dwell with prudence, and find out knowledge of witty inventions." *Proverbs 8:12*

"And thine ears shall hear a word behind thee, saying, This is the way, walk ye in it, when ye turn to the right hand, and when ye turn to the left." *Isaiah 30:21*

"At the noise of the tumult the people fled; at the lifting up of thyself the nations were scattered." *Isaiah 33:3*

"Behold, I will do a new thing; now it shall spring forth; shall ye not know it? I will even make a way in the wilderness, and rivers in the desert." *Isaiah 43:19*

"And I will give thee the treasures of darkness, and hidden riches of secret places, that thou mayest know that I, the Lord, which call thee by thy name, am the God of Israel." *Isaiah 45:3*

"Thou hast heard, see all this; and will not ye declare it? I have shewed thee new things from this time, even hidden things, and thou didst not know them. They are created now, and not from the beginning; even before the day when thou heardest them not; lest thou shouldest say, Behold, I knew them." *Isaiah 48:6-7*

"There Are Two Ways To Increase Wisdom: Mistakes And Mentors."

-MIKE MURDOCK

READ THE BIBLE THROUGH IN ONE YEAR: Psalms 81-83

Ignorance

June 21

"So foolish was I, and ignorant: I was as a beast before thee." *Psalm 73:22*

"His watchmen are blind: they are all ignorant, they are all dumb dogs, they cannot bark; sleeping, lying down, loving to slumber." *Isaiah 56:10*

"For they being ignorant of God's righteousness, and going about to establish their own righteousness, have not submitted themselves unto the righteousness of God." *Romans 10:3*

"For I would not, brethren, that ye should be ignorant of this mystery, lest ye should be wise in your own conceits; that blindness in part is happened to Israel, until the fulness of the Gentiles be come in." *Romans 11:25*

"But if any man be ignorant, let him be ignorant." *1 Corinthians 14:38*

"Who can have compassion on the ignorant, and on them that are out of the way; for that he himself also is compassed with infirmity." *Hebrews 5:2*

"Questions That Expose The Incompetence of Another Will Always Birth An Adversary."

-MIKE MURDOCK

READ THE BIBLE THROUGH IN ONE YEAR: Psalms 84-88

Imagination June 22

"And the Lord said, Behold, the people is one, and they have all one language; and this they begin to do: and now nothing will be restrained from them, which they have imagined to do." *Genesis 11:6*

"And thou, Solomon my son, know thou the God of thy father, and serve Him with a perfect heart and with a willing mind: for the Lord searcheth all hearts, and understandeth all the imaginations of the thoughts: if thou seek Him, He will be found of thee; but if thou forsake Him, He will cast thee off for ever."
1 Chronicles 28:9

"These six things doth the Lord hate;...An heart that deviseth wicked imaginations, feet that be swift in running to mischief." *Proverbs 6:16, 18*

"For as he thinketh in his heart, so is he."
Proverbs 23:7

"Casting down imaginations, and every high thing that exalteth itself against the knowledge of God, and bringing into captivity every thought to the obedience of Christ." *2 Corinthians 10:5*

"Memory Replays The Past—Imagination Preplays The Future."

-MIKE MURDOCK

READ THE BIBLE THROUGH IN ONE YEAR: Psalms 89-91

Impatience

June 23

"Wait on the Lord: be of good courage, and He shall strengthen thine heart: wait, I say, on the Lord."
Psalm 27:14

"The eyes of all wait upon thee; and thou givest them their meat in due season." *Psalm 145:15*

"And He said unto them, It is not for you to know the times or the seasons, which the Father hath put in His own power." *Acts 1:7*

"And not only so, but we glory in tribulations also: knowing that tribulation worketh patience; And patience, experience; and experience, hope." *Romans 5:3-4*

"But if we hope for that we see not, then do we with patience wait for it." *Romans 8:25*

"And let us not be weary in well doing: for in due season we shall reap, if we faint not." *Galatians 6:9*

"Knowing this, that the trying of your faith worketh patience." *James 1:3*

"But let patience have her perfect work, that ye may be perfect and entire, wanting nothing." *James 1:4*

"An Uncommon Dream Requires Uncommon Patience."

-MIKE MURDOCK

READ THE BIBLE THROUGH IN ONE YEAR: Psalms 92-94

Increase

June 24

"Trust not in oppression, and become not vain in robbery: if riches increase, set not your heart upon them." *Psalm 62:10*

"Honour the Lord with thy substance, and with the firstfruits of all thine increase." *Proverbs 3:9*

"For the seed shall be prosperous; the vine shall give her fruit, and the ground shall give her increase, and the Heavens shall give their dew; and I will cause the remnant of this people to possess all these things."

Zechariah 8:12

"And He said unto them, Take heed, and beware of covetousness: for a man's life consisteth not in the abundance of the things which he possesseth."

Luke 12:15

"Now he that ministereth seed to the sower both minister bread for your food, and multiply your seed sown, and increase the fruits of your righteousness."

2 Corinthians 9:10

"And the Lord make you to increase and abound in love one toward another, and toward all men, even as we do toward you." *1 Thessalonians 3:12*

"Every Decision Creates Increase or Decrease."

-MIKE MURDOCK

READ THE BIBLE THROUGH IN ONE YEAR: Psalms 95-97

Influence

June 25

"A good name is rather to be chosen than great riches, and loving favour rather than silver and gold."
Proverbs 22:1

"Ye are the salt of the earth." *Matthew 5:13*

"Ye are the light of the world. A city that is set on an hill cannot be hid." *Matthew 5:14*

"Let your light so shine before men, that they may see your good works, and glorify your Father which is in Heaven." *Matthew 5:16*

"And He said unto them, Go ye into all the world, and preach the gospel to every creature." *Mark 16:15*

"Know ye not that a little leaven leaveneth the whole lump?" *1 Corinthians 5:6*

"Be not deceived: evil communications corrupt good manners." *1 Corinthians 15:33*

"Your Adversity Is Always Proportionate To Your Potential Influence."

-MIKE MURDOCK

READ THE BIBLE THROUGH IN ONE YEAR: Psalms 98-100

Injustice

June 26

"No weapon that is formed against thee shall prosper; and every tongue that shall rise against thee in judgment thou shalt condemn. This is the heritage of the servants of the Lord, and their righteousness is of Me, saith the Lord."   *Isaiah 54:17*

"But I say unto you, Love your enemies, bless them that curse you, do good to them that hate you, and pray for them which despitefully use you, and persecute you."
Matthew 5:44

"...If thy brother trespass against thee, rebuke him; and if he repent, forgive him."   *Luke 17:3*

"When the chief priests therefore and officers saw Him, they cried out, saying, Crucify Him, crucify Him. Pilate saith unto them, Take ye Him, and crucify Him: for I find no fault in Him."   *John 19:6*

"And we know that all things work together for good to them that love God, to them who are the called according to His purpose."   *Romans 8:28*

"And the Lord shall deliver me from every evil work, and will preserve me unto His Heavenly kingdom: to Whom be glory for ever and ever. Amen."
2 Timothy 4:18

"Injustice Is Only As Powerful As Your Memory of It."
-MIKE MURDOCK

READ THE BIBLE THROUGH IN ONE YEAR: Psalms 101-103

Integrity

June 27

"A good man sheweth favour, and lendeth: he will guide his affairs with discretion."   *Psalm 112:5*

"The lip of truth shall be established for ever: but a lying tongue is but for a moment."   *Proverbs 12:19*

"Lying lips are abomination to the Lord: but they that deal truly are His delight."   *Proverbs 12:22*

"A righteous man hateth lying: but a wicked man is loathsome, and cometh to shame."   *Proverbs 13:5*

"The just man walketh in his integrity: his children are blessed after him."   *Proverbs 20:7*

"A good name is rather to be chosen than great riches, and loving favour rather than silver and gold."
Proverbs 22:1

"Be not a witness against thy neighbour without cause; and deceive not with thy lips." *Proverbs 24:28*

"The Reward of Integrity Is Self-Confidence."

-MIKE MURDOCK

READ THE BIBLE THROUGH IN ONE YEAR: Psalms 104-106

Integrity of God

June 28

"And, behold, I am with thee, and will keep thee in all places whither thou goest, and will bring thee again into this land; for I will not leave thee, until I have that which I have spoken to thee of." *Genesis 28:15*

"God is not a man, that He should lie; neither the son of man, that He should repent: hath He said, and shall He not do it? or hath He spoken, and shall He not make it good?" *Numbers 23:19*

"Every word of God is pure: He is a shield unto them that put their trust in Him. Add thou not unto His words, lest He reprove thee, and thou be found a liar."

Proverbs 30:5-6

"I have not spoken in secret, in a dark place of the earth: I said not unto the seed of Jacob, Seek ye Me in vain: I the Lord speak righteousness, I declare things that are right." *Isaiah 45:19*

"I the Lord have spoken it: it shall come to pass, and I will do it." *Ezekiel 24:14*

"God's Only Pain Is To Be Doubted, His Only Pleasure Is To Be Believed."

-MIKE MURDOCK

READ THE BIBLE THROUGH IN ONE YEAR: Psalms 107-111

Intercession June 29

"And I sought for a man among them, that should make up the hedge, and stand in the gap before Me for the land, that I should not destroy it: but I found none." *Ezekiel 22:30*

"Verily I say unto you, Whatsoever ye shall bind on earth shall be bound in Heaven: and whatsoever ye shall loose on earth shall be loosed in Heaven. Again I say unto you, That if two of you shall agree on earth as touching any thing that they shall ask, it shall be done for them of My Father which is in Heaven."
Matthew 18:18-19

"Likewise the Spirit also helpeth our infirmities: for we know not what we should pray for as we ought: but the Spirit itself maketh intercession for us with groanings which cannot be uttered." *Romans 8:26*

"Pray without ceasing." *1 Thessalonians 5:17*

"Wherefore He is able also to save them to the uttermost that come unto God by Him, seeing He ever liveth to make intercession for them." *Hebrews 7:25*

"God Never Responds To Pain; God Always Responds To Pursuit."

-MIKE MURDOCK

READ THE BIBLE THROUGH IN ONE YEAR: Psalms 112-114

Jealousy

June 30

"And when Rachel saw that she bare Jacob no children, Rachel envied her sister; and said unto Jacob, Give me children, or else I die." *Genesis 30:1*

"Thou shalt not covet thy neighbour's house, thou shalt not covet thy neighbour's wife, nor his manservant, nor his maidservant, nor his ox, nor his ass, nor any thing that is thy neighbour's." *Exodus 20:17*

"For jealousy is the rage of a man: therefore he will not spare in the day of vengeance. He will not regard any ransom; neither will he rest content, though thou givest many gifts." *Proverbs 6:34-35*

"Again, I considered all travail, and every right work, that for this a man is envied of his neighbour. This is also vanity and vexation of spirit." *Ecclesiastes 4:4*

"...jealousy is cruel as the grave: the coals thereof are coals of fire, which hath a most vehement flame."
Song of Solomon 8:6

"Giving thanks always for all things unto God and the Father in the name of our Lord Jesus Christ."
Ephesians 5:20

"Jealousy Occurs When You Believe Someone Else Received What You Earned."

-MIKE MURDOCK

READ THE BIBLE THROUGH IN ONE YEAR: Psalms 115-117

Jesus

July 1

"And she shall bring forth a son, and thou shalt call His name Jesus: for He shall save His people from their sins." *Matthew 1:21*

"Then spake Jesus again unto them, saying, I am the light of the world: he that followeth Me shall not walk in darkness, but shall have the light of life." *John 8:12*

"I am the good shepherd: the good shepherd giveth His life for the sheep." *John 10:11*

"Jesus said unto her, I am the resurrection, and the life: he that believeth in Me, though he were dead, yet shall he live." *John 11:25*

"Jesus saith unto him, I am the way, the truth, and the life: no man cometh unto the Father, but by Me." *John 14:6*

"For there is one God, and one mediator between God and men, the man Christ Jesus." *1 Timothy 2:5*

"His Mind Is Keener Than Yours; His Memory Is Longer Than Yours; His Shoulders Are Bigger Than Yours."

-MIKE MURDOCK

READ THE BIBLE THROUGH IN ONE YEAR: Psalms 118-120

Job

July 2

"Six days shalt thou labour, and do all thy work."
Exodus 20:9

"The Lord shall open unto thee His good treasure, the Heaven to give the rain unto thy land in His season, and to bless all the work of thine hand: and thou shalt lend unto many nations, and thou shalt not borrow."
Deuteronomy 28:12

"Also unto Thee, O Lord, belongeth mercy: for Thou renderest to every man according to his work."
Psalm 62:12

"And let the beauty of the Lord our God be upon us: and establish thou the work of our hands upon us; yea, the work of our hands establish thou it." *Psalm 90:17*

"But let every man prove his own work, and then shall he have rejoicing in himself alone, and not in another." *Galatians 6:4*

"For even when we were with you, this we commanded you, that if any would not work, neither should he eat." *2 Thessalonians 3:10*

"You Can Only Be Promoted By The Person Whose Instructions You Follow."

-MIKE MURDOCK

READ THE BIBLE THROUGH IN ONE YEAR: Psalms 121-123

Journalizing — July 3

"And thou shalt write upon the stones all the words of this law very plainly." *Deuteronomy 27:8*

"Now go, write it before them in a table, and note it in a book, that it may be for the time to come for ever and ever." *Isaiah 30:8*

"Thus speaketh the Lord God of Israel, saying, Write thee all the words that I have spoken unto thee in a book." *Jeremiah 30:2*

"And the Lord answered me, and said, Write the vision, and make it plain upon tables, that he may run that readeth it." *Habakkuk 2:2*

"For this is the covenant that I will make with the house of Israel after those days, saith the Lord; I will put My laws into their mind, and write them in their hearts: and I will be to them a God, and they shall be to Me a people." *Hebrews 8:10*

"And these things write we unto you, that your joy may be full." *1 John 1:4*

"A Short Pencil Is Better Than A Long Memory."
  -MIKE MURDOCK

READ THE BIBLE THROUGH IN ONE YEAR: Psalms 124-126

Joy

July 4

"...For this day is holy unto our Lord: neither be ye sorry; for the joy of the Lord is your strength."
Nehemiah 8:10

"But let all those that put their trust in Thee rejoice: let them ever shout for joy, because Thou defendest them: let them also that love Thy name be joyful in Thee." *Psalm 5:11*

"Thou wilt shew me the path of life: in Thy presence is fulness of joy; at Thy right hand there are pleasures for evermore." *Psalm 16:11*

"For His anger endureth but a moment; in His favour is life: weeping may endure for a night, but joy cometh in the morning." *Psalm 30:5*

"But the fruit of the Spirit is love, joy, peace, longsuffering, gentleness, goodness, faith." *Galatians 5:22*

"Joy Is The Fragrance Reserved For The Obedient."
-MIKE MURDOCK

READ THE BIBLE THROUGH IN ONE YEAR: Psalms 127-129

Judgments of God

July 5

"Let us hear the conclusion of the whole matter: Fear God, and keep His commandments: for this is the whole duty of man. For God shall bring every work into judgment, with every secret thing, whether it be good, or whether it be evil." *Ecclesiastes 12:13-14*

"But we are sure that the judgment of God is according to truth against them which commit such things. And thinkest thou this, O man, that judgest them which do such things, and doest the same, that thou shalt escape the judgment of God? But after thy hardness and impenitent heart treasurest up unto thyself wrath against the day of wrath and revelation of the righteous judgment of God." *Romans 2:2-3, 5*

"So then every one of us shall give account of himself to God." *Romans 14:12*

"Knowing therefore the terror of the Lord, we persuade men." *2 Corinthians 5:11*

"You Will Never Respect Someone You Are Capable of Deceiving."

-MIKE MURDOCK

READ THE BIBLE THROUGH IN ONE YEAR: Psalms 130-134

Kindness

July 6

"For His merciful kindness is great toward us: and the truth of the Lord endureth for ever. Praise ye the Lord."
Psalm 117:2

"She openeth her mouth with Wisdom; and in her tongue is the law of kindness." *Proverbs 31:26*

"Charity suffereth long, and is kind." *1 Corinthians 13:4*

"But in all things approving ourselves as the ministers of God, in much patience,...by knowledge, by longsuffering, by kindness, by the Holy Ghost, by love unfeigned." *2 Corinthians 6:4, 6*

"And be ye kind one to another, tenderhearted, forgiving one another, even as God for Christ's sake hath forgiven you." *Ephesians 4:32*

"...but Christ is all, and in all. Put on therefore, as the elect of God, holy and beloved, bowels of mercies, kindness, humbleness of mind, meekness, longsuffering." *Colossians 3:11-12*

"People Don't Always Remember What You Say — They Always Remember How They Felt When You Said It."

-MIKE MURDOCK

READ THE BIBLE THROUGH IN ONE YEAR: Psalms 135-137

Knowledge

July 7

"The fear of the Lord is the beginning of knowledge: but fools despise Wisdom and instruction." *Proverbs 1:7*

"Yea, if thou criest after knowledge, and liftest up thy voice for understanding; If thou seekest her as silver, and searchest for her as for hid treasures; Then shalt thou understand the fear of the Lord, and find the knowledge of God. For the Lord giveth Wisdom: out of His mouth cometh knowledge and understanding."

Proverbs 2:3-6

"Receive My instruction, and not silver; and knowledge rather than choice gold." *Proverbs 8:10*

"Wise men lay up knowledge: but the mouth of the foolish is near destruction." *Proverbs 10:14*

"He that hath knowledge spareth his words: and a man of understanding is of an excellent spirit."

Proverbs 17:27

"My people are destroyed for lack of knowledge: because thou hast rejected knowledge, I will also reject thee, that thou shalt be no priest to Me: seeing thou hast forgotten the law of thy God, I will also forget thy children." *Hosea 4:6*

"Your Ignorance Is The Only Weapon Your Enemy Can Use Against You."

-MIKE MURDOCK

READ THE BIBLE THROUGH IN ONE YEAR: Psalms 138-140

Laughter

July 8

"And Sarah said, God hath made me to laugh, so that all that hear will laugh with me." *Genesis 21:6*

"Thou wilt shew me the path of life: in Thy presence is fulness of joy; at Thy right hand there are pleasures for evermore." *Psalm 16:11*

"Then was our mouth filled with laughter, and our tongue with singing: then said they among the heathen, The Lord hath done great things for them." *Psalm 126:2*

"A merry heart doeth good like a medicine: but a broken spirit drieth the bones." *Proverbs 17:22*

"A time to weep, and a time to laugh; a time to mourn, and a time to dance." *Ecclesiastes 3:4*

"Sorrow is better than laughter: for by the sadness of the countenance the heart is made better." *Ecclesiastes 7:3*

"Blessed are ye that hunger now: for ye shall be filled. Blessed are ye that weep now: for ye shall laugh."
Luke 6:21

"Joy Is The Fruit of Order."

-MIKE MURDOCK

READ THE BIBLE THROUGH IN ONE YEAR: Psalms 141-143

Lawlessness — July 9

"This book of the law shall not depart out of thy mouth; but thou shalt meditate therein day and night, that thou mayest observe to do according to all that is written therein: for then thou shalt make thy way prosperous, and then thou shalt have good success." *Joshua 1:8*

"The law of his God is in his heart; none of his steps shall slide." *Psalm 37:31*

"Let every soul be subject unto the higher powers. For there is no power but of God: the powers that be are ordained of God. Whosoever therefore resisteth the power, resisteth the ordinance of God: and they that resist shall receive to themselves damnation. For rulers are not a terror to good works, but to the evil. Wilt thou then not be afraid of the power? do that which is good, and thou shalt have praise of the same: For he is the minister of God to thee for good. But if thou do that which is evil, be afraid; for he beareth not the sword in vain: for he is the minister of God, a revenger to execute wrath upon him that doeth evil. Wherefore ye must needs be subject, not only for wrath, but also for conscience sake." *Romans 13:1-5*

"The Product of Legitimate Authority And Law Is Order."

-MIKE MURDOCK

READ THE BIBLE THROUGH IN ONE YEAR: Psalms 144-146

Laziness

July 10

"Yet a little sleep, a little slumber, a little folding of the hands to sleep: So shall thy poverty come as one that travelleth, and thy want as an armed man."
Proverbs 6:10-11

"The hand of the diligent shall bear rule: but the slothful shall be under tribute." *Proverbs 12:24*

"The soul of the sluggard desireth, and hath nothing: but the soul of the diligent shall be made fat."
Proverbs 13:4

"Whatsoever thy hand findeth to do, do it with thy might." *Ecclesiastes 9:10*

"By much slothfulness the building decayeth; and through idleness of the hands the house droppeth through." *Ecclesiastes 10:18*

"For even when we were with you, this we commanded you, that if any would not work, neither should he eat."
2 Thessalonians 3:10

"Laziness Is Silent Defiance."

-MIKE MURDOCK

READ THE BIBLE THROUGH IN ONE YEAR: Psalms 147-149

Leadership

July 11

"Therefore now go, lead the people unto the place of which I have spoken unto thee: behold, Mine Angel shall go before thee." *Exodus 32:34*

"The steps of a good man are ordered by the Lord: and He delighteth in his way." *Psalm 37:23*

"Behold, I have given him for a witness to the people, a leader and commander to the people." *Isaiah 55:4*

"As a shepherd seeketh out his flock in the day that he is among his sheep that are scattered; so will I seek out my sheep, and will deliver them out of all places where they have been scattered in the cloudy and dark day."
Ezekiel 34:12

"And Jesus, when he came out, saw much people, and was moved with compassion toward them, because they were as sheep not having a shepherd: and he began to teach them many things." *Mark 6:34*

"Thou therefore, my son, be strong in the grace that is in Christ Jesus. And the things that thou hast heard of me among many witnesses, the same commit thou to faithful men, who shall be able to teach others also."
2 Timothy 2:1-2

"Leadership Is The Ability To Influence The Decisions of Others."

-MIKE MURDOCK

READ THE BIBLE THROUGH IN ONE YEAR: Psalm 150-Proverbs 2

Learning

July 12

"A wise man will hear, and will increase learning; and a man of understanding shall attain unto wise counsels."
Proverbs 1:5

"Give instruction to a wise man, and he will be yet wiser: teach a just man, and he will increase in learning."
Proverbs 9:9

"The wise in heart shall be called prudent: and the sweetness of the lips increaseth learning." *Proverbs 16:21*

"The heart of the wise teacheth his mouth, and addeth learning to his lips." *Proverbs 16:23*

"Learn to do well." *Isaiah 1:17*

"For whatsoever things were written aforetime were written for our learning, that we through patience and comfort of the scriptures might have hope."
Romans 15:4

"Ever learning, and never able to come to the knowledge of the truth." *2 Timothy 3:7*

"The Proof of Humility Is The Willingness To Reach."
-MIKE MURDOCK

READ THE BIBLE THROUGH IN ONE YEAR: Proverbs 3-7

Letter Writing

July 13

"And the Lord said unto Moses, Write this for a memorial in a book, and rehearse it in the ears of Joshua." *Exodus 17:14*

"And the Lord answered me, and said, Write the vision, and make it plain upon tables, that he may run that readeth it." *Habakkuk 2:2*

"It seemed good to me also, having had perfect understanding of all things from the very first, to write unto thee in order, most excellent Theophilus, That thou mightest know the certainty of those things, wherein thou hast been instructed." *Luke 1:3-4*

"And these things write we unto you, that your joy may be full." *1 John 1:4*

"My little children, these things write I unto you, that ye sin not." *1 John 2:1*

"Beloved, when I gave all diligence to write unto you of the common salvation, it was needful for me to write unto you, and exhort you that ye should earnestly contend for the faith which was once delivered unto the saints." *Jude 1:3*

"Every Letter You Write Is An Opportunity To Heal Another."

-MIKE MURDOCK

READ THE BIBLE THROUGH IN ONE YEAR: Proverbs 8-10

Life

July 14

"My son, attend to my words; incline thine ear unto my sayings. For they are life unto those that find them, and health to all their flesh." *Proverbs 4:20, 22*

"For whoso findeth Me findeth life, and shall obtain favour of the Lord." *Proverbs 8:35*

"Therefore I say unto you, Take no thought for your life, what ye shall eat, or what ye shall drink; nor yet for your body, what ye shall put on. Is not the life more than meat, and the body than raiment?" *Matthew 6:25*

"And He said unto them, Take heed, and beware of covetousness: for a man's life consisteth not in the abundance of the things which he possesseth."
Luke 12:15

"The thief cometh not, but for to steal, and to kill, and to destroy: I am come that they might have life, and that they might have it more abundantly." *John 10:10*

"When Christ, Who is our life, shall appear, then shall ye also appear with Him in glory." *Colossians 3:4*

"Life Is A Collection of Decisions That Decide The Joy You Experience."

-MIKE MURDOCK

READ THE BIBLE THROUGH IN ONE YEAR: Proverbs 11-13

Listening

July 15

"Observe and hear all these words which I command thee, that it may go well with thee, and with thy children after thee for ever, when thou doest that which is good and right in the sight of the Lord thy God."
Deuteronomy 12:28

"I will hear what God the Lord will speak: for He will speak peace unto His people, and to His saints: but let them not turn again to folly." *Psalm 85:8*

"In the multitude of words there wanteth not sin: but he that refraineth his lips is wise." *Proverbs 10:19*

"For by wise counsel thou shalt make thy war: and in multitude of counsellors there is safety." *Proverbs 24:6*

"Wherefore, my beloved brethren, let every man be swift to hear, slow to speak, slow to wrath." *James 1:19*

"He that hath an ear, let him hear what the Spirit saith unto the churches." *Revelation 2:7*

"The Willingness To Listen Is The First Step Toward Change."

-MIKE MURDOCK

READ THE BIBLE THROUGH IN ONE YEAR: Proverbs 14-16

Loneliness July 16

"And, behold, I am with thee, and will keep thee in all places whither thou goest, and will bring thee again into this land; for I will not leave thee, until I have done that which I have spoken to thee of."
Genesis 28:15

"And the Lord, He it is that doth go before thee; He will be with thee, He will not fail thee, neither forsake thee: fear not, neither be dismayed."
Deuteronomy 31:8

"Yea, though I walk through the valley of the shadow of death, I will fear no evil: for Thou art with me; Thy rod and Thy staff they comfort me." *Psalm 23:4*

"When my father and my mother forsake me, then the Lord will take me up." *Psalm 27:10*

"A man that hath friends must shew himself friendly: and there is a friend that sticketh closer than a brother." *Proverbs 18:24*

"I will never leave thee, nor forsake thee." *Hebrews 13:5*

"Loneliness Is Not The Absence of Affection, But The Absence of Direction."

-*MIKE MURDOCK*

READ THE BIBLE THROUGH IN ONE YEAR: Proverbs 17-19

Longevity

July 17

"Honour thy father and thy mother: that thy days may be long upon the land which the Lord thy God giveth thee." *Exodus 20:12*

"And God said to Solomon, Because this was in thine heart, and thou hast not asked riches, wealth, or honour, nor the life of thine enemies, neither yet hast asked long life; but hast asked Wisdom and knowledge for thyself, that thou mayest judge my people, over whom I have made thee king." *2 Chronicles 1:11*

"With long life will I satisfy him, and shew him my salvation." *Psalm 91:16*

"I will sing unto the Lord as long as I live: I will sing praise to my God while I have my being." *Psalm 104:33*

"My son, forget not My law; but let thine heart keep My commandments: For length of days, and long life, and peace, shall they add to thee." *Proverbs 3:1-2*

"Beloved, I wish above all things that thou mayest prosper and be in health, even as thy soul prospereth." *3 John 1:2*

"An Uncommon Future Will Require Uncommon Preparation."

-MIKE MURDOCK

READ THE BIBLE THROUGH IN ONE YEAR: Proverbs 20-22

Longsuffering — July 18

"But Thou, O Lord, art a God full of compassion, and gracious, longsuffering, and plenteous in mercy and truth." *Psalm 86:15*

"And shall not God avenge His own elect, which cry day and night unto Him, though He bear long with them?" *Luke 18:7*

"But the fruit of the Spirit is love, joy, peace, longsuffering, gentleness, goodness, faith." *Galatians 5:22*

"No man that warreth entangleth himself with the affairs of this life; that he may please Him Who hath chosen him to be a soldier." *2 Timothy 2:4*

"The Lord is not slack concerning His promise, as some men count slackness; but is longsuffering to us-ward, not willing that any should perish, but that all should come to repentance." *2 Peter 3:9*

"Your Ability To Forgive Determines The Quality of Your Life."

-MIKE MURDOCK

READ THE BIBLE THROUGH IN ONE YEAR: Proverbs 23-25

Loss

July 19

"Rest in the Lord, and wait patiently for Him: fret not thyself because of him who prospereth in his way, because of the man who bringeth wicked devices to pass. The steps of a good man are ordered by the Lord: and He delighteth in his way."   *Psalm 37:7, 23*

"Men do not despise a thief, if he steal to satisfy his soul when he is hungry; But if he be found, he shall restore sevenfold; he shall give all the substance of his house."   *Proverbs 6:30-31*

"And I will restore to you the years that the locust hath eaten, the cankerworm, and the caterpillar, and the palmerworm, My great army which I sent among you."   *Joel 2:25*

"The thief cometh not, but for to steal, and to kill, and to destroy: I am come that they might have life, and that they might have it more abundantly."   *John 10:10*

"Loss Is The Quickest Cure For Ingratitude."

-*MIKE MURDOCK*

READ THE BIBLE THROUGH IN ONE YEAR: Proverbs 26-30

Love

July 20

"Many waters cannot quench love, neither can the floods drown it: if a man would give all the substance of his house for love, it would utterly be condemned."
Song of Solomon 8:7

"For God so loved the world, that He gave His only begotten Son, that whosoever believeth in Him should not perish, but have everlasting life." *John 3:16*

"A new commandment I give unto you, That ye love one another; as I have loved you, that ye also love one another. By this shall all men know that ye are My disciples, if ye have love one to another." *John 13:34-35*

"And hope maketh not ashamed; because the love of God is shed abroad in our hearts by the Holy Ghost which is given unto us." *Romans 5:5*

"But the fruit of the Spirit is love, joy, peace, longsuffering, gentleness, goodness, faith." *Galatians 5:22*

"Husbands, love your wives, even as Christ also loved the church, and gave Himself for it." *Ephesians 5:25*

"The Proof of Love Is The Willingness To Change."

-MIKE MURDOCK

READ THE BIBLE THROUGH IN ONE YEAR: Proverbs 31-Ecclesiastes 2

Love of God — July 21

"He that hath My commandments, and keepeth them, he it is that loveth Me: and he that loveth Me shall be loved of My Father, and I will love him, and will manifest Myself to him." *John 14:21*

"For I am persuaded, that neither death, nor life, nor angels, nor principalities, nor powers, nor things present, nor things to come, Nor height, nor depth, nor any other creature, shall be able to separate us from the love of God, which is in Christ Jesus our Lord."
Romans 8:38-39

"And to know the love of Christ, which passeth knowledge, that ye might be filled with all the fulness of God." *Ephesians 3:19*

"But whoso keepeth His word, in him verily is the love of God perfected: hereby know we that we are in Him."
1 John 2:5

"Beloved, let us love one another: for love is of God; and every one that loveth is born of God, and knoweth God. He that loveth not knoweth not God; for God is love." *1 John 4:7, 10*

"What You Love Will Eventually Reward You."

-MIKE MURDOCK

READ THE BIBLE THROUGH IN ONE YEAR: Ecclesiastes 3-5

Loyalty

July 22

"Discretion shall preserve thee, understanding shall keep thee." *Proverbs 2:11*

"A talebearer revealeth secrets: but he that is of a faithful spirit concealeth the matter." *Proverbs 11:13*

"A man that hath friends must shew himself friendly: and there is a friend that sticketh closer than a brother." *Proverbs 18:24*

"Most men will proclaim every one his own goodness: but a faithful man who can find?" *Proverbs 20:6*

"Debate thy cause with thy neighbour himself; and discover not a secret to another." *Proverbs 25:9*

"As the cold of snow in the time of harvest, so is a faithful messenger to them that send him: for he refresheth the soul of his masters." *Proverbs 25:13*

"Confidence in an unfaithful man in time of trouble is like a broken tooth, and a foot out of joint."

Proverbs 25:19

"A faithful man shall abound with blessings: but he that maketh haste to be rich shall not be innocent."

Proverbs 28:20

"Give Someone What They Cannot Find Anywhere Else, And They Will Keep Returning."

-MIKE MURDOCK

READ THE BIBLE THROUGH IN ONE YEAR: Ecclesiastes 6-8

Lust

July 23

"Who can understand his errors? cleanse Thou me from secret faults. Keep back Thy servant also from presumptuous sins; let them not have dominion over me: then shall I be upright, and I shall be innocent from the great transgression. Let the words of my mouth, and the meditation of my heart, be acceptable in Thy sight, O Lord, my strength, and my redeemer." *Psalm 19:12-14*

"Create in me a clean heart, O God; and renew a right spirit within me." *Psalm 51:10*

"That ye put off concerning the former conversation the old man, which is corrupt according to the deceitful lusts; And be renewed in the spirit of your mind; And that ye put on the new man, which after God is created in righteousness and true holiness." *Ephesians 4:22-24*

"Let no man say when he is tempted, I am tempted of God: for God cannot be tempted with evil, neither tempteth he any man: But every man is tempted, when he is drawn away of his own lust, and enticed."
James 1:13-14

"What You Fail To Conquer Will Eventually Conquer You."

-MIKE MURDOCK

READ THE BIBLE THROUGH IN ONE YEAR: Ecclesiastes 9-11

Lying

July 24

"Through thy precepts I get understanding: therefore I hate every false way." *Psalm 119:104*

"The lip of truth shall be established for ever: but a lying tongue is but for a moment." *Proverbs 12:19*

"Lying lips are abomination to the Lord: but they that deal truly are his delight." *Proverbs 12:22*

"A righteous man hateth lying: but a wicked man is loathsome, and cometh to shame." *Proverbs 13:5*

"Trust ye not in a friend, put ye not confidence in a guide: keep the doors of thy mouth from her that lieth in thy bosom." *Micah 7:5*

"Wherefore putting away lying, speak every man truth with his neighbour: for we are members one of another." *Ephesians 4:25*

"But the fearful, and unbelieving, and the abominable, and murderers, and whoremongers, and sorcerers, and idolaters, and all liars, shall have their part in the lake which burneth with fire and brimstone: which is the second death." *Revelation 21:8*

"Those Who Lie For You Will Eventually Lie Against You."

-MIKE MURDOCK

READ THE BIBLE THROUGH IN ONE YEAR: Eccl. 12-Song of Solomon 2

Marriage

July 25

"And the Lord God said, It is not good that the man should be alone; I will make him an help meet for him. Therefore shall a man leave his father and his mother, and shall cleave unto his wife: and they shall be one flesh." *Genesis 2:18, 24*

"Two are better than one; because they have a good reward for their labour. For if they fall, the one will lift up his fellow: but woe to him that is alone when he falleth; for he hath not another to help him up. Again, if two lie together, then they have heat: but how can one be warm alone? And if one prevail against him, two shall withstand him; and a threefold cord is not quickly broken." *Ecclesiastes 4:9-12*

"Husbands, love your wives, even as Christ also loved the church, and gave Himself for it; So ought men to love their wives as their own bodies. He that loveth his wife loveth himself." *Ephesians 5:25, 28*

"Wives, submit yourselves unto your own husbands, as it is fit in the Lord. Husbands, love your wives, and be not bitter against them." *Colossians 3:18-19*

"God Will Never Authorize A Man To Marry A Woman Who Refuses To Follow; Nor A Woman To Marry A Man Who Refuses To Lead."

-MIKE MURDOCK

READ THE BIBLE THROUGH IN ONE YEAR: Song of Solomon 3-5

Meditation

July 26

"This book of the law shall not depart out of thy mouth; but thou shalt meditate therein day and night." *Joshua 1:8*

"Let the words of my mouth, and the meditation of my heart, be acceptable in Thy sight, O Lord, my strength, and my Redeemer." *Psalm 19:14*

"I will meditate also of all Thy work, and talk of Thy doings." *Psalm 77:12*

"For as he thinketh in his heart, so is he: Eat and drink, saith he to thee; but his heart is not with thee." *Proverbs 23:7*

"In the day of prosperity be joyful, but in the day of adversity consider." *Ecclesiastes 7:14*

"Finally, brethren, whatsoever things are true, whatsoever things are honest, whatsoever things are just, whatsoever things are pure, whatsoever things are lovely, whatsoever things are of good report; if there be any virtue, and if there be any praise, think on these things." *Philippians 4:8*

"What You Think About The Most Will Grow The Strongest In You."

-MIKE MURDOCK

READ THE BIBLE THROUGH IN ONE YEAR: Song of Solomon 6-Isaiah 2

Memorizing Scriptures

July 27

"And thou shalt teach them diligently unto thy children, and shalt talk of them when thou sittest in thine house, and when thou walkest by the way, and when thou liest down, and when thou risest up. And thou shalt bind them for a sign upon thine hand, and they shall be as frontlets between thine eyes. And thou shalt write them upon the posts of thy house, and on thy gates."
Deuteronomy 6:7-9

"Thy word have I hid in mine heart, that I might not sin against Thee." *Psalm 119:11*

"Jesus answered and said unto them, Ye do err, not knowing the scriptures, nor the power of God."
Matthew 22:29

"And that from a child thou hast known the holy scriptures, which are able to make thee wise unto salvation through faith which is in Christ Jesus."
2 Timothy 3:15

"What Enters You Determines What Exits You."
-MIKE MURDOCK

READ THE BIBLE THROUGH IN ONE YEAR: Isaiah 3-5

Mentorship — July 28

"Then one of the priests whom they had carried away from Samaria came and dwelt in Bethel, and taught them how they should fear the Lord." *2 Kings 17:28*

"Where no counsel is, the people fall: but in the multitude of counsellors there is safety." *Proverbs 11:14*

"And it came to pass, that, as He was praying in a certain place, when He ceased, one of His disciples said unto Him, Lord, teach us to pray, as John also taught his disciples." *Luke 11:1*

"And how I kept back nothing that was profitable unto you, but have shewed you, and have taught you publicly, and from house to house." *Acts 20:20*

"For this cause left I thee in Crete, that thou shouldest set in order the things that are wanting, and ordain elders in every city, as I had appointed thee." *Titus 1:5*

"Someone Has Heard What You Have Not; Someone Has Seen What You Have Not; Someone Knows What You Do Not. Your Success Depends On Your Willingness To Be Mentored By Them."

-MIKE MURDOCK

READ THE BIBLE THROUGH IN ONE YEAR: Isaiah 6-8

Mercy

July 29

"For Thou, Lord, art good, and ready to forgive; and plenteous in mercy unto all them that call upon Thee."
Psalm 86:5

"The Lord is merciful and gracious, slow to anger, and plenteous in mercy." *Psalm 103:8*

"Let not mercy and truth forsake thee: bind them about thy neck; write them upon the table of thine heart."
Proverbs 3:3

"He that despiseth his neighbour sinneth: but he that hath mercy on the poor, happy is he." *Proverbs 14:21*

"He that followeth after righteousness and mercy findeth life, righteousness, and honour." *Proverbs 21:21*

"Blessed are the merciful: for they shall obtain mercy."
Matthew 5:7

"But the Wisdom that is from above is first pure, then peaceable, gentle, and easy to be intreated, full of mercy and good fruits, without partiality, and without hypocrisy." *James 3:17*

"The Future of Every Relationship Is Decided By Mercy."

-MIKE MURDOCK

READ THE BIBLE THROUGH IN ONE YEAR: Isaiah 9-11

Millionaire Mentality

July 30

"...Let the Lord be magnified, which hath pleasure in the prosperity of His servant." *Psalm 35:27*

"If ye be willing and obedient, ye shall eat the good of the land." *Isaiah 1:19*

"Thus saith the Lord, thy Redeemer, the Holy One of Israel; I am the Lord thy God which teacheth thee to profit, which leadeth thee by the way that thou shouldest go." *Isaiah 48:17*

"The silver is Mine, and the gold is Mine, saith the Lord of hosts." *Haggai 2:8*

"Beloved, I wish above all things that thou mayest prosper and be in health, even as thy soul prospereth." *3 John 1:2*

"Money Does Not Change You...It Magnifies What You Already Are."

-MIKE MURDOCK

READ THE BIBLE THROUGH IN ONE YEAR: Isaiah 12-14

Ministry

July 31

"And if thou draw out thy soul to the hungry, and satisfy the afflicted soul; then shall thy light rise in obscurity, and thy darkness be as the noon day."   *Isaiah 58:10*

"And these signs shall follow them that believe; In My name shall they cast out devils; they shall speak with new tongues."   *Mark 16:17*

"How then shall they call on Him in Whom they have not believed? and how shall they believe in Him of Whom they have not heard? and how shall they hear without a preacher? And how shall they preach, except they be sent? as it is written, How beautiful are the feet of them that preach the gospel of peace, and bring glad tidings of good things!"   *Romans 10:14-15*

"...but our sufficiency is of God; Who also hath made us able ministers of the new testament."

2 Corinthians 3:5-6

"For God is not unrighteous to forget your work and labour of love, which ye have shewed toward His name, in that ye have ministered to the saints, and do minister."

Hebrews 6:10

"Your Reaction To Those In Trouble Determines How God Responds To You When You Are In Trouble."

-MIKE MURDOCK

READ THE BIBLE THROUGH IN ONE YEAR: Isaiah 15-17

Ministers

August 1

"...he that winneth souls is wise." *Proverbs 11:30*

"The Spirit of the Lord God is upon me; because the Lord hath anointed me to preach good tidings unto the meek; He hath sent me to bind up the brokenhearted, to proclaim liberty to the captives, and the opening of the prison to them that are bound; To proclaim the acceptable year of the Lord, and the day of vengeance of our God; to comfort all that mourn; To appoint unto them that mourn in Zion, to give unto them beauty for ashes, the oil of joy for mourning, the garment of praise for the spirit of heaviness; that they might be called trees of righteousness, the planting of the Lord, that He might be glorified. But ye shall be named the Priests of the Lord: men shall call you the Ministers of our God: ye shall eat the riches of the Gentiles, and in their glory shall ye boast yourselves." *Isaiah 61:1-3, 6*

"Knowing therefore the terror of the Lord, we persuade men." *2 Corinthians 5:11*

"Your Reaction To A Man of God Determines God's Reaction To You."

-MIKE MURDOCK

READ THE BIBLE THROUGH IN ONE YEAR: Isaiah 18-20

Miracles

August 2

"Ah Lord God! behold, thou hast made the Heaven and the earth by thy great power and stretched out arm, and there is nothing too hard for Thee." *Jeremiah 32:17*

"Ask, and it shall be given you; seek, and ye shall find; knock, and it shall be opened unto you." *Matthew 7:7*

"For verily I say unto you, That whosoever shall say unto this mountain, Be thou removed, and be thou cast into the sea; and shall not doubt in his heart, but shall believe that those things which he saith shall come to pass; he shall have whatsoever he saith. Therefore I say unto you, What things soever ye desire, when ye pray, believe that ye receive them, and ye shall have them." *Mark 11:23-24*

"How God anointed Jesus of Nazareth with the Holy Ghost and with power: Who went about doing good, and healing all that were oppressed of the devil; for God was with Him." *Acts 10:38*

"You Are Never As Far From A Miracle As It First Appears."

-MIKE MURDOCK

READ THE BIBLE THROUGH IN ONE YEAR: Isaiah 21-25

Missions

August 3

"...he that winneth souls is wise." *Proverbs 11:30*

"And He said unto them, Go ye into all the world, and preach the gospel to every creature." *Mark 16:15*

"But ye shall receive power, after that the Holy Ghost is come upon you: and ye shall be witnesses unto Me both in Jerusalem, and in all Judaea, and in Samaria, and unto the uttermost part of the earth." *Acts 1:8*

"How then shall they call on Him in Whom they have not believed? and how shall they believe in Him of Whom they have not heard? and how shall they hear without a preacher? And how shall they preach, except they be sent? as it is written, How beautiful are the feet of them that preach the gospel of peace, and bring glad tidings of good things!" *Romans 10:14-15*

"Knowing therefore the terror of the Lord, we persuade men." *2 Corinthians 5:11*

"Let him know, that he which converteth the sinner from the error of his way shall save a soul from death, and shall hide a multitude of sins." *James 5:20*

"He Who Withholds Bread Is Guilty of Murder."

-*MIKE MURDOCK*

READ THE BIBLE THROUGH IN ONE YEAR: Isaiah 26-28

Mistakes

August 4

"The beauty of Israel is slain upon Thy high places: how are the mighty fallen! Tell it not in Gath, publish it not in the streets of Askelon; lest the daughters of the Philistines rejoice, lest the daughters of the uncircumcised triumph." *2 Samuel 1:19-20*

"The steps of a good man are ordered by the Lord: and He delighteth in his way. Though he fall, he shall not be utterly cast down: for the Lord upholdeth him with His hand." *Psalm 37:23-24*

"Where no counsel is, the people fall: but in the multitude of counsellors there is safety." *Proverbs 11:14*

"For a just man falleth seven times, and riseth up again: but the wicked shall fall into mischief." *Proverbs 24:16*

"Come now, and let us reason together, saith the Lord: though your sins be as scarlet, they shall be as white as snow; though they be red like crimson, they shall be as wool." *Isaiah 1:18*

"All Men Fall, The Great Ones Get Back Up."

-MIKE MURDOCK

READ THE BIBLE THROUGH IN ONE YEAR: Isaiah 29-31

Misunderstandings August 5

"And I have filled him with the spirit of God, in Wisdom, and in understanding, and in knowledge, and in all manner of workmanship." *Exodus 31:3*

"For they are a nation void of counsel, neither is there any understanding in them." *Deuteronomy 32:28*

"And unto man He said, Behold, the fear of the Lord, that is Wisdom; and to depart from evil is understanding." *Job 28:28*

"I have more understanding than all my teachers: for thy testimonies are my meditation." *Psalm 119:99*

"The entrance of thy words giveth light; it giveth understanding unto the simple." *Psalm 119:130*

"Can two walk together, except they be agreed?" *Amos 3:3*

"Consider what I say; and the Lord give thee understanding in all things." *2 Timothy 2:7*

"Say What You Want Another To Hear."

-MIKE MURDOCK

READ THE BIBLE THROUGH IN ONE YEAR: Isaiah 32-34

Money

August 6

"A feast is made for laughter, and wine maketh merry: but money answereth all things." *Ecclesiastes 10:19*

"The silver is Mine, and the gold is Mine, saith the Lord of hosts." *Haggai 2:8*

"Give, and it shall be given unto you; good measure, pressed down, and shaken together, and running over, shall men give into your bosom. For with the same measure that ye mete withal it shall be measured to you again." *Luke 6:38*

"And He said unto them, Take heed, and beware of covetousness: for a man's life consisteth not in the abundance of the things which he possesseth." *Luke 12:15*

"For the love of money is the root of all evil: which while some coveted after, they have erred from the faith, and pierced themselves through with many sorrows." *1 Timothy 6:10*

"Beloved, I wish above all things that thou mayest prosper and be in health, even as thy soul prospereth." *3 John 1:2*

"Money Is Merely A Reward For Solving A Problem."
-*MIKE MURDOCK*

READ THE BIBLE THROUGH IN ONE YEAR: Isaiah 35-37

Moods

August 7

"A merry heart maketh a cheerful countenance: but by sorrow of the heart the spirit is broken." *Proverbs 15:13*

"All the days of the afflicted are evil: but he that is of a merry heart hath a continual feast." *Proverbs 15:15*

"He that is slow to anger is better than the mighty; and he that ruleth his spirit than he that taketh a city." *Proverbs 16:32*

"A merry heart doeth good like a medicine: but a broken spirit drieth the bones." *Proverbs 17:22*

"It is better to dwell in the wilderness, than with a contentious and an angry woman." *Proverbs 21:19*

"As he that taketh away a garment in cold weather, and as vinegar upon nitre, so is he that singeth songs to an heavy heart." *Proverbs 25:20*

"Where there is no vision, the people perish: but he that keepeth the law, happy is he." *Proverbs 29:18*

"When You Change Your Focus You Change Your Feelings."

-MIKE MURDOCK

READ THE BIBLE THROUGH IN ONE YEAR: Isaiah 38-40

Mothers

August 8

"Whoso curseth his father or his mother, his lamp shall be put out in obscure darkness." *Proverbs 20:20*

"Hearken unto thy father that begat thee, and despise not thy mother when she is old." *Proverbs 23:22*

"Thine own friend, and thy father's friend, forsake not; neither go into thy brother's house in the day of thy calamity: for better is a neighbour that is near than a brother far off." *Proverbs 27:10*

"Behold, every one that useth proverbs shall use this proverb against thee, saying, As is the mother, so is her daughter." *Ezekiel 16:44*

"For this cause shall a man leave his father and mother, and shall be joined unto his wife, and they two shall be one flesh." *Ephesians 5:31*

"Honour thy father and mother; (which is the first commandment with promise;) That it may be well with thee, and thou mayest live long on the earth."

Ephesians 6:2-3

"Your Reaction To Your Parents Determines God's Commitment To Your Prosperity."

-MIKE MURDOCK

READ THE BIBLE THROUGH IN ONE YEAR: Isaiah 41-43

Motivating Yourself

August 9

"Be strong and of a good courage, fear not, nor be afraid of them: for the Lord thy God, He it is that doth go with thee; He will not fail thee, nor forsake thee."

Deuteronomy 31:6

"And David was greatly distressed; for the people spake of stoning him, because the soul of all the people was grieved, every man for his sons and for his daughters: but David encouraged himself in the Lord his God." *1 Samuel 30:6*

"But He knoweth the way that I take: when He hath tried me, I shall come forth as gold. For He performeth the thing that is appointed for me: and many such things are with Him." *Job 23:10, 14*

"Delight thyself also in the Lord; and He shall give thee the desires of thine heart." *Psalm 37:4*

"In the day when I cried Thou answeredst me, and strengthenedst me with strength in my soul."

Psalm 138:3

"I can do all things through Christ which strengtheneth me." *Philippians 4:13*

"What You Keep Saying You Eventually Believe."

-MIKE MURDOCK

READ THE BIBLE THROUGH IN ONE YEAR: Isaiah 44-48

Music

August 10

"And it came to pass, when the evil spirit from God was upon Saul, that David took an harp, and played with his hand: so Saul was refreshed, and was well, and the evil spirit departed from him." *1 Samuel 16:23*

"It came even to pass, as the trumpeters and singers were as one, to make one sound to be heard in praising and thanking the Lord; and when they lifted up their voice with the trumpets and cymbals and instruments of music, and praised the Lord, saying, For He is good; for His mercy endureth for ever: that then the house was filled with a cloud, even the house of the Lord."
2 Chronicles 5:13

"Make a joyful noise unto the Lord, all ye lands. Serve the Lord with gladness: come before His presence with singing." *Psalm 100:1-2*

"Let the word of Christ dwell in you richly in all Wisdom; teaching and admonishing one another in psalms and hymns and spiritual songs, singing with grace in your hearts to the Lord." *Colossians 3:16*

"A Song Is The Protocol For Entering The Presence of God."

-MIKE MURDOCK

READ THE BIBLE THROUGH IN ONE YEAR: Isaiah 49-51

Negotiation — August 11

"And he said, Oh let not the Lord be angry, and I will speak yet but this once: Peradventure ten shall be found there. And He said, I will not destroy it for ten's sake. And the Lord went His way, as soon as He had left communing with Abraham: and Abraham returned unto his place."   *Genesis 18:32-33*

"A soft answer turneth away wrath: but grievous words stir up anger."   *Proverbs 15:1*

"Pleasant words are as an honeycomb, sweet to the soul, and health to the bones."   *Proverbs 16:24*

"Come now, and let us reason together, saith the Lord: though your sins be as scarlet, they shall be as white as snow; though they be red like crimson, they shall be as wool."   *Isaiah 1:18*

"And whosoever shall compel thee to go a mile, go with him twain."   *Matthew 5:41*

"And the Lord said, Hear what the unjust judge saith. And shall not God avenge His own elect, which cry day and night unto Him, though He bear long with them?"   *Luke 18:6-7*

"Those Willing To Wait Are The Qualified To Receive."

-MIKE MURDOCK

READ THE BIBLE THROUGH IN ONE YEAR: Isaiah 52-54

Networking August 12

"Come on, let us deal wisely with them; lest they multiply, and it come to pass, that, when there falleth out any war, they join also unto our enemies, and fight against us, and so get them up out of the land."
Exodus 1:10

"Thou shalt not plow with an ox and an ass together."
Deuteronomy 22:10

"And Saul sent to Jesse, saying, Let David, I pray thee, stand before me; for he hath found favour in my sight." *1 Samuel 16:22*

"Two are better than one; because they have a good reward for their labour. For if they fall, the one will lift up his fellow: but woe to him that is alone when he falleth; for he hath not another to help him up. Again, if two lie together, then they have heat: but how can one be warm alone? And if one prevail against him, two shall withstand him; and a threefold cord is not quickly broken." *Ecclesiastes 4:9-12*

"Whatever God Did Not Give You He Stored In Someone Near You And Love Is The Secret Code To That Treasure."

-MIKE MURDOCK

READ THE BIBLE THROUGH IN ONE YEAR: Isaiah 55-57

Obedience — August 13

"But if thou shalt indeed obey His voice, and do all that I speak; then I will be an enemy unto thine enemies, and an adversary unto thine adversaries. For Mine Angel shall go before thee." *Exodus 23:22-23*

"And all these blessings shall come on thee, and overtake thee, if thou shalt hearken unto the voice of the Lord thy God." *Deuteronomy 28:2*

"...Behold, to obey is better than sacrifice, and to hearken than the fat of rams." *1 Samuel 15:22*

"If ye be willing and obedient, ye shall eat the good of the land." *Isaiah 1:19*

"For as by one man's disobedience many were made sinners, so by the obedience of one shall many be made righteous." *Romans 5:19*

"Children, obey your parents in the Lord: for this is right." *Ephesians 6:1*

"And hereby we do know that we know Him, if we keep His commandments." *1 John 2:3*

"And whatsoever we ask, we receive of Him, because we keep His commandments, and do those things that are pleasing in His sight." *1 John 3:22*

"Obedience Is The Only Thing God Has Ever Required of Man."

-MIKE MURDOCK

READ THE BIBLE THROUGH IN ONE YEAR: Isaiah 58-60

Occults

August 14

"And it shall be, if thou do at all forget the Lord thy God, and walk after other gods, and serve them, and worship them, I testify against you this day that ye shall surely perish." *Deuteronomy 8:19*

"For rebellion is as the sin of witchcraft, and stubbornness is as iniquity and idolatry. Because thou hast rejected the word of the Lord, He hath also rejected thee from being king." *1 Samuel 15:23*

"And I will cut off witchcrafts out of thine hand; and thou shalt have no more soothsayers." *Micah 5:12*

"Many of them also which used curious arts brought their books together, and burned them before all men: and they counted the price of them, and found it fifty thousand pieces of silver." *Acts 19:19*

"Now the Spirit speaketh expressly, that in the latter times some shall depart from the faith, giving heed to seducing spirits, and doctrines of devils." *1 Timothy 4:1*

"Rejecting The Spirit of Truth Opens You To The Spirit of Error."

-MIKE MURDOCK

READ THE BIBLE THROUGH IN ONE YEAR: Isaiah 61-63

Offenses

August 15

" I have kept Thy precepts and Thy testimonies: for all my ways are before Thee." *Psalm 119:168*

"And blessed is he, whosoever shall not be offended in Me." *Matthew 11:6*

"But he turned, and said unto Peter, Get thee behind Me, satan: thou art an offence unto Me: for thou savourest not the things that be of God, but those that be of men." *Matthew 16:23*

"But whoso shall offend one of these little ones which believe in Me, it were better for him that a millstone were hanged about his neck, and that he were drowned in the depth of the sea." *Matthew 18:6*

"And herein do I exercise myself, to have always a conscience void of offence toward God, and toward men." *Acts 24:16*

"Giving no offence in any thing, that the ministry be not blamed." *2 Corinthians 6:3*

"Looking diligently lest any man fail of the grace of God; lest any root of bitterness springing up trouble you, and thereby many be defiled." *Hebrews 12:15*

"Your Success Is Determined By What You Are Willing To Ignore."

-MIKE MURDOCK

READ THE BIBLE THROUGH IN ONE YEAR: Isaiah 64-66

Offerings

August 16

"Take ye from among you an offering unto the Lord: whosoever is of a willing heart, let him bring it, an offering of the Lord; gold, and silver, and brass."
Exodus 35:5

"Give unto the Lord the glory due unto His name: bring an offering, and come into His courts." *Psalm 96:8*

"Honour the Lord with thy substance, and with the firstfruits of all thine increase: So shall thy barns be filled with plenty, and thy presses shall burst out with new wine." *Proverbs 3:9-10*

"Will a man rob God? Yet ye have robbed Me. But ye say, Wherein have we robbed Thee? In tithes and offerings. Bring ye all the tithes into the storehouse, that there may be meat in Mine house, and prove Me now herewith, saith the Lord of hosts, if I will not open you the windows of Heaven, and pour you out a blessing, that there shall not be room enough to receive it."
Malachi 3:8, 10

"Give, and it shall be given unto you; good measure, pressed down, and shaken together, and running over, shall men give into your bosom. For with the same measure that ye mete withal it shall be measured to you again." *Luke 6:38*

"When You Let Go of What Is In Your Hand, God Will Let Go of What Is In His Hand."

-MIKE MURDOCK

READ THE BIBLE THROUGH IN ONE YEAR: Jeremiah 1-5

Order

August 17

"Although my house be not so with God; yet He hath made with me an everlasting covenant, ordered in all things, and sure: for this is all my salvation, and all my desire, although He make it not to grow." *2 Samuel 23:5*

"In those days was Hezekiah sick unto death. And the prophet Isaiah the son of Amoz came to him, and said unto him, Thus saith the Lord, Set thine house in order; for thou shalt die, and not live." *2 Kings 20:1*

"But seek ye first the kingdom of God, and His righteousness; and all these things shall be added unto you." *Matthew 6:33*

"For they were about five thousand men. And He said to His disciples, Make them sit down by fifties in a company. And they did so, and made them all sit down." *Luke 9:14-15*

"Let all things be done decently and in order." *1 Corinthians 14:40*

"For this cause left I thee in Crete, that thou shouldest set in order the things that are wanting, and ordain elders in every city, as I had appointed thee." *Titus 1:5*

"God's Only Obsession Is Order."

-MIKE MURDOCK

READ THE BIBLE THROUGH IN ONE YEAR: Jeremiah 6-8

Overcoming August 18

"Be not overcome of evil, but overcome evil with good." *Romans 12:21*

"...Resist the devil, and he will flee from you." *James 4:7*

"Ye are of God, little children, and have overcome them: because greater is He that is in you, than he that is in the world." *1 John 4:4*

"To him that overcometh will I give to eat of the tree of life, which is in the midst of the paradise of God." *Revelation 2:7*

"To him that overcometh will I grant to sit with Me in My throne, even as I also overcame, and am set down with My Father in His throne." *Revelation 3:21*

"He that overcometh shall inherit all things; and I will be his God, and he shall be My son." *Revelation 21:7*

"What You Refuse To Overcome Eventually Overcomes You."

-MIKE MURDOCK

READ THE BIBLE THROUGH IN ONE YEAR: Jeremiah 9-11

Overload August 19

"And he shall speak great words against the most High, and shall wear out the saints of the most High, and think to change times and laws: and they shall be given into his hand until a time and times and the dividing of time." *Daniel 7:25*

"Come unto Me, all ye that labour and are heavy laden, and I will give you rest. Take My yoke upon you, and learn of Me; for I am meek and lowly in heart: and ye shall find rest unto your souls. For My yoke is easy, and My burden is light." *Matthew 11:28-30*

"There hath no temptation taken you but such as is common to man: but God is faithful, Who will not suffer you to be tempted above that ye are able; but will with the temptation also make a way to escape, that ye may be able to bear it." *1 Corinthians 10:13*

"Casting all your care upon Him; for He careth for you." *1 Peter 5:7*

"Ye are of God, little children, and have overcome them: because greater is He that is in you, than he that is in the world." *1 John 4:4*

"Stress Is The Proof You Are Attempting Something God Did Not Command."

-MIKE MURDOCK

READ THE BIBLE THROUGH IN ONE YEAR: Jeremiah 12-14

Pain

August 20

"For His anger endureth but a moment; in His favour is life: weeping may endure for a night, but joy cometh in the morning." *Psalm 30:5*

"Many are the afflictions of the righteous: but the Lord delivereth him out of them all." *Psalm 34:19*

"He healeth the broken in heart, and bindeth up their wounds." *Psalm 147:3*

"And one shall say unto Him, What are these wounds in Thine hands? Then He shall answer, Those with which I was wounded in the house of My friends."

Zechariah 13:6

"For we have not an high priest which cannot be touched with the feeling of our infirmities; but was in all points tempted like as we are, yet without sin."

Hebrews 4:15

"And God shall wipe away all tears from their eyes; and there shall be no more death, neither sorrow, nor crying, neither shall there be any more pain: for the former things are passed away." *Revelation 21:4*

"Pain Is Not Your Enemy—But Merely The Proof That You Have One."

-MIKE MURDOCK

READ THE BIBLE THROUGH IN ONE YEAR: Jeremiah 15-17

Parenting

August 21

"Only take heed to thyself, and keep thy soul diligently, lest thou forget the things which thine eyes have seen, and lest they depart from thy heart all the days of thy life: but teach them thy sons, and thy sons' sons."
Deuteronomy 4:9

"Lo, children are an heritage of the Lord." *Psalm 127:3*

"The just man walketh in his integrity: his children are blessed after him." *Proverbs 20:7*

"Train up a child in the way he should go: and when he is old, he will not depart from it." *Proverbs 22:6*

"Foolishness is bound in the heart of a child; but the rod of correction shall drive it far from him." *Proverbs 22:15*

"And all thy children shall be taught of the Lord; and great shall be the peace of thy children." *Isaiah 54:13*

"And, ye fathers, provoke not your children to wrath: but bring them up in the nurture and admonition of the Lord." *Ephesians 6:4*

"Anything You Permit Will Increase."

-MIKE MURDOCK

READ THE BIBLE THROUGH IN ONE YEAR: Jeremiah 18-20

Passion

August 22

"And David danced before the Lord with all his might; and David was girded with a linen ephod." *2 Samuel 6:14*

"As the hart panteth after the water brooks, so panteth my soul after Thee, O God." *Psalm 42:1*

"Whatsoever thy hand findeth to do, do it with thy might." *Ecclesiastes 9:10*

"And ye shall seek Me, and find Me, when ye shall search for Me with all your heart." *Jeremiah 29:13*

"Ask, and it shall be given you; seek, and ye shall find; knock, and it shall be opened unto you." *Matthew 7:7*

"Jesus said unto him, Thou shalt love the Lord thy God with all thy heart, and with all thy soul, and with all thy mind. This is the first and great commandment."
Matthew 22:37-38

"I have fought a good fight, I have finished my course, I have kept the faith." *2 Timothy 4:7*

"You Only Qualify For What You Pursue."

-MIKE MURDOCK

READ THE BIBLE THROUGH IN ONE YEAR: Jeremiah 21-23

Patience

August 23

"Rest in the Lord, and wait patiently for Him: fret not thyself because of him who prospereth in his way, because of the man who bringeth wicked devices to pass." *Psalm 37:7*

"The Lord is good unto them that wait for Him, to the soul that seeketh Him." *Lamentations 3:25*

"And not only so, but we glory in tribulations also: knowing that tribulation worketh patience; And patience, experience; and experience, hope." *Romans 5:3-4*

"Rejoicing in hope; patient in tribulation; continuing instant in prayer." *Romans 12:12*

"And let us not be weary in well doing: for in due season we shall reap, if we faint not." *Galatians 6:9*

"Knowing this, that the trying of your faith worketh patience. But let patience have her perfect work, that ye may be perfect and entire, wanting nothing." *James 1:3-4*

"Patience Is The Weapon That Forces Deception To Reveal Itself."

-MIKE MURDOCK

READ THE BIBLE THROUGH IN ONE YEAR: Jeremiah 24-28

Peace

August 24

"I will both lay me down in peace, and sleep: for Thou, Lord, only makest me dwell in safety." *Psalm 4:8*

"Great peace have they which love Thy law: and nothing shall offend them." *Psalm 119:165*

"Thou wilt keep him in perfect peace, whose mind is stayed on Thee: because He trusteth in Thee. Lord, Thou wilt ordain peace for us: for Thou also hast wrought all our works in us." *Isaiah 26:3, 12*

"Peace I leave with you, My peace I give unto you: not as the world giveth, give I unto you. Let not your heart be troubled, neither let it be afraid." *John 14:27*

"For to be carnally minded is death; but to be spiritually minded is life and peace." *Romans 8:6*

"If it be possible, as much as lieth in you, live peaceably with all men." *Romans 12:18*

"But the fruit of the Spirit is love, joy, peace, longsuffering, gentleness, goodness, faith." *Galatians 5:22*

"Peace Is Not The Absence of Conflict, It Is The Absence of Inner Conflict."

-MIKE MURDOCK

READ THE BIBLE THROUGH IN ONE YEAR: Jeremiah 29-31

Peacemakers August 25

"So that I come again to my father's house in peace; then shall the Lord be my God." *Genesis 28:21*

"A soft answer turneth away wrath: but grievous words stir up anger." *Proverbs 15:1*

"Whoso keepeth his mouth and his tongue keepeth his soul from troubles." *Proverbs 21:23*

"By long forbearing is a prince persuaded, and a soft tongue breaketh the bone." *Proverbs 25:15*

"Where no wood is, there the fire goeth out: so where there is no talebearer, the strife ceaseth." *Proverbs 26:20*

"Blessed are the peacemakers: for they shall be called the children of God." *Matthew 5:9*

"And the fruit of righteousness is sown in peace of them that make peace." *James 3:18*

"Peacemakers Do Not Fear Confrontation—They Simply Avoid Loss."

-MIKE MURDOCK

READ THE BIBLE THROUGH IN ONE YEAR: Jeremiah 32-34

People-Pressure

August 26

"If thy brother, the son of thy mother, or thy son, or thy daughter, or the wife of thy bosom, or thy friend, which is as thine own soul, entice thee secretly, saying, Let us go and serve other gods, which thou hast not known, thou, nor thy fathers; Thou shalt not consent unto him, nor hearken unto him." *Deuteronomy 13:6, 8*

"But they hearkened not: and Manasseh seduced them to do more evil than did the nations whom the Lord destroyed before the children of Israel." *2 Kings 21:9*

"My son, if sinners entice thee, consent thou not. My son, walk not thou in the way with them; refrain thy foot from their path." *Proverbs 1:10, 15*

"Make no friendship with an angry man; and with a furious man thou shalt not go." *Proverbs 22:24*

"Be not deceived: evil communications corrupt good manners." *1 Corinthians 15:33*

"Knowing therefore the terror of the Lord, we persuade men." *2 Corinthians 5:11*

"Every Relationship Takes You Toward Your Dreams or Away From Them."

-MIKE MURDOCK

READ THE BIBLE THROUGH IN ONE YEAR: Jeremiah 35-37

Persecution — August 27

"If they have persecuted Me, they will also persecute you." *John 15:20*

"Who shall separate us from the love of Christ? shall tribulation, or distress, or persecution, or famine, or nakedness, or peril, or sword? Nay, in all these things we are more than conquerors through Him that loved us." *Romans 8:35, 37*

"We are troubled on every side, yet not distressed; we are perplexed, but not in despair; Persecuted, but not forsaken; cast down, but not destroyed."
2 Corinthians 4:8-9

"Yea, and all that will live godly in Christ Jesus shall suffer persecution." *2 Timothy 3:12*

"But and if ye suffer for righteousness' sake, happy are ye: and be not afraid of their terror, neither be troubled."
1 Peter 3:14

"Anything Right Intimidates Everything Evil."
-MIKE MURDOCK

READ THE BIBLE THROUGH IN ONE YEAR: Jeremiah 38-40

Pitfalls

August 28

"Take heed to thyself, lest thou make a covenant with the inhabitants of the land whither thou goest, lest it be for a snare in the midst of thee." *Exodus 34:12*

"Surely He shall deliver thee from the snare of the fowler, and from the noisome pestilence." *Psalm 91:3*

"Thy word is a lamp unto my feet, and a light unto my path." *Psalm 119:105*

"The wicked have laid a snare for me: yet I erred not from Thy precepts." *Psalm 119:110*

"Wherefore let him that thinketh he standeth take heed lest he fall." *1 Corinthians 10:12*

"Be not deceived: evil communications corrupt good manners." *1 Corinthians 15:33*

"Lest satan should get an advantage of us: for we are not ignorant of his devices." *2 Corinthians 2:11*

"An Unrecognized Weakness Always Births A Tragedy."

-MIKE MURDOCK

READ THE BIBLE THROUGH IN ONE YEAR: Jeremiah 41-43

Planning August 29

"In all thy ways acknowledge Him, and He shall direct thy paths." *Proverbs 3:6*

"Go to the ant, thou sluggard; consider her ways, and be wise: Which having no guide, overseer, or ruler, Provideth her meat in the summer, and gathereth her food in the harvest." *Proverbs 6:6-8*

"Without counsel purposes are disappointed: but in the multitude of counsellors they are established."
Proverbs 15:22

"For I know the thoughts that I think toward you, saith the Lord, thoughts of peace, and not of evil, to give you an expected end." *Jeremiah 29:11*

"...Write the vision, and make it plain upon tables, that he may run that readeth it. For the vision is yet for an appointed time, but at the end it shall speak, and not lie: though it tarry, wait for it; because it will surely come, it will not tarry." *Habakkuk 2:2-3*

"For which of you, intending to build a tower, sitteth not down first, and counteth the cost, whether he have sufficient to finish it?" *Luke 14:28*

"A Plan Is A Written Map To Your Destination."
-MIKE MURDOCK

READ THE BIBLE THROUGH IN ONE YEAR: Jeremiah 44-46

Poverty

August 30

"This poor man cried, and the Lord heard him, and saved him out of all his troubles." *Psalm 34:6*

"I have been young, and now am old; yet have I not seen the righteous forsaken, nor His seed begging bread." *Psalm 37:25*

"Honour the Lord with thy substance,...shall thy barns be filled with plenty." *Proverbs 3:9-10*

"He becometh poor that dealeth with a slack hand: but the hand of the diligent maketh rich." *Proverbs 10:4*

"He that hath pity upon the poor lendeth unto the Lord; and that which he hath given will He pay him again." *Proverbs 19:17*

"He that tilleth his land shall have plenty of bread: but he that followeth after vain persons shall have poverty enough." *Proverbs 28:19*

"For the poor always ye have with you; but Me ye have not always." *John 12:8*

"All Poverty Can Be Traced To A Broken Law of God."
-MIKE MURDOCK

READ THE BIBLE THROUGH IN ONE YEAR: Jeremiah 47-51

Power

August 31

"O God, Thou art terrible out of Thy holy places: the God of Israel is He that giveth strength and power unto His people. Blessed be God." *Psalm 68:35*

"He hath shewed His people the power of His works, that He may give them the heritage of the heathen."
Psalm 111:6

"Death and life are in the power of the tongue: and they that love it shall eat the fruit thereof." *Proverbs 18:21*

"But ye shall receive power, after that the Holy Ghost is come upon you: and ye shall be witnesses unto Me both in Jerusalem, and in all Judaea, and in Samaria, and unto the uttermost part of the earth." *Acts 1:8*

"And with great power gave the apostles witness of the resurrection of the Lord Jesus: and great grace was upon them all." *Acts 4:33*

"For the kingdom of God is not in word, but in power."
1 Corinthians 4:20

"Power Is The Ability To Walk Away From Something You Desire To Protect Something Else You Love."

-MIKE MURDOCK

READ THE BIBLE THROUGH IN ONE YEAR: Jeremiah 52-Lamentations 2

Power of God

September 1

"That your faith should not stand in the Wisdom of men, but in the power of God." *1 Corinthians 2:5*

"But we have this treasure in earthen vessels, that the excellency of the power may be of God, and not of us." *2 Corinthians 4:7*

"For though He was crucified through weakness, yet He liveth by the power of God. For we also are weak in Him, but we shall live with Him by the power of God toward you." *2 Corinthians 13:4*

"Whereof I was made a minister, according to the gift of the grace of God given unto me by the effectual working of His power." *Ephesians 3:7*

"For God hath not given us the spirit of fear; but of power, and of love, and of a sound mind. Be not thou therefore ashamed of the testimony of our Lord, nor of me His prisoner: but be thou partaker of the afflictions of the gospel according to the power of God." *2 Timothy 1:7-8*

"What You Do First Will Determine What God Does Second."

-MIKE MURDOCK

READ THE BIBLE THROUGH IN ONE YEAR: Lamentations 3-5

Praise

September 2

"To the end that my glory may sing praise to Thee, and not be silent. O Lord my God, I will give thanks unto Thee for ever." *Psalm 30:12*

"Praise the Lord with harp: sing unto Him with the psaltery and an instrument of ten strings." *Psalm 33:2*

"I will bless the Lord at all times: His praise shall continually be in my mouth." *Psalm 34:1*

"I will praise the name of God with a song, and will magnify Him with thanksgiving." *Psalm 69:30*

"Let them praise His name in the dance: let them sing praises unto Him with the timbrel and harp."

Psalm 149:3

"Praise Him with the sound of the trumpet: praise Him with the psaltery and harp. Praise Him with the timbrel and dance: praise Him with stringed instruments and organs. Praise Him upon the loud cymbals: praise Him upon the high sounding cymbals. Let every thing that hath breath praise the Lord. Praise ye the Lord."

Psalm 150:3-6

"Your Present Focus Determines Your Present Joy."

-MIKE MURDOCK

READ THE BIBLE THROUGH IN ONE YEAR: Ezekiel 1-3

Prayer

September 3

"Seek the Lord and His strength, seek His face continually." *1 Chronicles 16:11*

"If My people, which are called by My name, shall humble themselves, and pray, and seek My face, and turn from their wicked ways; then will I hear from Heaven, and will forgive their sin, and will heal their land." *2 Chronicles 7:14*

"Watch and pray, that ye enter not into temptation: the spirit indeed is willing, but the flesh is weak." *Matthew 26:41*

"Continue in prayer, and watch in the same with thanksgiving." *Colossians 4:2*

"Pray without ceasing." *1 Thessalonians 5:17*

"The effectual fervent prayer of a righteous man availeth much." *James 5:16*

"The Secret of Your Future Is Hidden In Your Daily Routine."

-MIKE MURDOCK

READ THE BIBLE THROUGH IN ONE YEAR: Ezekiel 4-6

Prayer Language

September 4

"Likewise the Spirit also helpeth our infirmities: for we know not what we should pray for as we ought: but the Spirit itself maketh intercession for us with groanings which cannot be uttered." *Romans 8:26*

"For he that speaketh in an unknown tongue speaketh not unto men, but unto God: for no man understandeth him; howbeit in the Spirit he speaketh mysteries."
1 Corinthians 14:2

"For if I pray in an unknown tongue, my spirit prayeth, but my understanding is unfruitful. What is it then? I will pray with the Spirit, and I will pray with the understanding also: I will sing with the Spirit, and I will sing with the understanding also." *1 Corinthians 14:14-15*

"Praying always with all prayer and supplication in the Spirit, and watching thereunto with all perseverance and supplication for all saints." *Ephesians 6:18*

"But ye, beloved, building up yourselves on your most holy faith, praying in the Holy Ghost." *Jude 1:20*

"You Will Only Be Remembered For Your Obsession."
-MIKE MURDOCK

READ THE BIBLE THROUGH IN ONE YEAR: Ezekiel 7-9

Prejudice

September 5

"Therefore have I also made you contemptible and base before all the people, according as ye have not kept My ways, but have been partial in the law." *Malachi 2:9*

"For with what judgment ye judge, ye shall be judged: and with what measure ye mete, it shall be measured to you again." *Matthew 7:2*

"Judge not according to the appearance, but judge righteous judgment." *John 7:24*

"I charge thee before God, and the Lord Jesus Christ, and the elect angels, that thou observe these things without preferring one before another, doing nothing by partiality." *1 Timothy 5:21*

"Are ye not then partial in yourselves, and are become judges of evil thoughts?" *James 2:4*

"But the Wisdom that is from above is first pure, then peaceable, gentle, and easy to be intreated, full of mercy and good fruits, without partiality, and without hypocrisy." *James 3:17*

"Focus Creates Blindness."

-MIKE MURDOCK

READ THE BIBLE THROUGH IN ONE YEAR: Ezekiel 10-12

Presence of God

September 6

"As smoke is driven away, so drive them away: as wax melteth before the fire, so let the wicked perish at the presence of God."
Psalm 68:2

"The earth shook, the Heavens also dropped at the presence of God: even Sinai itself was moved at the presence of God, the God of Israel."
Psalm 68:8

"But it is good for me to draw near to God: I have put my trust in the Lord God, that I may declare all Thy works."
Psalm 73:28

"And the angel answering said unto him, I am Gabriel, that stand in the presence of God; and am sent to speak unto thee, and to shew thee these glad tidings."
Luke 1:19

"For Christ is not entered into the holy places made with hands, which are the figures of the true; but into Heaven itself, now to appear in the presence of God for us."
Hebrews 9:24

"When You Keep Doing Right Things, Right People Enter Your Life."

-MIKE MURDOCK

READ THE BIBLE THROUGH IN ONE YEAR: Ezekiel 13-17

Pride

September 7

"These six things doth the Lord hate: yea, seven are an abomination unto Him: A proud look, a lying tongue, and hands that shed innocent blood, An heart that deviseth wicked imaginations, feet that be swift in running to mischief, A false witness that speaketh lies, and he that soweth discord among brethren."

Proverbs 6:16-19

"When pride cometh, then cometh shame: but with the lowly is Wisdom." *Proverbs 11:2*

"Pride goeth before destruction, and an haughty spirit before a fall. Better it is to be of an humble spirit with the lowly, than to divide the spoil with the proud."

Proverbs 16:18-19

"And whosoever shall exalt himself shall be abased; and he that shall humble himself shall be exalted."

Matthew 23:12

"But He giveth more grace. Wherefore He saith, God resisteth the proud, but giveth grace unto the humble."

James 4:6

"The Proof of Humility Is The Desire To Change."

-MIKE MURDOCK

READ THE BIBLE THROUGH IN ONE YEAR: Ezekiel 18-20

Problem People

September 8

"Then the Lord said unto Moses, Go in unto Pharaoh, and tell him, Thus saith the Lord God of the Hebrews, Let My people go, that they may serve Me. And Pharaoh sent, and, behold, there was not one of the cattle of the Israelites dead. And the heart of Pharaoh was hardened, and he did not let the people go."
Exodus 9:1, 7

"Wherefore the people did chide with Moses, and said, Give us water that we may drink. And Moses said unto them, Why chide ye with me? wherefore do ye tempt the Lord?" *Exodus 17:2*

"And when the people complained, it displeased the Lord: and the Lord heard it; and His anger was kindled; and the fire of the Lord burnt among them, and consumed them that were in the uttermost parts of the camp." *Numbers 11:1*

"When Wrong People Leave, Right Things Happen."
-MIKE MURDOCK

READ THE BIBLE THROUGH IN ONE YEAR: Ezekiel 21-23

Problem-Solving

September 9

"I sought the Lord, and He heard me, and delivered me from all my fears." *Psalm 34:4*

"Let them be confounded and put to shame that seek after my soul: let them be turned back and brought to confusion that devise my hurt." *Psalm 35:4*

"I will say of the Lord, He is my refuge and my fortress: my God; in Him will I trust. He shall call upon me, and I will answer Him: I will be with Him in trouble; I will deliver Him, and honour Him." *Psalm 91:2, 15*

"For we have not an high priest which cannot be touched with the feeling of our infirmities; but was in all points tempted like as we are, yet without sin. Let us therefore come boldly unto the throne of grace, that we may obtain mercy, and find grace to help in time of need." *Hebrews 4:15-16*

"You Will Only Be Remembered In Life For Two Things: The Problems You Solve or The Ones You Create."

-MIKE MURDOCK

READ THE BIBLE THROUGH IN ONE YEAR: Ezekiel 24-26

Productivity September 10

"Wealth gotten by vanity shall be diminished: but he that gathereth by labour shall increase." *Proverbs 13:11*

"Of the increase of His government and peace there shall be no end, upon the throne of David, and upon his kingdom, to order it, and to establish it with judgment and with justice from henceforth even for ever. The zeal of the Lord of hosts will perform this." *Isaiah 9:7*

"Produce your cause, saith the Lord; bring forth your strong reasons, saith the King of Jacob." *Isaiah 41:21*

"And the tree of the field shall yield her fruit, and the earth shall yield her increase, and they shall be safe in their land, and shall know that I am the Lord, when I have broken the bands of their yoke, and delivered them out of the hand of those that served themselves of them." *Ezekiel 34:27*

"And I will multiply upon you man and beast; and they shall increase and bring fruit: and I will settle you after your old estates, and will do better unto you than at your beginnings: and ye shall know that I am the Lord."
Ezekiel 36:11

"The Quality of A Nation Is Revealed By The Quality of The Leader God Permits To Govern Them."

-MIKE MURDOCK

READ THE BIBLE THROUGH IN ONE YEAR: Ezekiel 27-29

Promises of God

September 11

"Wherefore Levi hath no part nor inheritance with his brethren; the Lord is his inheritance, according as the Lord thy God promised him." *Deuteronomy 10:9*

"Therefore it shall come to pass, that as all good things are come upon you, which the Lord your God promised you; so shall the Lord bring upon you all evil things, until He have destroyed you from off this good land which the Lord your God hath given you." *Joshua 23:15*

"He staggered not at the promise of God through unbelief; but was strong in faith, giving glory to God." *Romans 4:20*

"For all the promises of God in Him are yea, and in Him Amen, unto the glory of God by us." *2 Corinthians 1:20*

"Is the law then against the promises of God? God forbid: for if there had been a law given which could have given life, verily righteousness should have been by the law." *Galatians 3:21*

"If You Must Believe Somebody, Believe Somebody Good."

-MIKE MURDOCK

READ THE BIBLE THROUGH IN ONE YEAR: Ezekiel 30-32

Promotion September 12

"For I will promote thee unto very great honour, and I will do whatsoever thou sayest unto Me: come therefore, I pray thee, curse Me this people."
Numbers 22:17

"For promotion cometh neither from the east, nor from the west, nor from the south. But God is the judge: He putteth down one, and setteth up another." *Psalm 75:6-7*

"The wise shall inherit glory: but shame shall be the promotion of fools." *Proverbs 3:35*

"Wisdom is the principal thing; therefore get Wisdom: and with all thy getting get understanding. Exalt her, and she shall promote thee: she shall bring thee to honour, when thou dost embrace her. She shall give to thine head an ornament of grace: a crown of glory shall she deliver to thee." *Proverbs 4:7-9*

"I press toward the mark for the prize of the high calling of God in Christ Jesus." *Philippians 3:14*

"You Will Never Be Promoted Until You Become Overqualified For Your Present Position."

-MIKE MURDOCK

READ THE BIBLE THROUGH IN ONE YEAR: Ezekiel 33-35

Prosperity September 13

"If they obey and serve Him, they shall spend their days in prosperity, and their years in pleasures."
Job 36:11

"Blessed is the man that walketh not in the counsel of the ungodly, nor standeth in the way of sinners, nor sitteth in the seat of the scornful. But his delight is in the law of the Lord; and in His law doth he meditate day and night. And he shall be like a tree planted by the rivers of water, that bringeth forth his fruit in his season; his leaf also shall not wither; and whatsoever he doeth shall prosper." *Psalm 1:1-3*

"Let the Lord be magnified, which hath pleasure in the prosperity of His servant." *Psalm 35:27*

"Beloved, I wish above all things that thou mayest prosper and be in health, even as thy soul prospereth."
3 John 1:2

"Prosperity Is Having Enough of God's Provision To Complete His Instructions For Your Life."

-*MIKE MURDOCK*

READ THE BIBLE THROUGH IN ONE YEAR: Ezekiel 36-40

Protection of God

September 14

"The Lord is my shepherd; I shall not want. He maketh me to lie down in green pastures: He leadeth me beside the still waters. He restoreth my soul: He leadeth me in the paths of righteousness for His name's sake. Yea, though I walk through the valley of the shadow of death, I will fear no evil: for Thou art with me; Thy rod and Thy staff they comfort me."   *Psalm 23:1-4*

"He that dwelleth in the secret place of the most High shall abide under the shadow of the Almighty. He shall cover thee with His feathers, and under His wings shalt thou trust: His truth shall be thy shield and buckler. Thou shalt not be afraid for the terror by night; nor for the arrow that flieth by day; Nor for the pestilence that walketh in darkness; nor for the destruction that wasteth at noonday. A thousand shall fall at thy side, and ten thousand at thy right hand; but it shall not come nigh thee. There shall no evil befall thee, neither shall any plague come nigh thy dwelling. For He shall give His angels charge over thee, to keep thee in all thy ways."   *Psalm 91:1, 4-7, 10-11*

"Protection Is Produced Through Partnership."

-*MIKE MURDOCK*

READ THE BIBLE THROUGH IN ONE YEAR: Ezekiel 41-43

Protégés

September 15

"It is better to hear the rebuke of the wise, than for a man to hear the song of fools." *Ecclesiastes 7:5*

"And He saith unto them, Follow Me, and I will make you fishers of men." *Matthew 4:19*

"If any man serve Me, let him follow Me; and where I am, there shall also My servant be: if any man serve Me, him will My Father honour." *John 12:26*

"Those things, which ye have both learned, and received, and heard, and seen in Me, do: and the God of peace shall be with you." *Philippians 4:9*

"Children, obey your parents in all things: for this is well pleasing unto the Lord." *Colossians 3:20*

"For even hereunto were ye called: because Christ also suffered for us, leaving us an example, that ye should follow His steps." *1 Peter 2:21*

"Parasites Want What You Have *Earned*—
Protégés Want What You Have *Learned*."

-MIKE MURDOCK

READ THE BIBLE THROUGH IN ONE YEAR: Ezekiel 44-46

Protocol

September 16

"Enter into His gates with thanksgiving, and into His courts with praise: be thankful unto Him, and bless His name." *Psalm 100:4*

"And put a knife to thy throat, if thou be a man given to appetite." *Proverbs 23:2*

"Put not forth thyself in the presence of the king, and stand not in the place of great men: For better it is that it be said unto thee, Come up hither; than that thou shouldest be put lower in the presence of the prince whom thine eyes have seen." *Proverbs 25:6-7*

"Withdraw thy foot from thy neighbour's house; lest he be weary of thee, and so hate thee." *Proverbs 25:17*

"To every thing there is a season, and a time to every purpose under the Heaven." *Ecclesiastes 3:1*

"Recompense to no man evil for evil. Provide things honest in the sight of all men." *Romans 12:17*

"Let all things be done decently and in order."
1 Corinthians 14:40

"Every Environment Requires A Code of Conduct For Entering or Remaining In It."

-MIKE MURDOCK

READ THE BIBLE THROUGH IN ONE YEAR: Ezekiel 47-Daniel 1

Purity

September 17

"Now when Solomon had made an end of praying, the fire came down from Heaven, and consumed the burnt offering and the sacrifices; and the glory of the Lord filled the house." *2 Chronicles 7:1*

"Blessed are the pure in heart: for they shall see God." *Matthew 5:8*

"I beseech you therefore, brethren, by the mercies of God, that ye present your bodies a living sacrifice, holy, acceptable unto God, which is your reasonable service." *Romans 12:1*

"Know ye not that ye are the temple of God, and that the Spirit of God dwelleth in you?" *1 Corinthians 3:16*

"Abstain from all appearance of evil." *1 Thessalonians 5:22*

"Let no man despise thy youth; but be thou an example of the believers, in word, in conversation, in charity, in spirit, in faith, in purity." *1 Timothy 4:12*

"You Cannot Have A Great Life Unless You Have A Pure Life. You Cannot Have A Pure Life Unless You Have A Pure Mind. You Cannot Have A Pure Mind Unless You Wash It Daily With The Word of God."
-MIKE MURDOCK

READ THE BIBLE THROUGH IN ONE YEAR: Daniel 2-4

Quitting — September 18

"Be strong and of a good courage, fear not, nor be afraid of them: for the Lord thy God, He it is that doth go with thee; He will not fail thee, nor forsake thee."
Deuteronomy 31:6

"And ye shall be hated of all men for My name's sake: but he that endureth to the end shall be saved."
Matthew 10:22

"And Jesus said unto him, No man, having put his hand to the plough, and looking back, is fit for the kingdom of God." *Luke 9:62*

"Thou therefore endure hardness, as a good soldier of Jesus Christ." *2 Timothy 2:3*

"Blessed is the man that endureth temptation: for when he is tried, he shall receive the crown of life, which the Lord hath promised to them that love Him."
James 1:12

"You Have Already Been In Your Past. You Did Not Like It or You Would Have Stayed There."

-MIKE MURDOCK

READ THE BIBLE THROUGH IN ONE YEAR: Daniel 5-7

Racism

September 19

"Behold, how good and how pleasant it is for brethren to dwell together in unity!" *Psalm 133:1*

"A new commandment I give unto you, That ye love one another; as I have loved you, that ye also love one another." *John 13:34*

"Then Peter opened his mouth, and said, of a truth I perceive that God is no respecter of persons."*Acts 10:34*

"For by one Spirit are we all baptized into one body, whether we be Jews or Gentiles, whether we be bond or free; and have been all made to drink into one Spirit." *1 Corinthians 12:13*

"There is neither Jew nor Greek, there is neither bond nor free, there is neither male nor female: for ye are all one in Christ Jesus." *Galatians 3:28*

"But the fruit of the Spirit is love, joy, peace, longsuffering, gentleness, goodness, faith." *Galatians 5:22*

"Your Significance Is Not In Your Similarity To Another...But In Your Point of Difference From Another."

-MIKE MURDOCK

READ THE BIBLE THROUGH IN ONE YEAR: Daniel 8-10

Rapture   September 20

"Which also said, Ye men of Galilee, why stand ye gazing up into Heaven? this same Jesus, which is taken up from you into Heaven, shall so come in like manner as ye have seen Him go into Heaven."   *Acts 1:11*

"For this we say unto you by the word of the Lord, that we which are alive and remain unto the coming of the Lord shall not prevent them which are asleep. For the Lord Himself shall descend from Heaven with a shout, with the voice of the archangel, and with the trump of God: and the dead in Christ shall rise first: Then we which are alive and remain shall be caught up together with them in the clouds, to meet the Lord in the air: and so shall we ever be with the Lord. Wherefore comfort one another with these words." *1 Thessalonians 4:15-18*

"Beloved, now are we the sons of God, and it doth not yet appear what we shall be: but we know that, when He shall appear, we shall be like Him; for we shall see Him as He is. And every man that hath this hope in Him purifieth himself, even as He is pure."   *1 John 3:2-3*

"The First Time Christ Came He Was The Defendant. The Second Time Christ Comes He Will Be The Judge."

-MIKE MURDOCK

READ THE BIBLE THROUGH IN ONE YEAR: Daniel 11-Hosea 3

Reading

September 21

"Learn to do well; seek judgment, relieve the oppressed, judge the fatherless, plead for the widow." *Isaiah 1:17*

"Whereby, when ye read, ye may understand my knowledge in the mystery of Christ." *Ephesians 3:4*

"And when this epistle is read among you, cause that it be read also in the church of the Laodiceans; and that ye likewise read the epistle from Laodicea."

Colossians 4:16

"I charge you by the Lord that this epistle be read unto all the holy brethren." *1 Thessalonians 5:27*

"Till I come, give attendance to reading, to exhortation, to doctrine." *1 Timothy 4:13*

"Study to shew thyself approved unto God, a workman that needeth not to be ashamed, rightly dividing the word of truth." *2 Timothy 2:15*

"Blessed is he that readeth, and they that hear the words of this prophecy, and keep those things which are written therein: for the time is at hand." *Revelation 1:3*

"Reading Is Reaching, The Proof of Humility."

-MIKE MURDOCK

READ THE BIBLE THROUGH IN ONE YEAR: Hosea 4-6

Rebellion   September 22

"But if ye will not obey the voice of the Lord, but rebel against the commandment of the Lord, then shall the hand of the Lord be against you, as it was against your fathers." *1 Samuel 12:15*

"For rebellion is as the sin of witchcraft, and stubbornness is as iniquity and idolatry. Because thou hast rejected the word of the Lord, He hath also rejected thee from being king." *1 Samuel 15:23*

"Foolishness is bound in the heart of a child; but the rod of correction shall drive it far from him." *Proverbs 22:15*

"A whip for the horse, a bridle for the ass, and a rod for the fool's back." *Proverbs 26:3*

"If ye be willing and obedient, ye shall eat the good of the land: But if ye refuse and rebel, ye shall be devoured with the sword: for the mouth of the Lord hath spoken it." *Isaiah 1:19-20*

"Therefore thus saith the Lord; Behold, I will cast thee from off the face of the earth: this year thou shalt die, because thou hast taught rebellion against the Lord."
Jeremiah 28:16

"Correction Upward Is Rebellion."

-MIKE MURDOCK

READ THE BIBLE THROUGH IN ONE YEAR: Hosea 7-9

Reconciliation September 23

"Leave there thy gift before the altar, and go thy way; first be reconciled to thy brother, and then come and offer thy gift." *Matthew 5:24*

"But if ye forgive not men their trespasses, neither will your Father forgive your trespasses." *Matthew 6:15*

"If it be possible, as much as lieth in you, live peaceably with all men." *Romans 12:18*

"And all things are of God, Who hath reconciled us to Himself by Jesus Christ, and hath given to us the ministry of reconciliation; To wit, that God was in Christ, reconciling the world unto Himself, not imputing their trespasses unto them; and hath committed unto us the word of reconciliation."

2 Corinthians 5:18-19

"Brethren, if a man be overtaken in a fault, ye which are spiritual, restore such an one in the spirit of meekness; considering thyself, lest thou also be tempted."

Galatians 6:1

"Reconciliation Is Not The Ignoring of An Offense But The Forgiveness of An Offense."

-MIKE MURDOCK

READ THE BIBLE THROUGH IN ONE YEAR: Hosea 10-12

Recovery

September 24

"And David enquired at the Lord, saying, Shall I pursue after this troop? shall I overtake them? And He answered him, Pursue: for thou shalt surely overtake them, and without fail recover all." *1 Samuel 30:8*

"And she said unto her mistress, Would God my lord were with the prophet that is in Samaria! for He would recover him of his leprosy." *2 Kings 5:3*

"And I will restore to you the years that the locust hath eaten, the cankerworm, and the caterpillar, and the palmerworm, My great army which I sent among you."
Joel 2:25

"...they shall lay hands on the sick, and they shall recover." *Mark 16:18*

"The Spirit of the Lord is upon Me, because He hath anointed Me to preach the gospel to the poor;...and recovering of sight to the blind, to set at liberty them that are bruised." *Luke 4:18*

"And the servant of the Lord must not strive; but be gentle unto all men, apt to teach, patient, And that they may recover themselves out of the snare of the devil, who are taken captive by him at his will."
2 Timothy 2:24, 26

"Anything Broken Can Be Repaired;
Anything Closed Can Be Opened;
Anything Lost Can Be Recovered."

-MIKE MURDOCK

READ THE BIBLE THROUGH IN ONE YEAR: Hosea 13-Joel 1

Regrets

September 25

"It repenteth Me that I have set up Saul to be king: for he is turned back from following Me, and hath not performed My commandments. And it grieved Samuel; and he cried unto the Lord all night." *1 Samuel 15:11*

"For I will declare mine iniquity; I will be sorry for my sin." *Psalm 38:18*

"I thought on my ways, and turned my feet unto Thy testimonies." *Psalm 119:59*

"Remember ye not the former things, neither consider the things of old. Behold, I will do a new thing; now it shall spring forth; shall ye not know it? I will even make a way in the wilderness, and rivers in the desert."

Isaiah 43:18-19

"Brethren, I count not myself to have apprehended: but this one thing I do, forgetting those things which are behind, and reaching forth unto those things which are before." *Philippians 3:13*

"If we confess our sins, He is faithful and just to forgive us our sins, and to cleanse us from all unrighteousness."

1 John 1:9

"Those Without Regrets Have Made No Discoveries."

-MIKE MURDOCK

READ THE BIBLE THROUGH IN ONE YEAR: Joel 2-Amos 1

Rejection September 26

"For the Lord thy God is a merciful God; He will not forsake thee, neither destroy thee, nor forget the covenant of thy fathers which He sware unto them."
Deuteronomy 4:31

"When my father and my mother forsake me, then the Lord will take me up." *Psalm 27:10*

"Why art thou cast down, O my soul? and why art thou disquieted within me? hope in God: for I shall yet praise Him, Who is the health of my countenance, and my God." *Psalm 43:5*

"For the Lord will not cast off His people, neither will He forsake His inheritance." *Psalm 94:14*

"He is despised and rejected of men; a man of sorrows, and acquainted with grief: and we hid as it were our faces from Him; He was despised, and we esteemed Him not." *Isaiah 53:3*

"Thou shalt no more be termed Forsaken; neither shall thy land any more be termed Desolate." *Isaiah 62:4*

"You Can Only Overcome Rejection When Your Goals Are More Important Than Approval."

-MIKE MURDOCK

READ THE BIBLE THROUGH IN ONE YEAR: Amos 2-4

Relationships September 27

"Excellent speech becometh not a fool: much less do lying lips a prince." *Proverbs 17:7*

"A man that hath friends must shew himself friendly: and there is a friend that sticketh closer than a brother." *Proverbs 18:24*

"Two are better than one; because they have a good reward for their labour." *Ecclesiastes 4:9*

"Can two walk together, except they be agreed?" *Amos 3:3*

"Then they that feared the Lord spake often one to another: and the Lord hearkened, and heard it, and a book of remembrance was written before Him for them that feared the Lord, and that thought upon His name." *Malachi 3:16*

"Greater love hath no man than this, that a man lay down his life for his friends." *John 15:13*

"True Friends Have The Same Enemies."

-MIKE MURDOCK

READ THE BIBLE THROUGH IN ONE YEAR: Amos 5-9

Remembering September 28

"And the bow shall be in the cloud; and I will look upon it, that I may remember the everlasting covenant between God and every living creature of all flesh that is upon the earth." *Genesis 9:16*

"That ye may remember, and do all My commandments, and be holy unto your God." *Numbers 15:40*

"But thou shalt remember the Lord thy God: for it is He that giveth thee power to get wealth, that He may establish His covenant which He sware unto thy fathers, as it is this day." *Deuteronomy 8:18*

"I remember the days of old; I meditate on all Thy works; I muse on the work of Thy hands." *Psalm 143:5*

"Remember now thy Creator in the days of thy youth." *Ecclesiastes 12:1*

"Remember ye not the former things, neither consider the things of old." *Isaiah 43:18*

"...Remember my bonds." *Colossians 4:18*

"Those Without Your Memories Cannot Understand Your Goals."

-MIKE MURDOCK

READ THE BIBLE THROUGH IN ONE YEAR: Obadiah 1-Jonah 2

Renewing of The Mind

September 29

"Thou wilt keep him in perfect peace, whose mind is stayed on Thee: because he trusteth in Thee." *Isaiah 26:3*

"These were more noble than those in Thessalonica, in that they received the word with all readiness of mind, and searched the scriptures daily, whether those things were so." *Acts 17:11*

"And be not conformed to this world: but be ye transformed by the renewing of your mind, that ye may prove what is that good, and acceptable, and perfect, will of God." *Romans 12:2*

"Casting down imaginations, and every high thing that exalteth itself against the knowledge of God, and bringing into captivity every thought to the obedience of Christ." *2 Corinthians 10:5*

"Finally, brethren, whatsoever things are true, whatsoever things are honest, whatsoever things are just, whatsoever things are pure, whatsoever things are lovely, whatsoever things are of good report; if there be any virtue, and if there be any praise, think on these things." *Philippians 4:8*

"Your Memory Replays Your Past.
Your Imagination Preplays Your Future."

-MIKE MURDOCK

READ THE BIBLE THROUGH IN ONE YEAR: Jonah 3-Micah 1

Repentance September 30

"I came not to call the righteous, but sinners to repentance." *Luke 5:32*

"I tell you, Nay: but, except ye repent, ye shall all likewise perish." *Luke 13:3*

"Then Peter said unto them, Repent, and be baptized every one of you in the name of Jesus Christ for the remission of sins, and ye shall receive the gift of the Holy Ghost." *Acts 2:38*

"And the times of this ignorance God winked at; but now commandeth all men every where to repent." *Acts 17:30*

"The Lord is not slack concerning His promise, as some men count slackness; but is longsuffering to us-ward, not willing that any should perish, but that all should come to repentance." *2 Peter 3:9*

"If we confess our sins, He is faithful and just to forgive us our sins, and to cleanse us from all unrighteousness." *1 John 1:9*

"The Proof of Repentance Is Restitution."

-MIKE MURDOCK

READ THE BIBLE THROUGH IN ONE YEAR: Micah 2-4

Reputation

October 1

"A good name is rather to be chosen than great riches, and loving favour rather than silver and gold."

Proverbs 22:1

"Dead flies cause the ointment of the apothecary to send forth a stinking savour: so doth a little folly him that is in reputation for Wisdom and honour."

Ecclesiastes 10:1

"And His fame went throughout all Syria: and they brought unto Him all sick people that were taken with divers diseases and torments, and those which were possessed with devils, and those which were lunatick, and those that had the palsy; and He healed them."

Matthew 4:24

"Let your light so shine before men, that they may see your good works, and glorify your Father which is in Heaven."

Matthew 5:16

"And Jesus returned in the power of the Spirit into Galilee: and there went out a fame of Him through all the region round about."

Luke 4:14

"You Will Only Be Remembered In Life For Two Things: The Problems You Solve or The Ones You Create."

-MIKE MURDOCK

READ THE BIBLE THROUGH IN ONE YEAR: Micah 5-7

Respect

October 2

"And the Lord said unto Moses, Take thee Joshua the son of Nun, a man in whom is the spirit, and lay thine hand upon him; And thou shalt put some of thine honour upon him, that all the congregation of the children of Israel may be obedient." *Numbers 27:18, 20*

"Honour thy father and thy mother, as the Lord thy God hath commanded thee; that thy days may be prolonged, and that it may go well with thee, in the land which the Lord thy God giveth thee." *Deuteronomy 5:16*

"Wherefore the Lord God of Israel saith, I said indeed that thy house, and the house of thy father, should walk before Me for ever: but now the Lord saith, Be it far from Me; for them that honour Me I will honour, and they that despise Me shall be lightly esteemed."

1 Samuel 2:30

"A good name is rather to be chosen than great riches, and loving favour rather than silver and gold."

Proverbs 22:1

"...A prophet is not without honour, save in his own country, and in his own house." *Matthew 13:57*

"What You Respect Will Move Toward You. What You Do Not Respect Will Move Away From You."

-MIKE MURDOCK

READ THE BIBLE THROUGH IN ONE YEAR: Nahum 1-3

Rest

October 3

"And on the seventh day God ended His work which He had made; and He rested on the seventh day from all His work which He had made." *Genesis 2:2*

"Arise ye, and depart; for this is not your rest: because it is polluted, it shall destroy you, even with a sore destruction." *Micah 2:10*

"Come unto Me, all ye that labour and are heavy laden, and I will give you rest. Take My yoke upon you, and learn of Me; for I am meek and lowly in heart: and ye shall find rest unto your souls." *Matthew 11:28-29*

"And He said unto them, Come ye yourselves apart into a desert place, and rest a while: for there were many coming and going, and they had no leisure so much as to eat." *Mark 6:31*

"There remaineth therefore a rest to the people of God." *Hebrews 4:9*

"Tired Eyes Rarely See A Good Future."

-MIKE MURDOCK

READ THE BIBLE THROUGH IN ONE YEAR: Habakkuk 1-3

Restitution

October 4

"If a man shall steal an ox, or a sheep, and kill it, or sell it; he shall restore five oxen for an ox, and four sheep for a sheep. If a man shall cause a field or vineyard to be eaten, and shall put in his beast, and shall feed in another man's field; of the best of his own field, and of the best of his own vineyard, shall he make restitution. If fire break out, and catch in thorns, so that the stacks of corn, or the standing corn, or the field, be consumed therewith; he that kindled the fire shall surely make restitution. If a man shall deliver unto his neighbour money or stuff to keep, and it be stolen out of the man's house; if the thief be found, let him pay double."

Exodus 22:1, 5-7

"Men do not despise a thief, if he steal to satisfy his soul when he is hungry; But if he be found, he shall restore sevenfold; he shall give all the substance of his house."

Proverbs 6:30-31

"And Zacchaeus stood, and said unto the Lord: Behold, Lord, the half of my goods I give to the poor; and if I have taken any thing from any man by false accusation, I restore him fourfold." *Luke 19:8*

"The Proof of Repentance Is Restitution."

-MIKE MURDOCK

READ THE BIBLE THROUGH IN ONE YEAR: Zephaniah 1-Haggai 2

Restoration October 5

"Restore unto me the joy of Thy salvation; and uphold me with Thy free Spirit." *Psalm 51:12*

"Come now, and let us reason together, saith the Lord: though your sins be as scarlet, they shall be as white as snow; though they be red like crimson, they shall be as wool." *Isaiah 1:18*

"For I will restore health unto thee, and I will heal thee of thy wounds, saith the Lord; because they called thee an Outcast." *Jeremiah 30:17*

"Come, and let us return unto the Lord." *Hosea 6:1*

"And I will restore to you the years that the locust hath eaten, the cankerworm, and the caterpillar, and the palmerworm, My great army which I sent among you." *Joel 2:25*

"Brethren, if a man be overtaken in a fault, ye which are spiritual, restore such an one in the spirit of meekness; considering thyself, lest thou also be tempted." *Galatians 6:1*

"You Must Hate Your Present Before You Qualify For Your Future."

-MIKE MURDOCK

READ THE BIBLE THROUGH IN ONE YEAR: Zechariah 1-3

Resurrection of Christ

October 6

"Jesus said unto her, I am the Resurrection, and the Life: he that believeth in Me, though he were dead, yet shall he live." *John 11:25*

"For to this end Christ both died, and rose, and revived, that He might be Lord both of the dead and living." *Romans 14:9*

"And if Christ be not risen, then is our preaching vain, and your faith is also vain." *1 Corinthians 15:14*

"That I may know Him, and the power of His resurrection, and the fellowship of His sufferings, being made conformable unto His death." *Philippians 3:10*

"And to wait for His Son from Heaven, Whom He raised from the dead, even Jesus, which delivered us from the wrath to come." *1 Thessalonians 1:10*

"I am He that liveth, and was dead; and, behold, I am alive for evermore, Amen; and have the keys of hell and of death." *Revelation 1:18*

"Jesus Lived Through The Future So We Could Prepare For It."

-MIKE MURDOCK

READ THE BIBLE THROUGH IN ONE YEAR: Zechariah 4-6

Revenge

October 7

"Thou shalt not avenge, nor bear any grudge against the children of thy people, but thou shalt love thy neighbour as thyself: I am the Lord." *Leviticus 19:18*

"The Lord judge between me and thee, and the Lord avenge me of thee: but mine hand shall not be upon thee." *1 Samuel 24:12*

"But I say unto you, That ye resist not evil: but whosoever shall smite thee on thy right cheek, turn to him the other also." *Matthew 5:39*

"But if ye forgive not men their trespasses, neither will your Father forgive your trespasses."

Matthew 6:15

"Dearly beloved, avenge not yourselves, but rather give place unto wrath: for it is written, Vengeance is Mine; I will repay, saith the Lord." *Romans 12:19*

"Forgiveness Is Permitting God Alone To Penalize Another."

-MIKE MURDOCK

READ THE BIBLE THROUGH IN ONE YEAR: Zechariah 7-9

Revival

October 8

"If My people, which are called by My name, shall humble themselves, and pray, and seek My face, and turn from their wicked ways; then will I hear from Heaven, and will forgive their sin, and will heal their land." *2 Chronicles 7:14*

"Wilt Thou not revive us again: that Thy people may rejoice in Thee?" *Psalm 85:6*

"Though I walk in the midst of trouble, Thou wilt revive me: Thou shalt stretch forth Thine hand against the wrath of mine enemies, and Thy right hand shall save me." *Psalm 138:7*

"I dwell in the high and holy place, with him also that is of a contrite and humble spirit, to revive the spirit of the humble, and to revive the heart of the contrite ones."
Isaiah 57:15

"They that dwell under His shadow shall return; they shall revive as the corn, and grow as the vine: the scent thereof shall be as the wine of Lebanon." *Hosea 14:7*

"Miracles Do Not Go Where They Are Needed—They Go Where They Are Pursued."

-MIKE MURDOCK

READ THE BIBLE THROUGH IN ONE YEAR: Zechariah 10-12

Rewards

October 9

"Be ye strong therefore, and let not your hands be weak: for your work shall be rewarded."   *2 Chronicles 15:7*

"The Lord rewarded me according to my righteousness; according to the cleanness of my hands hath He recompensed me."   *Psalm 18:20*

"Seest thou a man diligent in his business? he shall stand before kings; he shall not stand before mean men."   *Proverbs 22:29*

"That thine alms may be in secret: and thy Father which seeth in secret Himself shall reward thee openly."
Matthew 6:4

"For the Son of man shall come in the glory of His Father with His angels; and then He shall reward every man according to his works."   *Matthew 16:27*

"For God is not unrighteous to forget your work and labour of love, which ye have shewed toward His name, in that ye have ministered to the saints, and do minister."
Hebrews 6:10

"The Problems You Solve Determine The Rewards You Receive."

-MIKE MURDOCK

READ THE BIBLE THROUGH IN ONE YEAR: Zechariah 13-Malachi 1

Rewards of Ritual

October 10

"Every day will I bless Thee; and I will praise Thy name for ever and ever." *Psalm 145:2*

"Blessed is the man that heareth Me, watching daily at My gates, waiting at the posts of My doors." *Proverbs 8:34*

"Now when Daniel knew that the writing was signed, he went into his house; and his windows being open in his chamber toward Jerusalem, he kneeled upon his knees three times a day, and prayed, and gave thanks before his God, as he did aforetime." *Daniel 6:10*

"These were more noble than those in Thessalonica, in that they received the word with all readiness of mind, and searched the scriptures daily, whether those things were so." *Acts 17:11*

"But exhort one another daily, while it is called To day; lest any of you be hardened through the deceitfulness of sin." *Hebrews 3:13*

"What You Do Daily Determines What You Become Permanently."

-*MIKE MURDOCK*

READ THE BIBLE THROUGH IN ONE YEAR: Malachi 2-4

Righteousness of God

October 11

"And ye shall be holy unto Me: for I the Lord am holy, and have severed you from other people, that ye should be Mine." *Leviticus 20:26*

"For the righteous Lord loveth righteousness; His countenance doth behold the upright." *Psalm 11:7*

"The fear of the Lord is clean, enduring for ever: the judgments of the Lord are true and righteous altogether." *Psalm 19:9*

"For the arms of the wicked shall be broken: but the Lord upholdeth the righteous." *Psalm 37:17*

"I have been young, and now am old; yet have I not seen the righteous forsaken, nor His seed begging bread." *Psalm 37:25*

"For the froward is abomination to the Lord: but His secret is with the righteous." *Proverbs 3:32*

"For He hath made Him to be sin for us, Who knew no sin; that we might be made the righteousness of God in Him." *2 Corinthians 5:21*

"What God Does Reveals What He Is."

-MIKE MURDOCK

READ THE BIBLE THROUGH IN ONE YEAR: Matthew 1-5

Romance

October 12

"Hatred stirreth up strifes: but love covereth all sins."
Proverbs 10:12

"Better is a dinner of herbs where love is, than a stalled ox and hatred therewith." *Proverbs 15:17*

"Two are better than one; because they have a good reward for their labour." *Ecclesiastes 4:9*

"Draw me, we will run after Thee: the king hath brought me into his chambers: we will be glad and rejoice in Thee, we will remember Thy love more than wine: the upright love Thee." *Song of Solomon 1:4*

"A garden enclosed is my sister, my spouse; a spring shut up, a fountain sealed." *Song of Solomon 4:12*

"Many waters cannot quench love, neither can the floods drown it: if a man would give all the substance of his house for love, it would utterly be contemned."
Song of Solomon 8:7

"The Proof of Love Is The Investment of Time."

-MIKE MURDOCK

READ THE BIBLE THROUGH IN ONE YEAR: Matthew 6-8

Salvation

October 13

"Come now, and let us reason together, saith the Lord: though your sins be as scarlet, they shall be as white as snow; though they be red like crimson, they shall be as wool." *Isaiah 1:18*

"For God so loved the world, that He gave His only begotten Son, that whosoever believeth in Him should not perish, but have everlasting life." *John 3:16*

"Neither is there salvation in any other: for there is none other name under Heaven given among men, whereby we must be saved." *Acts 4:12*

"For I am not ashamed of the gospel of Christ: for it is the power of God unto salvation to every one that believeth; to the Jew first, and also to the Greek."
Romans 1:16

"For with the heart man believeth unto righteousness; and with the mouth confession is made unto salvation."
Romans 10:10

"The Three Rewards of Reaching For Christ Are: Forgiveness, A Friend And A Future."

-MIKE MURDOCK

READ THE BIBLE THROUGH IN ONE YEAR: Matthew 9-11

Satan

October 14

"And He said unto them, I beheld satan as lightning fall from Heaven." *Luke 10:18*

"Ye are of your father the devil, and the lusts of your father ye will do. He was a murderer from the beginning, and abode not in the truth, because there is no truth in him. When he speaketh a lie, he speaketh of his own: for he is a liar, and the father of it." *John 8:44*

"Submit yourselves therefore to God. Resist the devil, and he will flee from you." *James 4:7*

"Be sober, be vigilant; because your adversary the devil, as a roaring lion, walketh about, seeking whom he may devour." *1 Peter 5:8*

"For this purpose the Son of God was manifested, that He might destroy the works of the devil." *1 John 3:8*

"And the great dragon was cast out, that old serpent, called the devil, and satan, which deceiveth the whole world: he was cast out into the earth, and his angels were cast out with him." *Revelation 12:9*

"Satan Resents Anything God Loves."

-MIKE MURDOCK

READ THE BIBLE THROUGH IN ONE YEAR: Matthew 12-14

Satanism

October 15

"Thou shalt have no other gods before Me."
Exodus 20:3

"For we wrestle not against flesh and blood, but against principalities, against powers, against the rulers of the darkness of this world, against spiritual wickedness in high places." *Ephesians 6:12*

"He that committeth sin is of the devil; for the devil sinneth from the beginning. For this purpose the Son of God was manifested, that He might destroy the works of the devil." *1 John 3:8*

"Ye are of God, little children, and have overcome them: because greater is He that is in you, than he that is in the world." *1 John 4:4*

"And the great dragon was cast out, that old serpent, called the devil, and satan, which deceiveth the whole world: he was cast out into the earth, and his angels were cast out with him." *Revelation 12:9*

"Warfare Is The Proof Your Enemy Has Discovered Your Future."

-MIKE MURDOCK

READ THE BIBLE THROUGH IN ONE YEAR: Matthew 15-17

Schedules

October 16

"The steps of a good man are ordered by the Lord: and He delighteth in his way." *Psalm 37:23*

"Seest thou a man diligent in his business? he shall stand before kings; he shall not stand before mean men." *Proverbs 22:29*

"A faithful man shall abound with blessings: but he that maketh haste to be rich shall not be innocent."
Proverbs 28:20

"She riseth also while it is yet night, and giveth meat to her household, and a portion to her maidens."
Proverbs 31:15

"To every thing there is a season, and a time to every purpose under the Heaven: A time to be born, and a time to die; a time to plant, and a time to pluck up that which is planted." *Ecclesiastes 3:1-2*

"Now when Daniel knew that the writing was signed, he went into his house; and his windows being open in his chamber toward Jerusalem, he kneeled upon his knees three times a day, and prayed, and gave thanks before his God, as he did aforetime." *Daniel 6:10*

"Walk in Wisdom toward them that are without, redeeming the time." *Colossians 4:5*

"When You Can Manage A Day, You Have Managed Your Life."

-MIKE MURDOCK

READ THE BIBLE THROUGH IN ONE YEAR: Matthew 18-20

Seasons

October 17

"And God said, Let there be lights in the firmament of the Heaven to divide the day from the night; and let them be for signs, and for seasons, and for days, and years." *Genesis 1:14*

"While the earth remaineth, seedtime and harvest, and cold and heat, and summer and winter, and day and night shall not cease." *Genesis 8:22*

"Then I will give you rain in due season, and the land shall yield her increase, and the trees of the field shall yield their fruit." *Leviticus 26:4*

"To every thing there is a season, and a time to every purpose under the Heaven." *Ecclesiastes 3:1*

"And He changeth the times and the seasons: He removeth kings, and setteth up kings: He giveth Wisdom unto the wise, and knowledge to them that know understanding." *Daniel 2:21*

"And let us not be weary in well doing: for in due season we shall reap, if we faint not." *Galatians 6:9*

"Your Past Decisions Have Created Your Present Season."

-MIKE MURDOCK

READ THE BIBLE THROUGH IN ONE YEAR: Matthew 21-23

Second Coming of Christ

October 18

"For as the lightning cometh out of the east, and shineth even unto the west; so shall also the coming of the Son of man be. And then shall appear the sign of the Son of man in Heaven: and then shall all the tribes of the earth mourn, and they shall see the Son of man coming in the clouds of Heaven with power and great glory. But of that day and hour knoweth no man, no, not the angels of Heaven, but My Father only. But as the days of Noe were, so shall also the coming of the Son of man be. And knew not until the flood came, and took them all away; so shall also the coming of the Son of man be."
Matthew 24:27, 30, 36-37, 39

"When the Son of man shall come in His glory, and all the holy angels with Him, then shall He sit upon the throne of His glory." *Matthew 25:31*

"In a moment, in the twinkling of an eye, at the last trump: for the trumpet shall sound, and the dead shall be raised incorruptible, and we shall be changed."
1 Corinthians 15:52

"His First Coming Was For Our Preparation; His Second Coming Is For Our Promotion."

-MIKE MURDOCK

READ THE BIBLE THROUGH IN ONE YEAR: Matthew 24-28

Seducing Spirits

October 19

"Lest satan should get an advantage of us: for we are not ignorant of his devices." *2 Corinthians 2:11*

"And no marvel; for satan himself is transformed into an angel of light. Therefore it is no great thing if his ministers also be transformed as the ministers of righteousness; whose end shall be according to their works." *2 Corinthians 11:14-15*

"Now the Spirit speaketh expressly, that in the latter times some shall depart from the faith, giving heed to seducing spirits, and doctrines of devils." *1 Timothy 4:1*

"Beloved, believe not every spirit, but try the spirits whether they are of God: because many false prophets are gone out into the world." *1 John 4:1*

"For they are the spirits of devils, working miracles, which go forth unto the kings of the earth and of the whole world, to gather them to the battle of that great day of God Almighty." *Revelation 16:14*

"Time Often Exposes What Interrogation Cannot."

-MIKE MURDOCK

READ THE BIBLE THROUGH IN ONE YEAR: Mark 1-3

Seed-Faith — October 20

"Honour the Lord with thy substance, and with the firstfruits of all thine increase: So shall thy barns be filled with plenty, and thy presses shall burst out with new wine." *Proverbs 3:9-10*

"Cast thy bread upon the waters: for thou shalt find it after many days. In the morning sow thy seed, and in the evening withhold not thine hand: for thou knowest not whether shall prosper, either this or that, or whether they both shall be alike good."
Ecclesiastes 11:1, 6

"Give, and it shall be given unto you; good measure, pressed down, and shaken together, and running over, shall men give into your bosom. For with the same measure that ye mete withal it shall be measured to you again." *Luke 6:38*

"But this I say, He which soweth sparingly shall reap also sparingly; and he which soweth bountifully shall reap also bountifully." *2 Corinthians 9:6*

"Seed-Faith Is Sowing Something God Gave To You To Create Something Else God Promised You."

-MIKE MURDOCK

READ THE BIBLE THROUGH IN ONE YEAR: Mark 4-6

Seedtime And Harvest

October 21

"While the earth remaineth, seedtime and harvest, and cold and heat, and summer and winter, and day and night shall not cease." *Genesis 8:22*

"Bring ye all the tithes into the storehouse, that there may be meat in Mine house, and prove Me now herewith, saith the Lord of hosts, if I will not open you the windows of Heaven, and pour you out a blessing, that there shall not be room enough to receive it."

Malachi 3:10

"Give, and it shall be given unto you; good measure, pressed down, and shaken together, and running over, shall men give into your bosom. For with the same measure that ye mete withal it shall be measured to you again." *Luke 6:38*

"But this I say, He which soweth sparingly shall reap also sparingly; and he which soweth bountifully shall reap also bountifully." *2 Corinthians 9:6*

"Be not deceived; God is not mocked: for whatsoever a man soweth, that shall he also reap. And let us not be weary in well doing: for in due season we shall reap, if we faint not." *Galatians 6:7, 9*

"The Quality of Your Seed Determines The Quality of Your Harvest."

-MIKE MURDOCK

READ THE BIBLE THROUGH IN ONE YEAR: Mark 7-9

Self-Confidence — October 22

"The Lord is my light and my salvation; whom shall I fear? the Lord is the strength of my life; of whom shall I be afraid?" *Psalm 27:1*

"It is better to trust in the Lord than to put confidence in man." *Psalm 118:8*

"For the Lord shall be thy confidence, and shall keep thy foot from being taken." *Proverbs 3:26*

"Behold, I have graven thee upon the palms of My hands." *Isaiah 49:16*

"Being confident of this very thing, that He which hath begun a good work in you will perform it until the day of Jesus Christ." *Philippians 1:6*

"I can do all things through Christ which strengtheneth me." *Philippians 4:13*

"...greater is He that is in you, than he that is in the world." *1 John 4:4*

"Information Always Breeds Confidence."

-MIKE MURDOCK

READ THE BIBLE THROUGH IN ONE YEAR: Mark 10-12

Self-Control — October 23

"Teach me, and I will hold my tongue: and cause me to understand wherein I have erred." *Job 6:24*

"He that is slow to anger is better than the mighty; and he that ruleth his spirit than he that taketh a city."
Proverbs 16:32

"He that hath no rule over his own spirit is like a city that is broken down, and without walls." *Proverbs 25:28*

"Neither yield ye your members as instruments of unrighteousness unto sin: but yield yourselves unto God, as those that are alive from the dead, and your members as instruments of righteousness unto God."
Romans 6:13

"I am crucified with Christ: nevertheless I live; yet not I, but Christ liveth in me: and the life which I now live in the flesh I live by the faith of the Son of God, Who loved me, and gave Himself for me." *Galatians 2:20*

"Ye are of God, little children, and have overcome them: because greater is He that is in you, than he that is in the world." *1 John 4:4*

"What You Can Walk Away From You Have Mastered."

-MIKE MURDOCK

READ THE BIBLE THROUGH IN ONE YEAR: Mark 13-15

Selfishness — October 24

"And thou shalt not glean thy vineyard, neither shalt thou gather every grape of thy vineyard; thou shalt leave them for the poor and stranger: I am the Lord your God." *Leviticus 19:10*

"There is that maketh himself rich, yet hath nothing: there is that maketh himself poor, yet hath great riches." *Proverbs 13:7*

"He that hath pity upon the poor lendeth unto the Lord; and that which he hath given will He pay him again." *Proverbs 19:17*

"And He said unto them, Take heed, and beware of covetousness: for a man's life consisteth not in the abundance of the things which he possesseth. So is he that layeth up treasure for himself, and is not rich toward God. For where your treasure is, there will your heart be also." *Luke 12:15, 21, 34*

"Look not every man on his own things, but every man also on the things of others." *Philippians 2:4*

"But whoso hath this world's good, and seeth his brother have need, and shutteth up his bowels of compassion from him, how dwelleth the love of God in him?" *1 John 3:17*

"Giving Is The Only Cure For Greed."

-MIKE MURDOCK

READ THE BIBLE THROUGH IN ONE YEAR: Mark 16-Luke 2

Servanthood — October 25

"Even as the Son of man came not to be ministered unto, but to minister, and to give His life a ransom for many." *Matthew 20:28*

"His lord said unto him, Well done, thou good and faithful servant: thou hast been faithful over a few things, I will make thee ruler over many things: enter thou into the joy of thy lord." *Matthew 25:21*

"And if ye have not been faithful in that which is another man's, who shall give you that which is your own?" *Luke 16:12*

"But ye shall not be so: but he that is greatest among you, let him be as the younger; and he that is chief, as he that doth serve." *Luke 22:26*

"Moreover it is required in stewards, that a man be found faithful." *1 Corinthians 4:2*

"For though I be free from all men, yet have I made myself servant unto all, that I might gain the more." *1 Corinthians 9:19*

"The Eventual Rewards of Submission Surpass The Immediate Rewards of Agreement."

-MIKE MURDOCK

READ THE BIBLE THROUGH IN ONE YEAR: Luke 3-7

Sex

October 26

"Wherewithal shall a young man cleanse his way? by taking heed thereto according to Thy word."
Psalm 119:9

"Flee fornication. Every sin that a man doeth is without the body; but he that committeth fornication sinneth against his own body." *1 Corinthians 6:18*

"What? know ye not that your body is the temple of the Holy Ghost which is in you, which ye have of God, and ye are not your own?" *1 Corinthians 6:19*

"Nevertheless, to avoid fornication, let every man have his own wife, and let every woman have her own husband." *1 Corinthians 7:2*

"There hath no temptation taken you but such as is common to man: but God is faithful, Who will not suffer you to be tempted above that ye are able; but will with the temptation also make a way to escape, that ye may be able to bear it." *1 Corinthians 10:13*

"Never Gaze At Something That Does Not Belong In Your Future."

-MIKE MURDOCK

READ THE BIBLE THROUGH IN ONE YEAR: Luke 8-10

Silence

October 27

"Whoso keepeth his mouth and his tongue keepeth his soul from troubles." *Proverbs 21:23*

"A time to rend, and a time to sew; a time to keep silence, and a time to speak." *Ecclesiastes 3:7*

"Better is an handful with quietness, than both the hands full with travail and vexation of spirit." *Ecclesiastes 4:6*

"Be not rash with thy mouth, and let not thine heart be hasty to utter any thing before God: for God is in Heaven, and thou upon earth: therefore let thy words be few." *Ecclesiastes 5:2*

"The words of wise men are heard in quiet more than the cry of him that ruleth among fools."

Ecclesiastes 9:17

"And that ye study to be quiet, and to do your own business, and to work with your own hands, as we commanded you." *1 Thessalonians 4:11*

"Wherefore, my beloved brethren, let every man be swift to hear, slow to speak, slow to wrath." *James 1:19*

"Silence Cannot Be Misquoted."

-MIKE MURDOCK

READ THE BIBLE THROUGH IN ONE YEAR: Luke 11-13

Sin

October 28

"If thou doest well, shalt thou not be accepted? and if thou doest not well, sin lieth at the door. And unto thee shall be his desire, and thou shalt rule over him."
Genesis 4:7

"For I will declare mine iniquity; I will be sorry for my sin." *Psalm 38:18*

"Thy word have I hid in mine heart, that I might not sin against Thee." *Psalm 119:11*

"For the wages of sin is death; but the gift of God is eternal life through Jesus Christ our Lord." *Romans 6:23*

"But if we walk in the light, as He is in the light, we have fellowship one with another, and the blood of Jesus Christ His Son cleanseth us from all sin. If we say that we have no sin, we deceive ourselves, and the truth is not in us." *1 John 1:7-8*

"My little children, these things write I unto you, that ye sin not. And if any man sin, we have an advocate with the Father, Jesus Christ the righteous." *1 John 2:1*

"The Willingness To Confess Births The Ability To Overcome."

-MIKE MURDOCK

READ THE BIBLE THROUGH IN ONE YEAR: Luke 14-16

Singing

October 29

"Serve the Lord with gladness: come before His presence with singing." *Psalm 100:2*

"Thy statutes have been my songs in the house of my pilgrimage." *Psalm 119:54*

"Then was our mouth filled with laughter, and our tongue with singing: then said they among the heathen, The Lord hath done great things for them." *Psalm 126:2*

"Sing, O ye Heavens; for the Lord hath done it: shout, ye lower parts of the earth: break forth into singing, ye mountains, O forest, and every tree therein: for the Lord hath redeemed Jacob, and glorified Himself in Israel." *Isaiah 44:23*

"Therefore the redeemed of the Lord shall return, and come with singing unto Zion; and everlasting joy shall be upon their head: they shall obtain gladness and joy; and sorrow and mourning shall flee away." *Isaiah 51:11*

"Is any among you afflicted? let him pray. Is any merry? let him sing psalms." *James 5:13*

"A Song Is A Corridor Into The Presence of God."

-MIKE MURDOCK

READ THE BIBLE THROUGH IN ONE YEAR: Luke 17-19

Slander

October 30

"Thou shalt hide them in the secret of Thy presence from the pride of man: Thou shalt keep them secretly in a pavilion from the strife of tongues." *Psalm 31:20*

"Whoso privily slandereth his neighbour, him will I cut off: him that hath an high look and a proud heart will not I suffer." *Psalm 101:5*

"He that hideth hatred with lying lips, and he that uttereth a slander, is a fool." *Proverbs 10:18*

"A false witness shall not be unpunished, and he that speaketh lies shall perish." *Proverbs 19:9*

"Blessed are ye, when men shall revile you, and persecute you, and shall say all manner of evil against you falsely, for My sake. Rejoice, and be exceeding glad: for great is your reward in Heaven: for so persecuted they the prophets which were before you." *Matthew 5:11-12*

"Let no corrupt communication proceed out of your mouth, but that which is good to the use of edifying, that it may minister grace unto the hearers." *Ephesians 4:29*

"Better To Experience An Injustice Than To Become A Slave To The Memory of It."

-MIKE MURDOCK

READ THE BIBLE THROUGH IN ONE YEAR: Luke 20-22

Solitude

October 31

"This is my rest for ever: here will I dwell; for I have desired it." *Psalm 132:14*

"To every thing there is a season, and a time to every purpose under the Heaven." *Ecclesiastes 3:1*

"And when He had sent the multitudes away, He went up into a mountain apart to pray: and when the evening was come, He was there alone." *Matthew 14:23*

"And He said unto them, Come ye yourselves apart into a desert place, and rest a while: for there were many coming and going, and they had no leisure so much as to eat." *Mark 6:31*

"But let every man prove his own work, and then shall he have rejoicing in himself alone, and not in another. For every man shall bear his own burden." *Galatians 6:4-5*

"And that ye study to be quiet, and to do your own business, and to work with your own hands, as we commanded you." *1 Thessalonians 4:11*

"Solitude Is The Silencing of Human Logic."

-*MIKE MURDOCK*

READ THE BIBLE THROUGH IN ONE YEAR: Luke 23-John 1

Sorrow

November 1

"For His anger endureth but a moment; in His favour is life: weeping may endure for a night, but joy cometh in the morning." *Psalm 30:5*

"Why art thou cast down, O my soul? and why art thou disquieted within me? hope thou in God: for I shall yet praise Him, Who is the health of my countenance, and my God." *Psalm 42:11*

"The Lord will perfect that which concerneth me: Thy mercy, O Lord, endureth for ever: forsake not the works of Thine own hands." *Psalm 138:8*

"He healeth the broken in heart, and bindeth up their wounds." *Psalm 147:3*

"A man hath joy by the answer of his mouth: and a word spoken in due season, how good is it!" *Proverbs 15:23*

"And we know that all things work together for good to them that love God, to them who are the called according to His purpose." *Romans 8:28*

"Casting all your care upon Him; for He careth for you." *1 Peter 5:7*

"Uncommon Pain Often Creates Uncommon People."
-MIKE MURDOCK

READ THE BIBLE THROUGH IN ONE YEAR: John 2-6

Soul-Winning November 2

"Ask of Me, and I shall give thee the heathen for thine inheritance, and the uttermost parts of the earth for thy possession." *Psalm 2:8*

"The fruit of the righteous is a tree of life; and he that winneth souls is wise." *Proverbs 11:30*

"...Go ye into all the world, and preach the gospel to every creature. He that believeth and is baptized shall be saved; but he that believeth not shall be damned." *Mark 16:15-16*

"Therefore said He unto them, The harvest truly is great, but the labourers are few: pray ye therefore the Lord of the harvest, that He would send forth labourers into His harvest." *Luke 10:2*

"How then shall they call on Him in Whom they have not believed? and how shall they believe in Him of Whom they have not heard? and how shall they hear without a preacher?" *Romans 10:14*

"Knowing therefore the terror of the Lord, we persuade men." *2 Corinthians 5:11*

"The Broken Become Masters At Mending."

-MIKE MURDOCK

READ THE BIBLE THROUGH IN ONE YEAR: John 7-9

Spirit of Error

November 3

"And the Lord said unto him, Wherewith? And he said, I will go forth, and I will be a lying spirit in the mouth of all his prophets." *1 Kings 22:22*

"Now the Spirit speaketh expressly, that in the latter times some shall depart from the faith, giving heed to seducing spirits, and doctrines of devils." *1 Timothy 4:1*

"Study to shew thyself approved unto God, a workman that needeth not to be ashamed, rightly dividing the word of truth." *2 Timothy 2:15*

"We are of God: he that knoweth God heareth us; he that is not of God heareth not us. Hereby know we the spirit of truth, and the spirit of error." *1 John 4:6*

"And the city had no need of the sun, neither of the moon, to shine in it: for the glory of God did lighten it, and the Lamb is the light thereof. And there shall in no wise enter into it any thing that defileth, neither whatsoever worketh abomination, or maketh a lie: but they which are written in the Lamb's book of life."
Revelation 21:23, 27

"The Opposite of Truth Is Confusion."

-MIKE MURDOCK

READ THE BIBLE THROUGH IN ONE YEAR: John 10-12

Spiritual Warfare

November 4

"There hath no temptation taken you but such as is common to man: but God is faithful, Who will not suffer you to be tempted above that ye are able; but will with the temptation also make a way to escape, that ye may be able to bear it." *1 Corinthians 10:13*

"For though we walk in the flesh, we do not war after the flesh: For the weapons of our warfare are not carnal, but mighty through God to the pulling down of strong holds." *2 Corinthians 10:3-4*

"For we wrestle not against flesh and blood, but against principalities, against powers, against the rulers of the darkness of this world, against spiritual wickedness in high places." *Ephesians 6:12*

"Fight the good fight of faith, lay hold on eternal life, whereunto thou art also called, and hast professed a good profession before many witnesses." *1 Timothy 6:12*

"Ye are of God, little children, and have overcome them: because greater is He that is in you, than he that is in the world." *1 John 4:4*

"When You Delay A Battle, You Delay Your Reward."
-MIKE MURDOCK

READ THE BIBLE THROUGH IN ONE YEAR: John 13-15

Strength

November 5

"For the joy of the Lord is your strength."
Nehemiah 8:10

"A wise man is strong; yea, a man of knowledge increaseth strength." *Proverbs 24:5*

"But they that wait upon the Lord shall renew their strength; they shall mount up with wings as eagles; they shall run, and not be weary; and they shall walk, and not faint." *Isaiah 40:31*

"And said, O man greatly beloved, fear not: peace be unto thee, be strong, yea, be strong. And when He had spoken unto me, I was strengthened, and said, Let my lord speak; for Thou hast strengthened me."
Daniel 10:19

"But ye shall receive power, after that the Holy Ghost is come upon you: and ye shall be witnesses unto Me both in Jerusalem, and in all Judaea, and in Samaria, and unto the uttermost part of the earth." *Acts 1:8*

"I can do all things through Christ which strengtheneth me." *Philippians 4:13*

"The Word of God Becomes The Energy of God In You."

-MIKE MURDOCK

READ THE BIBLE THROUGH IN ONE YEAR: John 16-18

Stress

November 6

"The Lord also will be a refuge for the oppressed, a refuge in times of trouble." *Psalm 9:9*

"My flesh and my heart faileth: but God is the strength of my heart, and my portion for ever." *Psalm 73:26*

"A thousand shall fall at thy side, and ten thousand at thy right hand; but it shall not come nigh thee. There shall no evil befall thee, neither shall any plague come nigh thy dwelling." *Psalm 91:7, 10*

"Peace I leave with you, My peace I give unto you: not as the world giveth, give I unto you. Let not your heart be troubled, neither let it be afraid." *John 14:27*

"There remaineth therefore a rest to the people of God." *Hebrews 4:9*

"Casting all your care upon Him; for He careth for you." *1 Peter 5:7*

"If You Have More Than You Can Organize, Prioritize or Supervise, You Have More Than God Intended."

-MIKE MURDOCK

READ THE BIBLE THROUGH IN ONE YEAR: John 19-21

Strife

November 7

"A wrathful man stirreth up strife: but he that is slow to anger appeaseth strife." *Proverbs 15:18*

"A froward man soweth strife: and a whisperer separateth chief friends." *Proverbs 16:28*

"It is an honour for a man to cease from strife: but every fool will be meddling." *Proverbs 20:3*

"Where no wood is, there the fire goeth out: so where there is no talebearer, the strife ceaseth." *Proverbs 26:20*

"Can two walk together, except they be agreed?" *Amos 3:3*

"If it be possible, as much as lieth in you, live peaceably with all men." *Romans 12:18*

"But foolish and unlearned questions avoid, knowing that they do gender strifes." *2 Timothy 2:23*

"For where envying and strife is, there is confusion and every evil work." *James 3:16*

"Strife Is The Proof of Disorder."

-MIKE MURDOCK

READ THE BIBLE THROUGH IN ONE YEAR: Acts 1-3

Struggle

November 8

"For a just man falleth seven times, and riseth up again: but the wicked shall fall into mischief."
Proverbs 24:16

"And ye shall be hated of all men for My name's sake: but he that endureth to the end shall be saved."
Matthew 10:22

"For we wrestle not against flesh and blood, but against principalities, against powers, against the rulers of the darkness of this world, against spiritual wickedness in high places." *Ephesians 6:12*

"Being confident of this very thing, that He which hath begun a good work in you will perform it until the day of Jesus Christ." *Philippians 1:6*

"But call to remembrance the former days, in which, after ye were illuminated, ye endured a great fight of afflictions." *Hebrews 10:32*

"Struggle Is The Proof You Have Not Yet Been Conquered."

-MIKE MURDOCK

READ THE BIBLE THROUGH IN ONE YEAR: Acts 4-8

Studying Your Bible

November 9

"But He answered and said, It is written, Man shall not live by bread alone, but by every word that proceedeth out of the mouth of God."   *Matthew 4:4*

"Search the scriptures; for in them ye think ye have eternal life: and they are they which testify of Me."
John 5:39

"For whatsoever things were written aforetime were written for our learning, that we through patience and comfort of the scriptures might have hope."
Romans 15:4

"Study to shew thyself approved unto God, a workman that needeth not to be ashamed, rightly dividing the word of truth."   *2 Timothy 2:15*

"All scripture is given by inspiration of God, and is profitable for doctrine, for reproof, for correction, for instruction in righteousness: That the man of God may be perfect, throughly furnished unto all good works."   *2 Timothy 3:16-17*

"Successful Men Do Daily What Unsuccessful Men Do Occasionally."

-MIKE MURDOCK

READ THE BIBLE THROUGH IN ONE YEAR: Acts 9-11

Submission November 10

"And whosoever shall compel thee to go a mile, go with him twain." *Matthew 5:41*

"No man can serve two masters: for either he will hate the one, and love the other; or else he will hold to the one, and despise the other. Ye cannot serve God and mammon." *Matthew 6:24*

"Submitting yourselves one to another in the fear of God. Wives, submit yourselves unto your own husbands, as unto the Lord. For the husband is the head of the wife, even as Christ is the head of the church: and He is the saviour of the body. Therefore as the church is subject unto Christ, so let the wives be to their own husbands in every thing." *Ephesians 5:21-24*

"Put them in mind to be subject to principalities and powers, to obey magistrates, to be ready to every good work." *Titus 3:1*

"Submission Begins When Agreement Ends."

-*MIKE MURDOCK*

READ THE BIBLE THROUGH IN ONE YEAR: Acts 12-14

Success

November 11

"And he said unto me, The Lord, before whom I walk, will send His angel with thee, and prosper thy way."
Genesis 24:40

"Keep therefore the words of this covenant, and do them, that ye may prosper in all that ye do."
Deuteronomy 29:9

"Only be thou strong and very courageous, that thou mayest observe to do according to all the law, which Moses My servant commanded thee: turn not from it to the right hand or to the left, that thou mayest prosper whithersoever thou goest. This book of the law shall not depart out of thy mouth; but thou shalt meditate therein day and night, that thou mayest observe to do according to all that is written therein: for then thou shalt make thy way prosperous, and then thou shalt have good success." *Joshua 1:7-8*

"Pray for the peace of Jerusalem: they shall prosper that love thee." *Psalm 122:6*

"Success Is The Fragrance of Joy When A Goal Has Been Achieved."

-MIKE MURDOCK

READ THE BIBLE THROUGH IN ONE YEAR: Acts 15-17

Suffering

November 12

"For His anger endureth but a moment; in His favour is life: weeping may endure for a night, but joy cometh in the morning." *Psalm 30:5*

"And shall not God avenge His own elect, which cry day and night unto Him, though He bear long with them?" *Luke 18:7*

"And they departed from the presence of the council, rejoicing that they were counted worthy to suffer shame for His name." *Acts 5:41*

"If we suffer, we shall also reign with Him: if we deny Him, He also will deny us." *2 Timothy 2:12*

"Choosing rather to suffer affliction with the people of God, than to enjoy the pleasures of sin for a season." *Hebrews 11:25*

"For it is better, if the will of God be so, that ye suffer for well doing, than for evil doing." *1 Peter 3:17*

"Wherefore let them that suffer according to the will of God commit the keeping of their souls to Him in well doing, as unto a faithful Creator." *1 Peter 4:19*

"Never Complain About Your Present—If You Are Unwilling To Walk Toward Your Future."

-MIKE MURDOCK

READ THE BIBLE THROUGH IN ONE YEAR: Acts 18-20

Suicidal Thoughts

November 13

"For His anger endureth but a moment; in His favour is life: weeping may endure for a night, but joy cometh in the morning." *Psalm 30:5*

"I shall not die, but live, and declare the works of the Lord." *Psalm 118:17*

"Casting down imaginations, and every high thing that exalteth itself against the knowledge of God, and bringing into captivity every thought to the obedience of Christ." *2 Corinthians 10:5*

"But I have all, and abound: I am full, having received of Epaphroditus the things which were sent from you, an odour of a sweet smell, a sacrifice acceptable, wellpleasing to God." *Philippians 4:18*

"Blessed is the man that endureth temptation: for when he is tried, he shall receive the crown of life, which the Lord hath promised to them that love Him." *James 1:12*

"Your Life Will Always Move In The Direction of Your Most Dominant Thought."

-MIKE MURDOCK

READ THE BIBLE THROUGH IN ONE YEAR: Acts 21-23

Survival

November 14

"And the Lord commanded us to do all these statutes, to fear the Lord our God, for our good always, that He might preserve us alive, as it is at this day."
Deuteronomy 6:24

"I sought the Lord, and He heard me, and delivered me from all my fears." *Psalm 34:4*

"Unless Thy law had been my delights, I should then have perished in mine affliction." *Psalm 119:92*

"Where no counsel is, the people fall: but in the multitude of counsellors there is safety." *Proverbs 11:14*

"So shall they fear the name of the Lord from the west, and His glory from the rising of the sun. When the enemy shall come in like a flood, the Spirit of the Lord shall lift up a standard against him." *Isaiah 59:19*

"Call unto Me, and I will answer thee, and shew thee great and mighty things, which thou knowest not."
Jeremiah 33:3

"You Never Receive A Miracle Until You Need One."
-MIKE MURDOCK

READ THE BIBLE THROUGH IN ONE YEAR: Acts 24-26

Talents And Skills

November 15

"A man's gift maketh room for him, and bringeth him before great men." *Proverbs 18:16*

"His lord said unto him, Well done, good and faithful servant; thou hast been faithful over a few things, I will make thee ruler over many things: enter thou into the joy of thy lord." *Matthew 25:23*

"But he that knew not, and did commit things worthy of stripes, shall be beaten with few stripes. For unto whomsoever much is given, of him shall be much required: and to whom men have committed much, of him they will ask the more." *Luke 12:48*

"From which some having swerved have turned aside unto vain jangling." *1 Timothy 1:6*

"Every good gift and every perfect gift is from above, and cometh down from the Father of lights, with Whom is no variableness, neither shadow of turning." *James 1:17*

"What You Love The Most Is A Clue To The Gift You Contain."

-MIKE MURDOCK

READ THE BIBLE THROUGH IN ONE YEAR: Acts 27-Romans 3

Talking

November 16

"A man hath joy by the answer of his mouth: and a word spoken in due season, how good is it!" *Proverbs 15:23*

"The heart of the righteous studieth to answer: but the mouth of the wicked poureth out evil things."
Proverbs 15:28

"Righteous lips are the delight of kings; and they love him that speaketh right." *Proverbs 16:13*

"Pleasant words are as an honeycomb, sweet to the soul, and health to the bones." *Proverbs 16:24*

"Death and life are in the power of the tongue: and they that love it shall eat the fruit thereof." *Proverbs 18:21*

"Every man shall kiss his lips that giveth a right answer." *Proverbs 24:26*

"By long forbearing is a prince persuaded, and a soft tongue breaketh the bone." *Proverbs 25:15*

"The words of a wise man's mouth are gracious."
Ecclesiastes 10:12

"Wherefore, my beloved brethren, let every man be swift to hear, slow to speak, slow to wrath." *James 1:19*

"Your Words Decide Your Future."

-MIKE MURDOCK

READ THE BIBLE THROUGH IN ONE YEAR: Romans 4-6

Teaching

November 17

"Behold, I have taught you statutes and judgments, even as the Lord my God commanded me, that ye should do so in the land whither ye go to possess it. Keep therefore and do them; for this is your Wisdom and your understanding in the sight of the nations, which shall hear all these statutes, and say, Surely this great nation is a wise and understanding people." *Deuteronomy 4:5-6*

"Whosoever therefore shall break one of these least commandments, and shall teach men so, he shall be called the least in the kingdom of Heaven: but whosoever shall do and teach them, the same shall be called great in the kingdom of Heaven." *Matthew 5:19*

"Go ye therefore, and teach all nations, baptizing them in the name of the Father, and of the Son, and of the Holy Ghost: Teaching them to observe all things whatsoever I have commanded you: and, lo, I am with you alway, even unto the end of the world. Amen."
Matthew 28:19-20

"And daily in the temple, and in every house, they ceased not to teach and preach Jesus Christ." *Acts 5:42*

"You Will Only Remember Something You Teach."
-MIKE MURDOCK

READ THE BIBLE THROUGH IN ONE YEAR: Romans 7-9

Teamwork November 18

"Behold, how good and how pleasant it is for brethren to dwell together in unity!" *Psalm 133:1*

"Two are better than one; because they have a good reward for their labour. For if they fall, the one will lift up his fellow: but woe to him that is alone when he falleth; for he hath not another to help him up. And if one prevail against him, two shall withstand him; and a threefold cord is not quickly broken."

Ecclesiastes 4:9-10, 12

"Can two walk together, except they be agreed?"

Amos 3:3

"Again I say unto you, That if two of you shall agree on earth as touching any thing that they shall ask, it shall be done for them of My Father which is in Heaven."

Matthew 18:19

"And they went forth, and preached every where, the Lord working with them, and confirming the word with signs following." *Mark 16:20*

"For we are labourers together with God: ye are God's husbandry, ye are God's building." *1 Corinthians 3:9*

"Two Are Necessary For Multiplication."

-MIKE MURDOCK

READ THE BIBLE THROUGH IN ONE YEAR: Romans 10-12

Tears

November 19

"Turn again, and tell Hezekiah the captain of My people, Thus saith the Lord, the God of David thy father, I have heard thy prayer, I have seen thy tears: behold, I will heal thee: on the third day thou shalt go up unto the house of the Lord." *2 Kings 20:5*

"For His anger endureth but a moment; in His favour is life: weeping may endure for a night, but joy cometh in the morning." *Psalm 30:5*

"Thou tellest my wanderings: put Thou my tears into Thy bottle: are they not in Thy book?" *Psalm 56:8*

"They that sow in tears shall reap in joy." *Psalm 126:5*

"Jesus wept." *John 11:35*

"Casting all your care upon Him; for He careth for you." *1 Peter 5:7*

"And God shall wipe away all tears from their eyes; and there shall be no more death, neither sorrow, nor crying, neither shall there be any more pain: for the former things are passed away." *Revelation 21:4*

"Those Without Your Memories Will Rarely Understand Your Tears."

-MIKE MURDOCK

READ THE BIBLE THROUGH IN ONE YEAR: Romans 13-15

Temptation November 20

"Thy word have I hid in mine heart, that I might not sin against Thee." *Psalm 119:11*

"There hath no temptation taken you but such as is common to man: but God is faithful, Who will not suffer you to be tempted above that ye are able; but will with the temptation also make a way to escape, that ye may be able to bear it." *1 Corinthians 10:13*

"Put on the whole armour of God, that ye may be able to stand against the wiles of the devil. Above all, taking the shield of faith, wherewith ye shall be able to quench all the fiery darts of the wicked." *Ephesians 6:11, 16*

"My brethren, count it all joy when ye fall into divers temptations." *James 1:2*

"Submit yourselves therefore to God. Resist the devil, and he will flee from you." *James 4:7*

"The Lord knoweth how to deliver the godly out of temptations." *2 Peter 2:9*

"What You Are Willing To Walk Away From You Have Conquered."

-MIKE MURDOCK

READ THE BIBLE THROUGH IN ONE YEAR: Romans 16-1 Corinthians 2

Ten Commandments

November 21

"Thou shalt have no other gods before Me."
Exodus 20:3

"Thou shalt not make unto thee any graven image."
Exodus 20:4

"Thou shalt not take the name of the Lord thy God in vain." *Exodus 20:7*

"Remember the sabbath day, to keep it holy."
Exodus 20:8

"Honour thy father and thy mother." *Exodus 20:12*

"Thou shalt not kill." *Exodus 20:13*

"Thou shalt not commit adultery." *Exodus 20:14*

"Thou shalt not steal." *Exodus 20:15*

"Thou shalt not bear false witness against thy neighbour." *Exodus 20:16*

"Thou shalt not covet." *Exodus 20:17*

"Each Act of Obedience Shortens The Distance To Any Miracle You Are Pursuing."

-MIKE MURDOCK

READ THE BIBLE THROUGH IN ONE YEAR: 1 Corinthians 3-5

Terrorism

November 22

"Thou shalt not be afraid for the terror by night; nor for the arrow that flieth by day." *Psalm 91:5*

"For He shall give His angels charge over thee, to keep thee in all thy ways." *Psalm 91:11*

"In righteousness shalt thou be established: thou shalt be far from oppression; for thou shalt not fear: and from terror; for it shall not come near thee." *Isaiah 54:14*

"For we wrestle not against flesh and blood, but against principalities, against powers, against the rulers of the darkness of this world, against spiritual wickedness in high places." *Ephesians 6:12*

"For God hath not given us the spirit of fear; but of power, and of love, and of a sound mind." *2 Timothy 1:7*

"But and if ye suffer for righteousness' sake, happy are ye: and be not afraid of their terror, neither be troubled." *1 Peter 3:14*

"What You Hate Reveals What You Were Created To Destroy."

-MIKE MURDOCK

READ THE BIBLE THROUGH IN ONE YEAR: 1 Corinthians 6-10

Testings

November 23

"And let us not be weary in well doing: for in due season we shall reap, if we faint not." *Galatians 6:9*

"I can do all things through Christ which strengtheneth me." *Philippians 4:13*

"Thou therefore endure hardness, as a good soldier of Jesus Christ." *2 Timothy 2:3*

"Behold, we count them happy which endure. Ye have heard of the patience of Job, and have seen the end of the Lord; that the Lord is very pitiful, and of tender mercy." *James 5:11*

"That the trial of your faith, being much more precious than of gold that perisheth, though it be tried with fire, might be found unto praise and honour and glory at the appearing of Jesus Christ." *1 Peter 1:7*

"Beloved, think it not strange concerning the fiery trial which is to try you, as though some strange thing happened unto you: But rejoice, inasmuch as ye are partakers of Christ's sufferings; that, when His glory shall be revealed, ye may be glad also with exceeding joy." *1 Peter 4:12-13*

"Endurance Demoralizes An Adversary."

-MIKE MURDOCK

READ THE BIBLE THROUGH IN ONE YEAR: 1 Corinthians 11-13

Thanksgiving November 24

"Then Hezekiah answered and said, Now ye have consecrated yourselves unto the Lord, come near and bring sacrifices and thank offerings into the house of the Lord. And the congregation brought in sacrifices and thank offerings; and as many as were of a free heart burnt offerings." *2 Chronicles 29:31*

"Offer unto God thanksgiving; and pay thy vows unto the most High." *Psalm 50:14*

"I will praise the name of God with a song, and will magnify Him with thanksgiving." *Psalm 69:30*

"Enter into His gates with thanksgiving, and into His courts with praise: be thankful unto Him, and bless His name." *Psalm 100:4*

"Sing unto the Lord with thanksgiving; sing praise upon the harp unto our God." *Psalm 147:7*

"I thank my God upon every remembrance of you, Always in every prayer of mine for you all making request with joy." *Philippians 1:3-4*

"Be careful for nothing; but in every thing by prayer and supplication with thanksgiving let your requests be made known unto God." *Philippians 4:6*

"The Quickest Cure For Ingratitude Is Loss."

-MIKE MURDOCK

READ THE BIBLE THROUGH IN ONE YEAR: 1 Corinthians 14-16

The Cross — November 25

"...Whosoever will come after Me, let him deny himself, and take up his cross, and follow Me." *Mark 8:34*

"For the preaching of the cross is to them that perish foolishness; but unto us which are saved it is the power of God." *1 Corinthians 1:18*

"And being found in fashion as a man, He humbled Himself, and became obedient unto death, even the death of the cross." *Philippians 2:8*

"Neither by the blood of goats and calves, but by His own blood He entered in once into the holy place, having obtained eternal redemption for us."
Hebrews 9:12

"Looking unto Jesus the Author and Finisher of our faith; Who for the joy that was set before Him endured the cross, despising the shame, and is set down at the right hand of the throne of God." *Hebrews 12:2*

"Who His own self bare our sins in His own body on the tree, that we, being dead to sins, should live unto righteousness: by Whose stripes ye were healed."
1 Peter 2:24

"Satan's Greatest Failure Was The Crucifixion of Christ."

-MIKE MURDOCK

READ THE BIBLE THROUGH IN ONE YEAR: 2 Corinthians 1-3

The Secret Place

November 26

"One thing have I desired of the Lord, that will I seek after; that I may dwell in the house of the Lord all the days of my life, to behold the beauty of the Lord, and to enquire in His temple." *Psalm 27:4*

"He that dwelleth in the secret place of the most High shall abide under the shadow of the Almighty."
Psalm 91:1

"But thou, when thou prayest, enter into thy closet, and when thou hast shut thy door, pray to thy Father which is in secret; and thy Father which seeth in secret shall reward thee openly." *Matthew 6:6*

"...couldest not thou watch one hour? Watch ye and pray, lest ye enter into temptation. The spirit truly is ready, but the flesh is weak." *Mark 14:37-38*

"And it came to pass in those days, that He went out into a mountain to pray, and continued all night in prayer to God." *Luke 6:12*

"Where You Are Determines What You Hear. What You Hear Determines What You Believe."

-MIKE MURDOCK

READ THE BIBLE THROUGH IN ONE YEAR: 2 Corinthians 4-6

The Tongue — November 27

"Death and life are in the power of the tongue: and they that love it shall eat the fruit thereof." *Proverbs 18:21*

"Whoso keepeth his mouth and his tongue keepeth his soul from troubles." *Proverbs 21:23*

"Let no corrupt communication proceed out of your mouth, but that which is good to the use of edifying, that it may minister grace unto the hearers. Let all bitterness, and wrath, and anger, and clamour, and evil speaking, be put away from you, with all malice."
Ephesians 4:29, 31

"But the tongue can no man tame; it is an unruly evil, full of deadly poison." *James 3:8*

"For he that will love life, and see good days, let him refrain his tongue from evil, and his lips that they speak no guile." *1 Peter 3:10*

"You Will Never Reach The Palace Talking Like A Peasant."

-MIKE MURDOCK

READ THE BIBLE THROUGH IN ONE YEAR: 2 Corinthians 7-9

Thought-Life November 28

"Commit thy works unto the Lord, and thy thoughts shall be established." *Proverbs 16:3*

"For to be carnally minded is death; but to be spiritually minded is life and peace." *Romans 8:6*

"And be not conformed to this world: but be ye transformed by the renewing of your mind, that ye may prove what is that good, and acceptable, and perfect, will of God." *Romans 12:2*

"And be renewed in the spirit of your mind."

Ephesians 4:23

"Finally, brethren, whatsoever things are true, whatsoever things are honest, whatsoever things are just, whatsoever things are pure, whatsoever things are lovely, whatsoever things are of good report; if there be any virtue, and if there be any praise, think on these things." *Philippians 4:8*

"For this is the covenant that I will make with the house of Israel after those days, saith the Lord; I will put My laws into their mind, and write them in their hearts: and I will be to them a God, and they shall be to Me a people." *Hebrews 8:10*

"Your Mind Is The Dark Room Where Your Self-Portrait Is Developed."

-MIKE MURDOCK

READ THE BIBLE THROUGH IN ONE YEAR: 2 Corinthians 10-12

Time

November 29

"And the Lord appointed a set time, saying, To morrow the Lord shall do this thing in the land." *Exodus 9:5*

"And satan answered the Lord, and said, Skin for skin, yea, all that a man hath will he give for his life." *Job 2:4*

"O remember that my life is wind: mine eye shall no more see good." *Job 7:7*

"...no man is sure of life." *Job 24:22*

"The Spirit of God hath made me, and the breath of the Almighty hath given me life." *Job 33:4*

"The fear of the Lord is the beginning of Wisdom: and the knowledge of the holy is understanding. For by Me thy days shall be multiplied, and the years of thy life shall be increased." *Proverbs 9:10-11*

"Then shall the dust return to the earth as it was: and the spirit shall return unto God Who gave it."

Ecclesiastes 12:7

"Whereas ye know not what shall be on the morrow. For what is your life? It is even a vapour, that appeareth for a little time, and then vanisheth away." *James 4:14*

"Every Moment Is The Arrival of A Gift Box; Joy Is The Reward For Discerning The Divine Gift It Contains."

-MIKE MURDOCK

READ THE BIBLE THROUGH IN ONE YEAR: 2 Corinthians 13-Galatians 4

Time-Management

November 30

"And the Lord appointed a set time, saying, To morrow the Lord shall do this thing in the land." *Exodus 9:5*

"Six days thou shalt work, but on the seventh day thou shalt rest: in earing time and in harvest thou shalt rest." *Exodus 34:21*

"To every thing there is a season, and a time to every purpose under the Heaven." *Ecclesiastes 3:1*

"I said in mine heart, God shall judge the righteous and the wicked: for there is a time there for every purpose and for every work." *Ecclesiastes 3:17*

"Walk in Wisdom toward them that are without, redeeming the time." *Colossians 4:5*

"Whereas ye know not what shall be on the morrow. For what is your life? It is even a vapour, that appeareth for a little time, and then vanisheth away." *James 4:14*

"Your Respect For Time Is A Prediction of Your Financial Future."

-MIKE MURDOCK

READ THE BIBLE THROUGH IN ONE YEAR: Galatians 5-Ephesians 1

Timing

December 1

"To every thing there is a season, and a time to every purpose under the Heaven: A time to be born, and a time to die; a time to plant, and a time to pluck up that which is planted; A time to kill, and a time to heal; a time to break down, and a time to build up; A time to weep, and a time to laugh; a time to mourn, and a time to dance; A time to cast away stones, and a time to gather stones together; a time to embrace, and a time to refrain from embracing; A time to get, and a time to lose; a time to keep, and a time to cast away; A time to rend, and a time to sew; a time to keep silence, and a time to speak; A time to love, and a time to hate; a time of war, and a time of peace." *Ecclesiastes 3:1-8*

"I said in mine heart, God shall judge the righteous and the wicked: for there is a time there for every purpose and for every work." *Ecclesiastes 3:17*

"But seek ye first the kingdom of God, and His righteousness; and all these things shall be added unto you." *Matthew 6:33*

"Let all things be done decently and in order." *1 Corinthians 14:40*

"Doing The Right Thing At The Wrong Time Becomes The Wrong Thing."

-MIKE MURDOCK

READ THE BIBLE THROUGH IN ONE YEAR: Ephesians 2-4

Tithing

December 2

"And all the tithe of the land, whether of the seed of the land, or of the fruit of the tree, is the Lord's: it is holy unto the Lord. And concerning the tithe of the herd, or of the flock, even of whatsoever passeth under the rod, the tenth shall be holy unto the Lord." *Leviticus 27:30, 32*

"Thou shalt truly tithe all the increase of thy seed, that the field bringeth forth year by year. And thou shalt eat before the Lord thy God, in the place which He shall choose to place His name there, the tithe of thy corn, of thy wine, and of thine oil, and the firstlings of thy herds and of thy flocks; that thou mayest learn to fear the Lord thy God always." *Deuteronomy 14:22-23*

"Bring ye all the tithes into the storehouse, that there may be meat in Mine house, and prove Me now herewith, saith the Lord of hosts, if I will not open you the windows of Heaven, and pour you out a blessing, that there shall not be room enough to receive it."

Malachi 3:10

"But this I say, he which soweth sparingly shall reap also sparingly; and he which soweth bountifully shall reap also bountifully." *2 Corinthians 9:6*

"Tithe Is Not The Payment of A Debt, It Is The Acknowledgment of A Debt."

-MIKE MURDOCK

READ THE BIBLE THROUGH IN ONE YEAR: Ephesians 5-Philippians 1

Tragedy

December 3

"For His anger endureth but a moment; in His favour is life: weeping may endure for a night, but joy cometh in the morning." *Psalm 30:5*

"He healeth the broken in heart, and bindeth up their wounds." *Psalm 147:3*

"In the day of prosperity be joyful, but in the day of adversity consider: God also hath set the one over against the other, to the end that man should find nothing after him." *Ecclesiastes 7:14*

"Although the fig tree shall not blossom, neither shall fruit be in the vines; the labour of the olive shall fail, and the fields shall yield no meat; the flock shall be cut off from the fold, and there shall be no herd in the stalls: Yet I will rejoice in the Lord, I will joy in the God of my salvation." *Habakkuk 3:17-18*

"And we know that all things work together for good to them that love God, to them who are the called according to His purpose." *Romans 8:28*

"Be not forgetful to entertain strangers: for thereby some have entertained angels unawares." *Hebrews 13:2*

"Miracles Can Happen As Quickly As Tragedies."

-*MIKE MURDOCK*

READ THE BIBLE THROUGH IN ONE YEAR: Philippians 2-4

Trouble

December 4

"And ye, in any wise keep yourselves from the accursed thing, lest ye make yourselves accursed, when ye take of the accursed thing, and make the camp of Israel a curse, and trouble it." *Joshua 6:18*

"But when they in their trouble did turn unto the Lord God of Israel, and sought Him, He was found of them." *2 Chronicles 15:4*

"For in the time of trouble He shall hide me in His pavilion: in the secret of His tabernacle shall He hide me; He shall set me up upon a rock." *Psalm 27:5*

"I will be glad and rejoice in Thy mercy: for Thou hast considered my trouble; Thou hast known my soul in adversities." *Psalm 31:7*

"In the day of my trouble I will call upon Thee: for Thou wilt answer me." *Psalm 86:7*

"...but the just shall come out of trouble." *Proverbs 12:13*

"Who comforteth us in all our tribulation, that we may be able to comfort them which are in any trouble, by the comfort wherewith we ourselves are comforted of God." *2 Corinthians 1:4*

"Trouble Is Not A Tragedy To Escape; But Rather A School To Learn."

-MIKE MURDOCK

READ THE BIBLE THROUGH IN ONE YEAR: Colossians 1-3

Trust

December 5

"Some trust in chariots, and some in horses: but we will remember the name of the Lord our God." *Psalm 20:7*

"In God have I put my trust: I will not be afraid what man can do unto me." *Psalm 56:11*

"It is better to trust in the Lord than to put confidence in man. It is better to trust in the Lord than to put confidence in princes." *Psalm 118:8-9*

"Put not your trust in princes, nor in the son of man, in whom there is no help." *Psalm 146:3*

"Trust in the Lord with all thine heart; and lean not unto thine own understanding. In all thy ways acknowledge Him, and He shall direct thy paths." *Proverbs 3:5-6*

"He that trusteth in his own heart is a fool: but whoso walketh wisely, he shall be delivered." *Proverbs 28:26*

"And let us not be weary in well doing: for in due season we shall reap, if we faint not." *Galatians 6:9*

"There remaineth therefore a rest to the people of God." *Hebrews 4:9*

"Trust God; Love Men."

-MIKE MURDOCK

READ THE BIBLE THROUGH IN ONE YEAR: Colossians 4-1 Thessalonians 2

Truth

December 6

"And the woman said to Elijah, Now by this I know that thou art a man of God, and that the word of the Lord in thy mouth is truth." *1 Kings 17:24*

"Thy righteousness is an everlasting righteousness, and Thy law is the truth." *Psalm 119:142*

"Thou art near, O Lord; and all Thy commandments are truth." *Psalm 119:151*

"Jesus saith unto him, I am the way, the truth, and the life: no man cometh unto the Father, but by Me." *John 14:6*

"Howbeit when He, the Spirit of truth, is come, He will guide you into all truth: for He shall not speak of Himself; but whatsoever He shall hear, that shall He speak: and He will shew you things to come." *John 16:13*

"Sanctify them through Thy truth: Thy word is truth." *John 17:17*

"Truth Is The Most Powerful Thing On Earth Because It Is The Only Thing That Cannot Be Changed."

-MIKE MURDOCK

READ THE BIBLE THROUGH IN ONE YEAR: 1 Thess. 3-2 Thess. 2

Understanding December 7

"The entrance of Thy words giveth light; it giveth understanding unto the simple." *Psalm 119:130*

"A wise man will hear, and will increase learning; and a man of understanding shall attain unto wise counsels." *Proverbs 1:5*

"For the Lord giveth Wisdom: out of His mouth cometh knowledge and understanding." *Proverbs 2:6*

"Happy is the man that findeth Wisdom, and the man that getteth understanding." *Proverbs 3:13*

"The Lord by Wisdom hath founded the earth; by understanding hath He established the Heavens."
Proverbs 3:19

"Wisdom is the principal thing; therefore get Wisdom: and with all thy getting get understanding."
Proverbs 4:7

"In the lips of him that hath understanding Wisdom is found: but a rod is for the back of him that is void of understanding." *Proverbs 10:13*

"Understanding is a wellspring of life unto him that hath it: but the instruction of fools is folly."
Proverbs 16:22

"There Are Two Ways To Get Wisdom: Mistakes And Mentors."

-MIKE MURDOCK

READ THE BIBLE THROUGH IN ONE YEAR: 2 Thess. 3-1 Timothy 2

Unity

December 8

"Behold, how good and how pleasant it is for brethren to dwell together in unity!" *Psalm 133:1*

"Where no wood is, there the fire goeth out: so where there is no talebearer, the strife ceaseth."
Proverbs 26:20

"Two are better than one; because they have a good reward for their labour." *Ecclesiastes 4:9*

"If it be possible, as much as lieth in you, live peaceably with all men." *Romans 12:18*

"For God is not the Author of confusion, but of peace, as in all churches of the saints." *1 Corinthians 14:33*

"With all lowliness and meekness, with longsuffering, forbearing one another in love; Endeavouring to keep the unity of the Spirit in the bond of peace."
Ephesians 4:2-3

"Unity Is Not The Blindness of Our Difference But The Celebration of Our Difference."

-MIKE MURDOCK

READ THE BIBLE THROUGH IN ONE YEAR: 1 Timothy 3-5

Unthankfulness December 9

"I thought on my ways, and turned my feet unto Thy testimonies." *Psalm 119:59*

"Pride goeth before destruction, and an haughty spirit before a fall." *Proverbs 16:18*

"And He turned to the woman, and said unto Simon, Seest thou this woman? I entered into thine house, thou gavest Me no water for My feet: but she hath washed My feet with tears, and wiped them with the hairs of her head. Thou gavest Me no kiss: but this woman since the time I came in hath not ceased to kiss My feet. My head with oil thou didst not anoint: but this woman hath anointed My feet with ointment. Wherefore I say unto thee, Her sins, which are many, are forgiven; for she loved much: but to whom little is forgiven, the same loveth little." *Luke 7:44-47*

"Do all things without murmurings and disputings." *Philippians 2:14*

"And let the peace of God rule in your hearts, to the which also ye are called in one body; and be ye thankful." *Colossians 3:15*

"The Unthankful Are Always The Unhappy."

-MIKE MURDOCK

READ THE BIBLE THROUGH IN ONE YEAR: 1 Timothy 6-2 Timothy 2

Victory

December 10

"The Lord shall cause thine enemies that rise up against thee to be smitten before thy face: they shall come out against thee one way, and flee before thee seven ways."
Deuteronomy 28:7

"Through God we shall do valiantly: for He it is that shall tread down our enemies." *Psalm 60:12*

"Thou through Thy commandments hast made me wiser than mine enemies: for they are ever with me."
Psalm 119:98

"Blessed be the Lord my strength, which teacheth my hands to war, and my fingers to fight." *Psalm 144:1*

"Ye are of God, little children, and have overcome them: because greater is He that is in you, than he that is in the world." *1 John 4:4*

"For whatsoever is born of God overcometh the world: and this is the victory that overcometh the world, even our faith." *1 John 5:4*

"And they overcame him by the blood of the Lamb, and by the word of their testimony; and they loved not their lives unto the death." *Revelation 12:11*

"The Proof of A Victorious Life Is Joy."

-MIKE MURDOCK

READ THE BIBLE THROUGH IN ONE YEAR: 2 Timothy 3-Titus 1

Violence

December 11

"The Lord trieth the righteous: but the wicked and him that loveth violence His soul hateth." *Psalm 11:5*

"Great deliverance giveth He to his king; and sheweth mercy to His anointed, to David, and to His seed for evermore." *Psalm 18:50*

"There shall no evil befall thee, neither shall any plague come nigh thy dwelling. For He shall give His angels charge over thee, to keep thee in all thy ways."
Psalm 91:10-11

"Make no friendship with an angry man; and with a furious man thou shalt not go." *Proverbs 22:24*

"Thus saith the Lord; Execute ye judgment and righteousness, and deliver the spoiled out of the hand of the oppressor: and do no wrong, do no violence to the stranger, the fatherless, nor the widow, neither shed innocent blood in this place." *Jeremiah 22:3*

"...Do violence to no man, neither accuse any falsely; and be content with your wages." *Luke 3:14*

"Your Reaction To People Determines God's Reaction To You."

-MIKE MURDOCK

READ THE BIBLE THROUGH IN ONE YEAR: Titus 2-Philemon 1

Vision

December 12

"Where there is no vision, the people perish: but he that keepeth the law, happy is he." *Proverbs 29:18*

"Enlarge the place of thy tent, and let them stretch forth the curtains of thine habitations: spare not, lengthen thy cords, and strengthen thy stakes; For thou shalt break forth on the right hand and on the left; and thy seed shall inherit the Gentiles, and make the desolate cities to be inhabited." *Isaiah 54:2-3*

"And I Daniel alone saw the vision: for the men that were with me saw not the vision; but a great quaking fell upon them, so that they fled to hide themselves. Therefore I was left alone, and saw this great vision, and there remained no strength in me: for my comeliness was turned in me into corruption, and I retained no strength." *Daniel 10:7-8*

"Write the vision, and make it plain upon tables, that he may run that readeth it." *Habakkuk 2:2*

"An Uncommon Dream Will Require Uncommon Faith."

-MIKE MURDOCK

READ THE BIBLE THROUGH IN ONE YEAR: Hebrews 1-3

Visualization December 13

"And the Lord said, Behold, the people is one, and they have all one language; and this they begin to do: and now nothing will be restrained from them, which they have imagined to do." *Genesis 11:6*

"And the Lord answered me, and said, Write the vision, and make it plain upon tables, that he may run that readeth it. For the vision is yet for an appointed time, but at the end it shall speak, and not lie: though it tarry, wait for it; because it will surely come, it will not tarry."
Habakkuk 2:2-3

"He staggered not at the promise of God through unbelief; but was strong in faith, giving glory to God; And being fully persuaded that, what He had promised, He was able also to perform." *Romans 4:20-21*

"Set your affection on things above, not on things on the earth." *Colossians 3:2*

"By faith he forsook Egypt, not fearing the wrath of the king: for he endured, as seeing Him Who is invisible."
Hebrews 11:27

"When Your Heart Decides The Destination Your Mind Will Design The Map To Reach It."

-MIKE MURDOCK

READ THE BIBLE THROUGH IN ONE YEAR: Hebrews 4-8

Voice of God — December 14

"And it shall come to pass, if thou shalt hearken diligently unto the voice of the Lord thy God, to observe and to do all His commandments which I command thee this day, that the Lord thy God will set thee on high above all nations of the earth: And all these blessings shall come on thee, and overtake thee, if thou shalt hearken unto the voice of the Lord thy God."

Deuteronomy 28:1-2

"Moreover all these curses shall come upon thee, and shall pursue thee, and overtake thee, till thou be destroyed; because thou hearkenedst not unto the voice of the Lord thy God, to keep His commandments and His statutes which He commanded thee."

Deuteronomy 28:45

"The voice of the Lord is powerful; the voice of the Lord is full of majesty. The voice of the Lord breaketh the cedars;...The voice of the Lord divideth the flames of fire. The voice of the Lord shaketh the wilderness."

Psalm 29:4-5, 7-8

"When You Ask God For A Miracle, He Will Always Give You An Instruction."

-MIKE MURDOCK

READ THE BIBLE THROUGH IN ONE YEAR: Hebrews 9-11

Vows

December 15

"If a man vow a vow unto the Lord, or swear an oath to bind his soul with a bond; he shall not break his word, he shall do according to all that proceedeth out of his mouth." *Numbers 30:2*

"When thou shalt vow a vow unto the Lord thy God, thou shalt not slack to pay it: for the Lord thy God will surely require it of thee; and it would be sin in thee. That which is gone out of thy lips thou shalt keep and perform; even a freewill offering, according as thou hast vowed unto the Lord thy God, which thou hast promised with thy mouth." *Deuteronomy 23:21, 23*

"Offer unto God thanksgiving; and pay thy vows unto the most High." *Psalm 50:14*

"When thou vowest a vow unto God, defer not to pay it; for He hath no pleasure in fools: pay that which thou hast vowed. Better is it that thou shouldest not vow, than that thou shouldest vow and not pay."
Ecclesiastes 5:4-5

"The Proof of Integrity Is A Fulfilled Vow."

-*MIKE MURDOCK*

READ THE BIBLE THROUGH IN ONE YEAR: Hebrews 12-James 1

Waiting On God

December 16

"And one kid of the goats for a sin offering; beside the continual burnt offering, and the meat offering thereof, and their drink offerings." *Numbers 29:19*

"Rest in the Lord, and wait patiently for Him: fret not thyself because of him who prospereth in his way, because of the man who bringeth wicked devices to pass." *Psalm 37:7*

"But they that wait upon the Lord shall renew their strength; they shall mount up with wings as eagles; they shall run, and not be weary; and they shall walk, and not faint." *Isaiah 40:31*

"The Lord is good unto them that wait for Him, to the soul that seeketh Him. It is good that a man should both hope and quietly wait for the salvation of the Lord." *Lamentations 3:25-26*

"And let us not be weary in well doing: for in due season we shall reap, if we faint not." *Galatians 6:9*

"The Proof of Respect Is The Investment of Time."

-*MIKE MURDOCK*

READ THE BIBLE THROUGH IN ONE YEAR: James 2-4

Walking In The Spirit

December 17

"And Jesus being full of the Holy Ghost returned from Jordan, and was led by the Spirit into the wilderness."
Luke 4:1

"For as many as are led by the Spirit of God, they are the sons of God." *Romans 8:14*

"This I say then, Walk in the Spirit, and ye shall not fulfil the lust of the flesh." *Galatians 5:16*

"If we live in the Spirit, let us also walk in the Spirit."
Galatians 5:25

"He that hath an ear, let him hear what the Spirit saith unto the churches; To him that overcometh will I give to eat of the tree of life, which is in the midst of the paradise of God." *Revelation 2:7*

"Where You Are Determines What You See."
-MIKE MURDOCK

READ THE BIBLE THROUGH IN ONE YEAR: James 5-1 Peter 2

Water Baptism

December 18

"And Jesus, when He was baptized, went up straightway out of the water: and, lo, the Heavens were opened unto Him, and He saw the Spirit of God descending like a dove, and lighting upon Him." *Matthew 3:16*

"And I knew Him not: but He that sent me to baptize with water, the same said unto me, Upon Whom thou shalt see the Spirit descending, and remaining on Him, the same is He which baptizeth with the Holy Ghost." *John 1:33*

"Then Peter said unto them, Repent, and be baptized every one of you in the name of Jesus Christ for the remission of sins, and ye shall receive the gift of the Holy Ghost." *Acts 2:38*

"Then they that gladly received his word were baptized: and the same day there were added unto them about three thousand souls." *Acts 2:41*

"Water Baptism Is An Outward Profession of An Inward Confession."

-MIKE MURDOCK

READ THE BIBLE THROUGH IN ONE YEAR: 1 Peter 3-5

Weakness December 19

"Wait on the Lord: be of good courage, and He shall strengthen thine heart: wait, I say, on the Lord."
Psalm 27:14

"He giveth power to the faint; and to them that have no might he increaseth strength." *Isaiah 40:29*

"But ye shall receive power, after that the Holy Ghost is come upon you: and ye shall be witnesses unto Me both in Jerusalem, and in all Judaea, and in Samaria, and unto the uttermost part of the earth." *Acts 1:8*

"For which cause we faint not; but though our outward man perish, yet the inward man is renewed day by day."
2 Corinthians 4:16

"And He said unto me, My grace is sufficient for thee: for My strength is made perfect in weakness. Most gladly therefore will I rather glory in my infirmities, that the power of Christ may rest upon me."
2 Corinthians 12:9

"I can do all things through Christ which strengtheneth me." *Philippians 4:13*

"Your Best Friend Loves You The Way You Are...Your Mentor Loves You Too Much To Leave You That Way."
-MIKE MURDOCK

READ THE BIBLE THROUGH IN ONE YEAR: 2 Peter 1-3

Wealth

December 20

"But thou shalt remember the Lord thy God: for it is He that giveth thee power to get wealth, that He may establish His covenant which He sware unto thy fathers, as it is this day." *Deuteronomy 8:18*

"Let them shout for joy, and be glad, that favour My righteous cause: yea, let them say continually, Let the Lord be magnified, which hath pleasure in the prosperity of His servant." *Psalm 35:27*

"Praise ye the Lord. Blessed is the man that feareth the Lord, that delighteth greatly in His commandments. Wealth and riches shall be in His house: and His righteousness endureth for ever." *Psalm 112:1,3*

"Wealth gotten by vanity shall be diminished: but he that gathereth by labour shall increase." *Proverbs 13:11*

"Every man also to whom God hath given riches and wealth, and hath given him power to eat thereof, and to take his portion, and to rejoice in his labour; this is the gift of God." *Ecclesiastes 5:19*

"A feast is made for laughter, and wine maketh merry: but money answereth all things." *Ecclesiastes 10:19*

"Wealth Is When You Have A Lot of Something You Love."

-MIKE MURDOCK

READ THE BIBLE THROUGH IN ONE YEAR: 1 John 1-5

Will of God December 21

"Not every one that saith unto Me, Lord, Lord, shall enter into the kingdom of Heaven; but he that doeth the will of My Father which is in Heaven." *Matthew 7:21*

"And be not conformed to this world: but be ye transformed by the renewing of your mind, that ye may prove what is that good, and acceptable, and perfect, will of God." *Romans 12:2*

"Wherefore be ye not unwise, but understanding what the will of the Lord is." *Ephesians 5:17*

"Not with eyeservice, as menpleasers; but as the servants of Christ, doing the will of God from the heart." *Ephesians 6:6*

"Epaphras, who is one of you, a servant of Christ, saluteth you, always labouring fervently for you in prayers, that ye may stand perfect and complete in all the will of God." *Colossians 4:12*

"Wherefore let them that suffer according to the will of God commit the keeping of their souls to Him in well doing, as unto a faithful Creator." *1 Peter 4:19*

"The Will of God Is An Attitude, Not A Place."

-MIKE MURDOCK

READ THE BIBLE THROUGH IN ONE YEAR: 2 John -Jude

Winning

December 22

"Through God we shall do valiantly: for He it is that shall tread down our enemies." *Psalm 60:12*

"Nay, in all these things we are more than conquerors through Him that loved us." *Romans 8:37*

"...which always causeth us to triumph in Christ." *2 Corinthians 2:14*

"I can do all things through Christ which strengtheneth me." *Philippians 4:13*

"If we suffer, we shall also reign with Him: if we deny Him, He also will deny us." *2 Timothy 2:12*

"I have fought a good fight, I have finished my course, I have kept the faith: Henceforth there is laid up for me a crown of righteousness, which the Lord, the righteous judge, shall give me at that day: and not to me only, but unto all them also that love His appearing."
2 Timothy 4:7-8

"Winners Are Just Ex-Losers Who Got Mad."

-MIKE MURDOCK

READ THE BIBLE THROUGH IN ONE YEAR: Revelation 1-3

Wisdom

December 23

"Behold, Thou desirest truth in the inward parts: and in the hidden part Thou shalt make me to know Wisdom."
Psalm 51:6

"So teach us to number our days, that we may apply our hearts unto Wisdom." *Psalm 90:12*

"For the Lord giveth Wisdom: out of His mouth cometh knowledge and understanding." *Proverbs 2:6*

"Wisdom is the principal thing; therefore get Wisdom: and with all thy getting get understanding."
Proverbs 4:7

"For Wisdom is a defence, and money is a defence: but the excellency of knowledge is, that Wisdom giveth life to them that have it." *Ecclesiastes 7:12*

"If any of you lack Wisdom, let him ask of God, that giveth to all men liberally, and upbraideth not; and it shall be given him." *James 1:5*

"But the Wisdom that is from above is first pure, then peaceable, gentle, and easy to be intreated, full of mercy and good fruits, without partiality, and without hypocrisy." *James 3:17*

"Every Problem In Your Life Is Simply A Wisdom Problem."

-MIKE MURDOCK

READ THE BIBLE THROUGH IN ONE YEAR: Revelation 4-5

Witchcraft

December 24

"There shall not be found among you any one that maketh his son or his daughter to pass through the fire, or that useth divination, or an observer of times, or an enchanter, or a witch." *Deuteronomy 18:10*

"For rebellion is as the sin of witchcraft, and stubbornness is as iniquity and idolatry. Because thou hast rejected the word of the Lord, He hath also rejected thee from being king." *1 Samuel 15:23*

"And he caused his children to pass through the fire in the valley of the son of Hinnom: also he observed times, and used enchantments, and used witchcraft, and dealt with a familiar spirit, and with wizards: he wrought much evil in the sight of the Lord, to provoke Him to anger." *2 Chronicles 33:6*

"Idolatry, witchcraft, hatred, variance, emulations, wrath, strife, seditions, heresies, Envyings, murders, drunkenness, revellings, and such like: of the which I tell you before, as I have also told you in time past, that they which do such things shall not inherit the kingdom of God." *Galatians 5:20-21*

"Any Moment Out of The Spirit Is An Invitation To An Evil Spirit."

-MIKE MURDOCK

READ THE BIBLE THROUGH IN ONE YEAR: Revelation 6-7

Witnessing December 25

"Ask of Me, and I shall give thee the heathen for thine inheritance, and the uttermost parts of the earth for thy possession." *Psalm 2:8*

"...he that winneth souls is wise." *Proverbs 11:30*

"And He said unto them, Go ye into all the world, and preach the gospel to every creature." *Mark 16:15*

"And daily in the temple, and in every house, they ceased not to teach and preach Jesus Christ." *Acts 5:42*

"How then shall they call on Him in Whom they have not believed? and how shall they believe in Him of Whom they have not heard? and how shall they hear without a preacher? And how shall they preach, except they be sent? as it is written, How beautiful are the feet of them that preach the gospel of peace, and bring glad tidings of good things!" *Romans 10:14-15*

"Knowing therefore the terror of the Lord, we persuade men." *2 Corinthians 5:11*

"The Willingness To Protect Is A Portrait of Your Passion."

-MIKE MURDOCK

READ THE BIBLE THROUGH IN ONE YEAR: Revelation 8-9

Word of God

December 26

"The law of his God is in his heart; none of his steps shall slide." *Psalm 37:31*

"Thy word have I hid in mine heart, that I might not sin against Thee." *Psalm 119:11*

"Thou through Thy commandments hast made me wiser than mine enemies: for they are ever with me." *Psalm 119:98*

"I have more understanding than all my teachers: for Thy testimonies are my meditation. I understand more than the ancients, because I keep Thy precepts." *Psalm 119:99-100*

"All scripture is given by inspiration of God, and is profitable for doctrine, for reproof, for correction, for instruction in righteousness." *2 Timothy 3:16*

"The Workings of God In Your Life Are Not Proportionate To Your *Need* of Him, But of Your *Knowledge* of Him."

-*MIKE MURDOCK*

READ THE BIBLE THROUGH IN ONE YEAR: Revelation 10-11

Words December 27

"Every day they wrest my words: all their thoughts are against me for evil." *Psalm 56:5*

"There is that speaketh like the piercings of a sword: but the tongue of the wise is health." *Proverbs 12:18*

"Righteous lips are the delight of kings; and they love him that speaketh right." *Proverbs 16:13*

"Pleasant words are as an honeycomb, sweet to the soul, and health to the bones." *Proverbs 16:24*

"Seest thou a man that is hasty in his words? there is more hope of a fool than of him." *Proverbs 29:20*

"The words of a wise man's mouth are gracious."
Ecclesiastes 10:12

"For in many things we offend all. If any man offend not in word, the same is a perfect man, and able also to bridle the whole body." *James 3:2*

"The Kindest Word Is An Unkind Word Unsaid."
-*MIKE MURDOCK*

READ THE BIBLE THROUGH IN ONE YEAR: Revelation 12-16

Work

December 28

"For thou shalt eat the labour of thine hands: happy shalt thou be, and it shall be well with thee."   *Psalm 128:2*

"Wealth gotten by vanity shall be diminished: but he that gathereth by labour shall increase."*Proverbs 13:11*

"Seest thou a man diligent in his business? he shall stand before kings; he shall not stand before mean men."   *Proverbs 22:29*

"Every man also to whom God hath given riches and wealth, and hath given him power to eat thereof, and to take his portion, and to rejoice in his labour; this is the gift of God."   *Ecclesiastes 5:19*

"For even when we were with you, this we commanded you, that if any would not work, neither should he eat."
2 Thessalonians 3:10

"The Problems You Solve Determine The Reward You Receive."

-MIKE MURDOCK

READ THE BIBLE THROUGH IN ONE YEAR: Revelation 17-18

Worry

December 29

"Fret not thyself because of evildoers, neither be thou envious against the workers of iniquity." *Psalm 37:1*

"In God I will praise His word, in God I have put my trust; I will not fear what flesh can do unto me."
Psalm 56:4

"Fret not thyself because of evil men, neither be thou envious at the wicked." *Proverbs 24:19*

"Finally, brethren, whatsoever things are true, whatsoever things are honest, whatsoever things are just, whatsoever things are pure, whatsoever things are lovely, whatsoever things are of good report; if there be any virtue, and if there be any praise, think on these things." *Philippians 4:8*

"There remaineth therefore a rest to the people of God."
Hebrews 4:9

"For there are three that bear record in Heaven, the Father, the Word, and the Holy Ghost: and these three are one." *1 John 5:7*

"When You Do Your Best, God Does The Rest."

-MIKE MURDOCK

READ THE BIBLE THROUGH IN ONE YEAR: Revelation 19-20

Worship

December 30

"For thou shalt worship no other god: for the Lord, Whose name is Jealous, is a jealous God."

Exodus 34:14

"Give unto the Lord the glory due unto His name; worship the Lord in the beauty of holiness."

Psalm 29:2

"Enter into His gates with thanksgiving, and into His courts with praise: be thankful unto Him, and bless His name." *Psalm 100:4*

"Praise ye the Lord. Sing unto the Lord a new song, and His praise in the congregation of saints."

Psalm 149:1

"But the hour cometh, and now is, when the true worshippers shall worship the Father in spirit and in truth: for the Father seeketh such to worship Him. God is a Spirit: and they that worship Him must worship Him in spirit and in truth." *John 4:23-24*

"Worship Is The Correction of Focus."

-MIKE MURDOCK

READ THE BIBLE THROUGH IN ONE YEAR: Revelation 21-22

Zeal

December 31

"But take diligent heed to do the commandment and the law, which Moses the servant of the Lord charged you, to love the Lord your God, and to walk in all His ways, and to keep His commandments, and to cleave unto Him, and to serve Him with all your heart and with all your soul." *Joshua 22:5*

"...he that hasteth with his feet sinneth." *Proverbs 19:2*

"Seest thou a man diligent in his business? he shall stand before kings; he shall not stand before mean men." *Proverbs 22:29*

"Whatsoever thy hand findeth to do, do it with thy might." *Ecclesiastes 9:10*

"Brethren, my heart's desire and prayer to God for Israel is, that they might be saved. For I bear them record that they have a zeal of God, but not according to knowledge. For they being ignorant of God's righteousness, and going about to establish their own righteousness, have not submitted themselves unto the righteousness of God." *Romans 10:1-3*

"Zeal Without Respect For Protocol Will Cause Tragedies."

-MIKE MURDOCK

READ THE BIBLE THROUGH IN ONE YEAR: Well Done!!!

DR. MIKE MURDOCK

- Has embraced his Assignment to Pursue...Proclaim... and Publish the Wisdom of God to help people achieve their dreams and goals.
- Preached his first public sermon at the age of 8.
- Preached his first evangelistic crusade at the age of 15.
- Began full-time evangelism at the age of 19, which has continued since 1966.
- Has traveled and spoken to more than 17,000 audiences in 100 countries, including East and West Africa, Asia, Europe and South America.
- Noted author of over 300 books, including best sellers, *Wisdom for Winning*, *Dream Seeds*, *The Double Diamond Principle*, *The Law of Recognition* and *The Holy Spirit Handbook*.
- Created the popular *Topical Bible* series for Businessmen, Mothers, Fathers, Teenagers; *The One-Minute Pocket Bible* series, and *The Uncommon Life* series.
- The Creator of the Master 7 Mentorship Program, an Achievement Program for Believers.
- Has composed thousands of songs such as "I Am Blessed," "You Can Make It," "God Rides On Wings of Love" and "Jesus, Just The Mention of Your Name," recorded by many gospel artists.
- Is the Founder and Senior Pastor of The Wisdom Center, in Fort Worth, Texas...a Church with International Ministry around the world.
- Host of *Wisdom Keys with Mike Murdock,* a weekly TV Program seen internationally.
- Has appeared often on TBN, CBN, BET, Daystar, Inspirational Network, LeSea Broadcasting and other television network programs.
- Has led over 3,000 to accept the call into full-time ministry.

DECISION

Will You Accept Jesus As Your Personal Savior Today?

The Bible says, "That if thou shalt confess with thy mouth the Lord Jesus, and shalt believe in thine heart that God hath raised Him from the dead, thou shalt be saved," (Romans 10:9).

Pray this prayer from your heart today! *"Dear Jesus, I believe that You died for me and rose again on the third day. I confess I am a sinner...I need Your love and forgiveness...Come into my heart. Forgive my sins. I receive Your eternal life. Confirm Your love by giving me peace, joy and supernatural love for others. Amen."*

☐ Yes, Mike, I made a decision to accept Christ as my personal Savior today. Please send me my free gift of your book *31 Keys to a New Beginning* to help me with my new life in Christ.

NAME _____

ADDRESS _____

CITY _____ STATE _____ ZIP _____

PHONE ( ) _____ E-MAIL _____

Mail To: **The Wisdom Center** DFC
4051 Denton Hwy. · Fort Worth, TX 76117
1-817-759-BOOK · 1-817-759-2665 · 1-817-759-0300
MikeMurdockBooks.com

Unless otherwise indicated, all Scripture quotations are taken from the King James Version of the Bible.
Inmate's Topical Bible
ISBN 1-56394-270-4 / B-176
Copyright © 2003 by **MIKE MURDOCK**
All publishing rights belong exclusively to Wisdom International
Editor/Publisher: Deborah Murdock Johnson
Published by The Wisdom Center · 4051 Denton Hwy. · Fort Worth, Texas 76117
1-817-759-BOOK · 1-817-759-2665 · 1-817-759-0300
MikeMurdockBooks.com
Printed in the United States of America. All rights reserved under International Copyright Law. Contents and/or cover may not be reproduced in whole or in part in any form without the expressed written consent of the publisher.

Clip and Mail

JOIN THE Wisdom Key 3000 TODAY!

Will You Become My Ministry Partner In The Work of God?

Dear Friend,

God has connected us!

I have asked The Holy Spirit for 3000 Special Partners who will plant a monthly Seed of $58.00 to help me bring the Gospel around the world. (58 represents 58 kinds of blessings in the Bible.)

Will you become my monthly Faith Partner in The Wisdom Key 3000? Your monthly Seed of $58.00 is so powerful in helping heal broken lives. When you sow into the work of God, 4 Miracle Harvests are guaranteed in Scripture, Isaiah 58...

- Uncommon <u>Health</u> (Isaiah 58)
- Uncommon <u>Wisdom For Decision-Making</u> (Isaiah 58)
- Uncommon <u>Financial Favor</u> (Isaiah 58)
- Uncommon <u>Family Restoration</u> (Isaiah 58)

Your Faith Partner,

Mike Murdock

P.S. Please clip the coupon attached and return it to me today, so I can rush the Wisdom Key Partnership Pak to you...or call me at 1-817-759-0300.

PP-03

☐ **Yes, Mike, I want to join The Wisdom Key 3000.**
Please rush The Wisdom Key Partnership Pak to me today!

☐ *Enclosed is my first monthly Seed-Faith Promise of:*
☐ **$58** ☐ **Other $**_____

☐ CHECK ☐ MONEY ORDER ☐ AMEX ☐ DISCOVER ☐ MASTERCARD ☐ VISA

Credit Card # _____ Exp. ___/___

Signature _____

Name _____ Birth Date ___/___

Address _____

City _____ State _____ Zip _____

Phone _____ E-Mail _____

WK304

Your Seed-Faith Offerings are used to support The Wisdom Center, and all of its programs. The Wisdom Center reserves the right to redirect funds as needed in order to carry out our charitable purpose. In the event The Wisdom Center receives more funds for the project than needed, the excess will be used for another worthy outreach. (Your transactions may be electronically deposited.)

THE WISDOM CENTER
4051 Denton Highway • Fort Worth, TX 76117

1-817-759-BOOK
1-817-759-2665
1-817-759-0300

— You Will Love Our Website..! —
MikeMurdockBooks.com

Miracle 7 BOOK PAK!

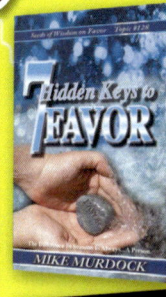

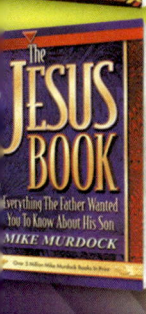
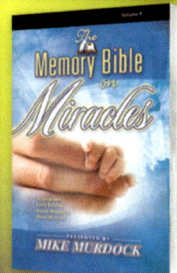
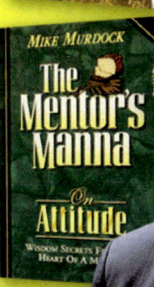

DR. MIKE MURDOCK

- **Dream Seeds** (Book/B-11/106pg/$12)
- **7 Hidden Keys to Favor** (Book/B-119/32pg/$7)
- **Seeds of Wisdom on Miracles** (Book/B-15/32pg/$5)
- **Seeds of Wisdom on Prayer** (Book/B-23/32pg/$5)
- **The Jesus Book** (Book/B-27/166pg/$10)
- **The Memory Bible on Miracles** (Book/B-208/32pg/$5)
- **The Mentor's Manna on Attitude** (Book/B-58/32pg/$5)

*Each Wisdom Book may be purchased separately if so desired.

The Wisdom Center
Miracle 7 Book Pak!
Only $30 $45 Value
WBL-24
Wisdom Is The Principal Thing

Add 20% For S/H

Quantity Prices Available Upon Request

THE WISDOM CENTER
4051 Denton Highway · Fort Worth, TX 76117
1-817-759-BOOK
1-817-759-2665
1-817-759-0300

You Will Love Our Website..!
WisdomOnline.com

A

CRISIS 7 BOOK PAK!

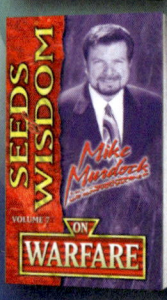
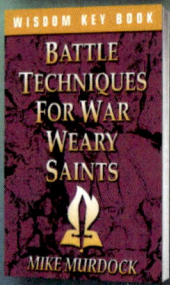

DR. MIKE MURDOCK

1. **The Survival Bible** (Book/B-29/248pg/$12)
2. **Wisdom For Crisis Times** (Book/B-40/112pg/$9)
3. **Seeds of Wisdom on Motivating Yourself** (Book/B-171/32pg/$5)
4. **Seeds of Wisdom on Overcoming** (Book/B-17/32pg/$5)
5. **Seeds of Wisdom on Warfare** (Book/B-19/32pg/$5)
6. **Battle Techniques For War-Weary Saints** (Book/B-07/32pg/$5)
7. **Seeds of Wisdom on Adversity** (Book/B-21/32pg/$5)

Each Wisdom Book may be purchased separately if so desired.

The Wisdom Center
Crisis 7 Book Pak!
Only $30
$46 Value
WBL-25
Wisdom Is The Principal Thing

Add 20% For S/H

Quantity Prices Available Upon Request

B

THE WISDOM CENTER
4051 Denton Highway · Fort Worth, TX 76117

1-817-759-BOOK
1-817-759-2665
1-817-759-0300

You Will Love Our Website..!
WisdomOnline.com

Money 7 BOOK PAK!

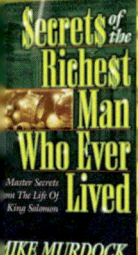
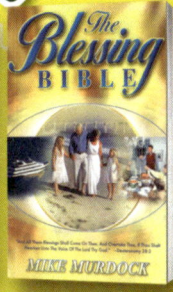
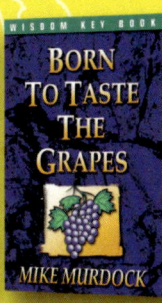
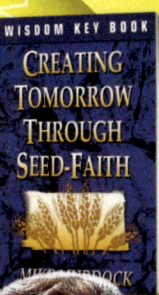
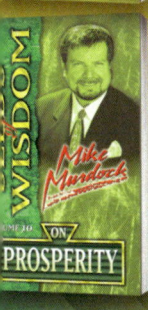

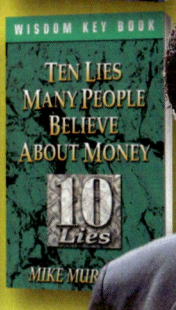

DR. MIKE MURDOCK

- **Secrets of the Richest Man Who Ever Lived** (Book/B-99/179pg/$10)
- **The Blessing Bible** (Book/B-28/252pg/$10)
- **Born To Taste The Grapes** (Book/B-65/32pg/$3)
- **Creating Tomorrow Through Seed-Faith** (Book/B-06/32pg/$5)
- **Seeds of Wisdom on Prosperity** (Book/B-22/32pg/$5)
- **Seven Obstacles To Abundant Success** (Book/B-64/32pg/$5)
- **Ten Lies Many People Believe About Money** (Book/B-04/32pg/$5)

The Wisdom Center
Money 7 Book Pak!
Only $30
WBL-30
$43 Value
Wisdom Is The Principal Thing

Each Wisdom Book may be purchased separately if so desired.

Add 20% For S/H

THE WISDOM CENTER
4051 Denton Highway · Fort Worth, TX 76117

1-817-759-BOOK
1-817-759-2665
1-817-759-0300

—You Will Love Our Website..!—
WisdomOnline.com

C

Career 7
Book Pak For Business People!

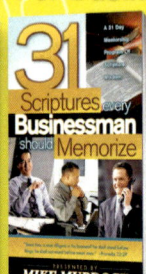

DR. MIKE MURDOCK

❶ **The Businessman's Topical Bible** (Book/B-33/384pg/$10)

❷ **31 Secrets for Career Success** (Book/B-44/112pg/$12)

❸ **31 Scriptures Every Businessman Should Memorize** (Book/B-141/32pg/$5)

❹ **7 Overlooked Keys To Effective Goal-Setting** (Book/B-127/32pg/$7)

❺ **7 Rewards of Problem Solving** (Book/B-118/32pg/$8)

❻ **How To Double Your Productivity In 24 Hours** (Book/B-137/32pg/$7)

❼ **The Mentor's Manna on Achievement** (Book/B-79/32pg/$5)

Each Wisdom Book may be purchased separately if so desired.

The Wisdom Center
Career 7 Book Pak!
Only $30 $54 Value
WBL-27
Wisdom Is The Principal Thing

Add 20% For S/H

THE WISDOM CENTER
4051 Denton Highway · Fort Worth, TX 76117
1-817-759-BOOK
1-817-759-2665
1-817-759-0300

You Will Love Our Website..!
WisdomOnline.com

Unforgettable Woman 4 Book Pak!

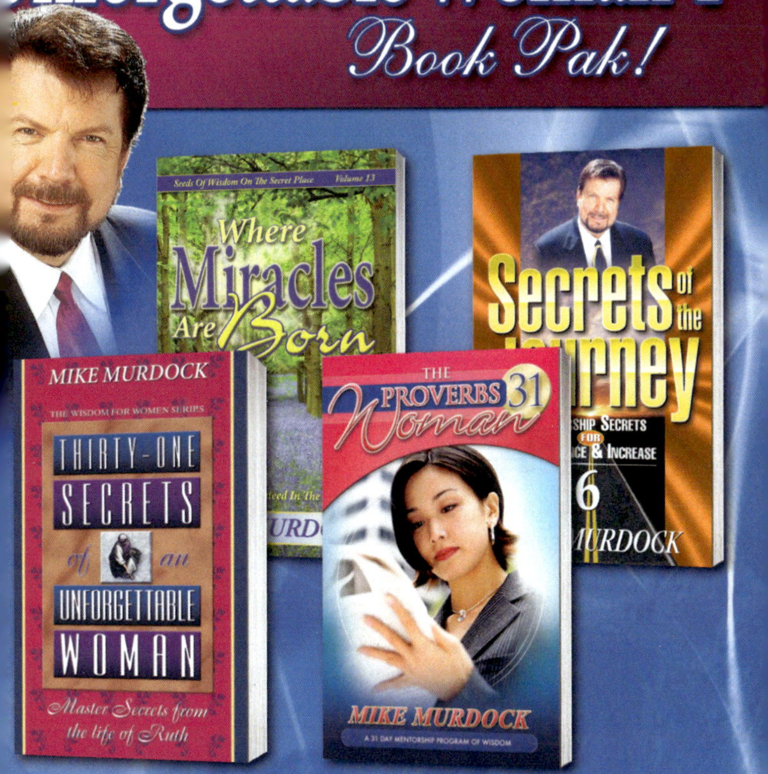

❶ **Where Miracles Are Born** (Book/B-115/32pg/$7)
❷ **Secrets of The Journey, Vol. 6** (Book/B-102/32pg/$5)
❸ **Thirty-One Secrets of an Unforgettable Woman** (Book/B-57/140pg/$12)
❹ **The Proverbs 31 Woman** (Book/B-49/70pg/$7)

Wisdom Book may be purchased separately if so desired.

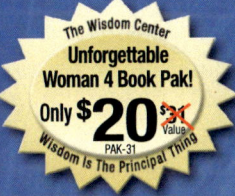

The Wisdom Center
Unforgettable Woman 4 Book Pak!
Only $20 $31 Value
PAK-31
Wisdom Is The Principal Thing

Add 20% For S/H

THE WISDOM CENTER
4051 Denton Highway · Fort Worth, TX 76117
1-817-759-BOOK
1-817-759-2665
1-817-759-0300

You Will Love Our Website..!
WISDOMONLINE.COM

E

Millionaire-Talk

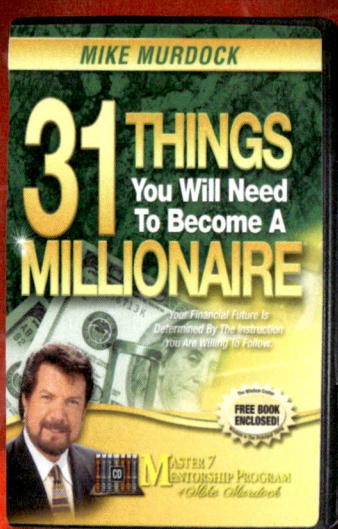

DR. MIKE MURDOCK

MY GIFT OF APPRECIATION
GIFT of Appreciation
Wisdom Is The Principal Thing

31 Things You Will Need To Become A Millionaire (2-CD's/SOWL-116)

Topics Include:
- You Will Need Financial Heroes
- Your Willingness To Negotiate Everything
- You Must Have The Ability To Transfer Your Enthusiasm, Your Vision To Others
- Know Your Competition
- Be Willing To Train Your Team Personally As To Your Expectations
- Hire Professionals To Do A Professional's Job

I have asked the Lord for 3,000 special partners who will sow an extra Seed of $58 towards o Television Outreach Ministry. Your Seed is so appreciated! Remember to request your Gift CD 2 Disc Volume, 31 Things You Will Need To Become A Millionaire, when you write this week

F — **THE WISDOM CENTER** 4051 Denton Highway · Fort Worth, TX 76117
1-817-759-BOOK
1-817-759-2665
1-817-759-0300

You Will Love Our Website..!
WisdomOnline.com

The Businessman's Devotional 4 Book Pak!

① **7 Rewards of Problem Solving** (Book/B-118/32pg/$8)
② **How To Make Your Dreams Come True!** (Book/B-143/32pg/$7)
③ **1 Minute Businessman's Devotional**
   (Book/B-42/224pg/$12)
④ **31 Greatest Chapters In The Bible**
   (Book/B-54/138pg/$10)

The Wisdom Center
The Businessman's Devotional 4 Book Pak!
Only $20
3X Value
PAK-22
Wisdom Is The Principal Thing

Add 20% For S/H

THE WISDOM CENTER
4051 Denton Highway · Fort Worth, TX 76117

1-817-759-BOOK
1-817-759-2665
1-817-759-0300

You Will Love Our Website..!
WisdomOnline.com

G

CHAMPIONS 4 Book Pak!

1. **Secrets of The Journey, Vol. 3** (Book/B-94/32pg/$5)
2. **How To Make Your Dreams Come True!** (Book/B-143/32pg/$7)
3. **Wisdom For Crisis Times** (Book/B-40/112pg/$9)
4. **The Making of A Champion** (Book/B-59/128pg/$10)

The Wisdom Center
Champions 4 Book Pak!
Only $20
PAK-23
Wisdom Is The Principal Thing

Each Wisdom Book may be purchased separately if so desired.

Add 20% For S/H

H THE WISDOM CENTER
4051 Denton Highway · Fort Worth, TX 76117
1-817-759-BOOK
1-817-759-2665
1-817-759-0300

You Will Love Our Website..!
WISDOMONLINE.COM

Increase 4 Book Pak!

- The Book That Changed My Life... (Book/B-117/32pg/$7)
- Secrets of The Journey, Vol. 2 (Book/B-93/32pg/$5)
- 7 Keys to 1000 Times More (Book/B-104/128pg/$10)
- 31 Secrets for Career Success (Book/B-44/112pg/$12)

The Wisdom Center
Increase 4 Book Pak!
Only $20 $34 Value
PAK-26
Wisdom Is The Principal Thing

Wisdom Book may be purchased separately if so desired.

Add 20% For S/H

THE WISDOM CENTER
4051 Denton Highway · Fort Worth, TX 76117
1-817-759-BOOK
1-817-759-2665
1-817-759-0300

You Will Love Our Website..!
WISDOMONLINE.COM

The Mentorship 7 Book Pak

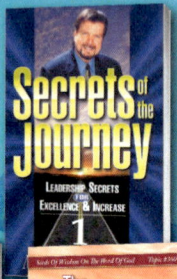

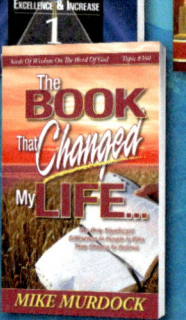
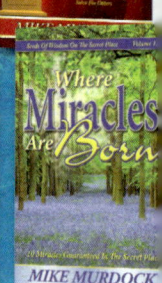

❶ **31 Facts About Wisdom**
(Book/B-46/32pg/$7)

❷ **Secrets of The Journey, Vol. 1**
(Book/B-92/32pg/$5)

❸ **7 Rewards of Problem Solving** (Book/B-118/32pg/$8)

❹ **How To Make Your Dreams Come True!** (Book/B-143/32pg/$7)

❺ **The Wisdom Key Devotional**
(Book/B-165/60pg/$10)

❻ **The Book That Changed My Life**
(Book/B-117/32pg/$7)

❼ **Where Miracles Are Born**
(Book/B-115/32pg/$7)

All 7 Books For One Great Price!

Each Wisdom Book may be purchased separately if so desired.

The Wisdom Center
The Mentorship 7 Book Pak!
Only $20 $52 Value
PAK-25
Wisdom Is The Principal Thing

Add 20% For S/H

THE WISDOM CENTER
4051 Denton Highway · Fort Worth, TX 76117

1-817-759-BOOK
1-817-759-2665
1-817-759-0300

You Will Love Our Website..!
WISDOMONLINE.COM

The Double Diamond Devotional 4 Book Pak!

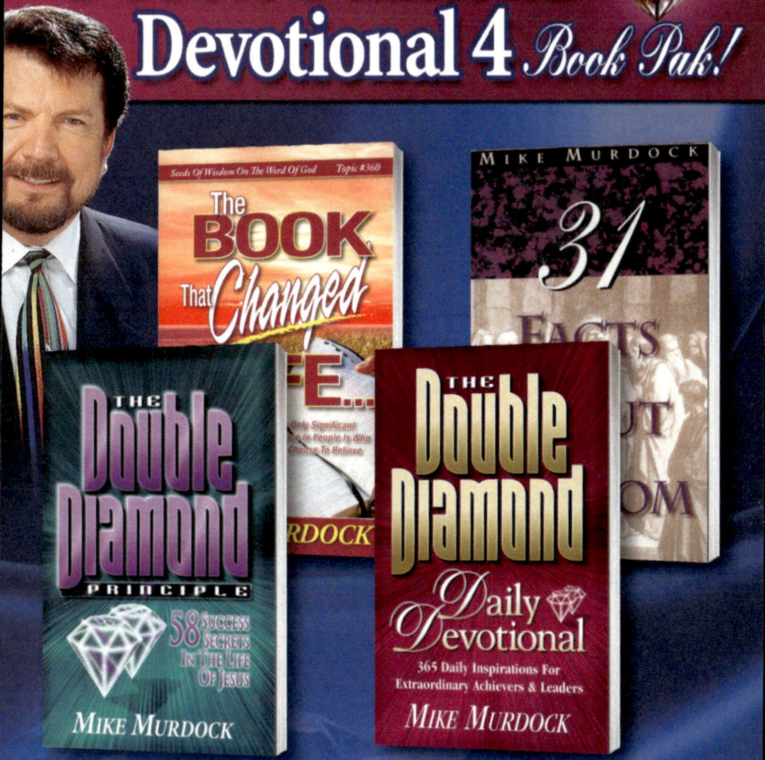

1. **The Book That Changed My Life...** (Book/B-117/32pg/$7)
2. **31 Facts About Wisdom** (Book/B-46/32pg/$7)
3. **The Double Diamond Principle** (Book/B-39/148pg/$9)
4. **The Double Diamond Daily Devotional** (Book/B-72/378pg/$15)

The Wisdom Center
The Double Diamond Devotional 4 Book Pak!
Only $20 $38 Value
PAK-29
Wisdom Is The Principal Thing

Wisdom Book may be purchased separately if so desired.　　Add 20% For S/H

THE WISDOM CENTER
4051 Denton Highway · Fort Worth, TX 76117
1-817-759-BOOK
1-817-759-2665
1-817-759-0300

You Will Love Our Website..!
WisdomOnline.com　K

THE WISDOM BIBLE
Partnership Edition

Over 120 Wisdom Study Guides Included Such As:

- 10 Qualities of Uncommon Achievers
- 18 Facts You Should Know About The Anointing
- 21 Facts To Help You Identify Those Assigned To You
- 31 Facts You Should Know About Your Assignment
- 8 Keys That Unlock Victory In Every Attack
- 22 Defense Techniques To Remember During Seasons of Personal Attack
- 20 Wisdom Keys And Techniques To Remember During An Uncommon Battle
- 11 Benefits You Can Expect From God
- 31 Facts You Should Know About Favor
- The Covenant of 58 Blessings
- 7 Keys To Receiving Your Miracle
- 16 Facts You Should Remember About Contentious People
- 5 Facts Solomon Taught About Contracts
- 7 Facts You Should Know About Conflict
- 6 Steps That Can Unlock Your Self-Confidence
- And Much More!

Your Partnership makes such a difference in The Wisdom Center Outreach Ministries. I wanted to place a Gift in your hand that could last a lifetime for you and your family...**The Wisdom Study Bible.**

40 Years of Personal Notes...this Partnership Edition Bible contains 160 pages of my Personal Study Notes...that could forever change your Bible Study of The Word of God. This **Partnership Edition...**is my personal **Gift of Appreciation** when you sow your Sponsorship Seed of $1,000 for our Television Outreach Ministry. An Uncommon Seed Always Creates An Uncommon Harvest!

Mike

Thank you from my heart for your Seed of Obedience (Luke 6:38).

THE WISDOM CENTER
4051 Denton Highway • Fort Worth, TX 76117
1-817-759-BOOK
1-817-759-2665
1-817-759-0300

You Will Love Our Website..!
WISDOMONLINE.COM

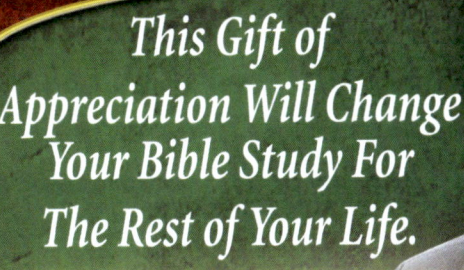

Prosperity Secrets 4 Book Pak!

1. **Secrets of The Journey, Vol. 5** (Book/B-96/32pg/$5)
2. **How To Make Your Dreams Come True!** (Book/B-143/32pg/$7)
3. **31 Reasons People Do Not Receive Their Financial Harvest** (Book/B-82/252pg/$15)
4. **Secrets of the Richest Man Who Ever Lived** (Book/B-99/179pg/$10)

Each Wisdom Book may be purchased separately if so desired.

The Wisdom Center
Prosperity Secrets 4 Book Pak!
Only $20
$37 Value
PAK-28
Wisdom Is The Principal Thing

Add 20% For S/H

THE WISDOM CENTER
4051 Denton Highway · Fort Worth, TX 76117

1-817-759-BOOK
1-817-759-2665
1-817-759-0300

—You Will Love Our Website..!—
WisdomOnline.com

YOUR ASSIGNMENT IS YOUR DISTINCTION FROM OTHERS.

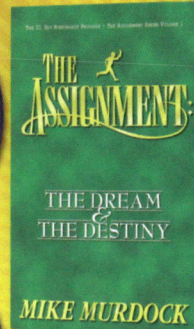
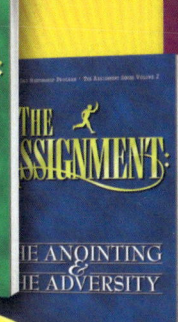
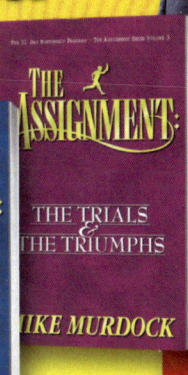
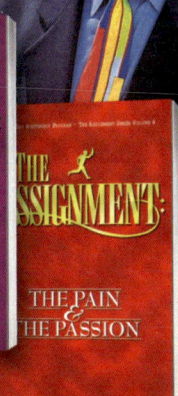

Assignment 4 Book Pak!

Uncommon Wisdom For Discovering Your Life Assignment.

1. **The Dream & The Destiny**
   Vol 1 (Book/B-74/164 pg/$15)
2. **The Anointing & The Adversity**
   Vol 2 (Book/B-75/192 pg/$10)
3. **The Trials & The Triumphs**
   Vol 3 (Book/B-97/160 pg/$10)
4. **The Pain & The Passion**
   Vol 4 (Book/B-98/144 pg/$10)

Each Wisdom Book may be purchased separately if so desired.

The Wisdom Center
Assignment 4 Book Pak!
Only $30 $45 Value
WBL-14
Wisdom Is The Principal Thing

Add 20% For S/H

THE WISDOM CENTER
4051 Denton Highway · Fort Worth, TX 76117
1-817-759-BOOK
1-817-759-2665
1-817-759-0300

You Will Love Our Website..!
WisdomOnline.com

O

JOIN THE Wisdom Key 3000 TODAY!

Will You Become My Ministry Partner In The Work Of God?

Dear Friend,

God has connected us!

I have asked The Holy Spirit for 3000 Special Partners who will plant a monthly Seed of $58.00 to help me bring the gospel around the world. (58 represents 58 kinds of blessings in the Bible.)

Will you become my monthly Faith Partner in The Wisdom Key 3000? Your monthly Seed of $58.00 is so powerful in helping heal broken lives. When you sow into the work of God, 4 Miracle Harvests are guaranteed in Scripture, Isaiah 58...

- Uncommon Health (Isaiah 58)
- Uncommon Wisdom For Decision-Making (Isaiah 58)
- Uncommon Financial Favor (Isaiah 58)
- Uncommon Family Restoration (Isaiah 58)

Your Faith Partner,

Mike Murdock

P.S. Please clip the coupon attached and return it to me today, so I can rush the Wisdom Key Partnership Pak to you...or call me at 1-817-759-0300.

PP-03

☐ **Yes, Mike, I want to join The Wisdom Key 3000. Please rush The Wisdom Key Partnership Pak to me today!**

☐ **Enclosed is my first monthly Seed-Faith Promise of:**
☐ $58 ☐ Other $_____.

☐ CHECK ☐ MONEY ORDER ☐ AMEX ☐ DISCOVER ☐ MASTERCARD ☐ VISA

Credit Card # _____ Exp. ___/___

Signature _____

Name _____ Birth Date ___/___

Address _____

City _____ State _____ Zip _____

Phone _____ E-Mail _____

Your Seed-Faith Offerings are used to support The Wisdom Center, and all of its programs. The Wisdom Center reserves the right to redirect funds as needed in order to carry out our charitable purpose. In the event The Wisdom Center receives more funds for the project than needed, the excess will be used for another worthy outreach. (Your transactions may be electronically deposited.)

WK304

THE WISDOM CENTER
4051 Denton Highway · Fort Worth, TX 76117
1-817-759-BOOK
1-817-759-2665
1-817-759-0300

You Will Love Our Website..!
WisdomOnline.com

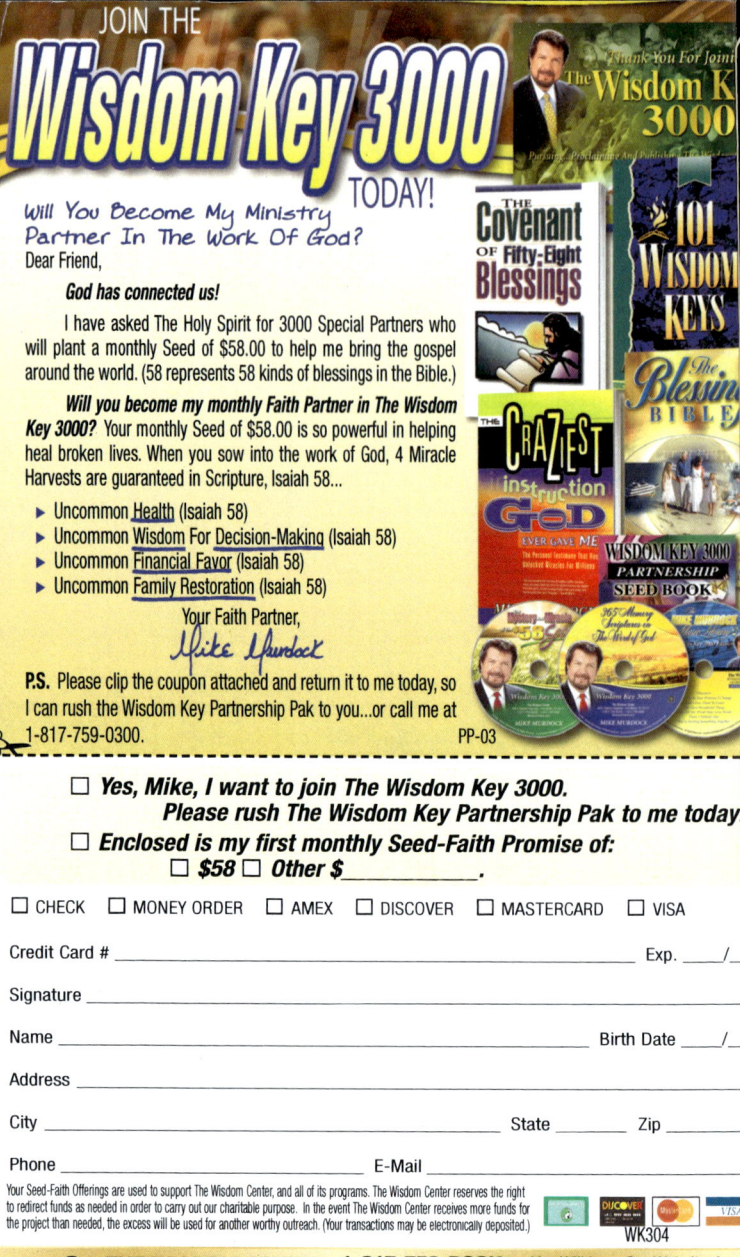